Critical Perspectives on Work And Employment

Series editors:
Irena Grugulis, Durham University Business School, UK
Caroline Lloyd, School of Social Sciences, Cardiff University, UK
Chris Smith, Royal Holloway University of London School of Management, UK
Chris Warhurst, University of Sydney Business School, Australia

Critical Perspectives on Work and Employment combines the best empirical research with leading edge, critical debate on key issues and developments in the field of work and employment. Extremely well regarded and popular, the series is linked to the highly successful *International Labour Process Conference*.

Formerly edited by David Knights, Hugh Willmott, Chris Smith and Paul Thompson, each volume in the series includes contributions from a range of disciplines, including the sociology of work and employment, business and management studies, human resources management, industrial relations and organisational analysis.

Further details of the *International Labour Process Conference* can be found at www.ilpc.org.uk

Published:

Carol Wolkowitz, Rachel Lara Cohen, Teela Sanders and Kate Hardy
BODY/SEX/WORK

Chris Warhurst, Françoise Carré, Patricia Findlay and Chris Tilly
ARE BAD JOBS INEVITABLE?

Irena Grugulis and Ödül Bozkurt
RETAIL WORK

Paul Thompson and Chris Smith
WORKING LIFE

Alan McKinlay and Chris Smith
CREATIVE LABOUR

Maeve Houlihan and Sharon Bolton
WORK MATTERS

Chris Warhurst, Doris Ruth Eikhof and Axel Hunschild
WORK LESS, LIVE MORE?

Bill Harley, Jeff Hyman and Paul Thompson
PARTICIPATION AND DEMOCRACY AT WORK

Chris Warhurst, Irena Grugulis and Ewart Keep
THE SKILLS THAT MATTER

Andrew Sturdy, Irena Grugulis and Hugh Willmott
CUSTOMER SERVICE

Craig Prichard, Richard Hull, Mike Chumer and Hugh Willmott
MANAGING KNOWLEDGE

Alan Felstead and Nick Jewson
GLOBAL TRENDS IN FLEXIBLE LABOUR

Paul Thompson and Chris Warhurst
WORKPLACES OF THE FUTURE

More details of the publications in this series can be found at http://www.palgrave.com/business/cpwe

---

Critical Perspectives on Work and Employment Series
Series Standing Order ISBN 978–0230–23017–0

You can receive future titles in this series as they are published by placing a standing order. Please contact your bookseller or, in case of difficulty, write to us at the address below with your name and address, the title of the series and the ISBN quoted above.

Customer Services Department, Macmillan Distribution Ltd
Houndmills, Basingstoke, Hampshire RG21 6XS, England

Body/Sex/Work

Intimate, Embodied and Sexualized Labour

Edited by

Carol Wolkowitz
Reader, Department of Sociology,
University of Warwick, UK

Rachel Lara Cohen
Senior Lecturer, Sociology Department,
City University London, UK

Teela Sanders
Reader, School of Sociology
and Social Policy, University of Leeds, UK

Kate Hardy
Lecturer, University of Leeds Business School,
University of Leeds, UK

palgrave
macmillan

First published 2013 by
PALGRAVE MACMILLAN

Palgrave Macmillan in the UK is an imprint of Macmillan Publishers Limited, registered in England, company number 785998, of Houndmills, Basingstoke, Hampshire RG21 6XS.

Palgrave Macmillan in the US is a division of St Martin's Press LLC, 175 Fifth Avenue, New York, NY 10010.

Palgrave Macmillan is the global academic imprint of the above companies and has companies and representatives throughout the world.

Palgrave® and Macmillan® are registered trademarks in the United States, the United Kingdom, Europe and other countries.

ISBN: 978–1–137–02190–8

This book is printed on paper suitable for recycling and made from fully managed and sustained forest sources. Logging, pulping and manufacturing processes are expected to conform to the environmental regulations of the country of origin.

A catalogue record for this book is available from the British Library.

A catalog record for this book is available from the Library of Congress.

10 9 8 7 6 5 4 3 2 1
22 21 20 19 18 17 16 15 14 13

Printed in China

Contents

List of Illustrations   *vii*

Acknowledgements   *viii*

Notes on Contributors   *ix*

Part I   Theorizing Body/Sex Work   **1**

1   **The Body/Sex/Work Nexus: A Critical Perspective
    on Body Work and Sex Work**   **3**
    Rachel Lara Cohen, Kate Hardy, Teela Sanders and Carol Wolkowitz

2   **Touching Moments: An Analysis of the Skilful Search for
    Dignity within Body Work Interactions**   **28**
    Marek Korczynski

3   **Equal to Any Other, but Not the Same as Any Other:
    The Politics of Sexual Labour, the Body and Intercorporeality**   **43**
    Kate Hardy

**Part II   The Socio-Economic and Legal
            Context of Body/Sex Work**   **59**

4   **Legal Constructions of Body Work**   **61**
    Ann Stewart

5   **Gender, Emotional Labour and Interactive Body Work:
    Negotiating Flesh and Fantasy in Sex Workers'
    Labour Practices**   **77**
    Barbara G. Brents and Crystal A. Jackson

6   The Frontline Costs of the Southern Cross Decline   93
    Joe Greener

7   Hairdressing/Undressing: Comparing Labour Relations
    in Self-Employed Body Work   110
    Teela Sanders, Rachel Lara Cohen and Kate Hardy

Part III   Sexualizing and Desexualizing Bodies in
           the Labour Process   127

8   Altered Bodies, Engineered Careers: A Comparison of Body
    Technologies in Corporate and Do-It-Yourself Pornographic
    Productions   129
    Lori L. Fazzino

9   From Erotic Capital to Erotic Knowledge: Body, Gender
    and Sexuality as Symbolic Skills in Phone Sex Work   146
    Giulia Selmi

10 'What Does a Manicure Have to Do With Sex?': Racialized
    Sexualization of Body Labour in Routine Beauty Services   160
    Miliann Kang

11 Touch in Holistic Massage: Ambiguities and Boundaries   175
    Carrie Purcell

Part IV   Disciplining and Resistant Bodies   191

12 Racing Bodies   193
    Janet Miller

13 Body Work and Ageing: The Biomedicalization of
    Nutrition Practices   207
    Giulia Rodeschini

14 Getting the Bodies of the Workers to the Bodies of
    the Clients: The Role of Rotas in Domiciliary Care   223
    Gemma Wibberley

15 Saliva, Semen and Sanity: Flat-Working Women in
    Hong Kong and Bodily Management Strategies   239
    Olive Cheung

Index   255

List of Illustrations

Tables

2.1   Three types of body work interaction and tensions in
the social meaning of the body of the service-recipient   33

8.1   Commonly used body technologies   131

8.2   Variables recorded for content analysis   135

14.1   Joanna's rota for the day   228

14.2   Joanna's real rota   230

Figure

8.1   Percentage of body technologies represented on the DIY site   138

Acknowledgements

Many of the chapters in this volume were presented at our stream at the annual International Labour Process Conference, held in Leeds, England, in March 2011, called Body/Sex/Work: Exploring the Diversification of Corporeal and Sexual Labour. We are grateful to Daniel Muzio, Jennifer Tomlinson and Steve Vincent, the conference organizers, for bringing so many people together and enabling us to put together a popular and lively stream. Other chapters were presented as papers at a September 2011 conference on Body Work in Health and Social Care, supported by the Sociology of Health and Illness Foundation and the British Sociological Association Study Group on Ageing, Body and Society. Two chapters are based on papers first presented at an ESRC-funded research seminar series on body work held at the Universities of Warwick and Kent from 2007 to 2009. We thank all these people and organizations for their support.

We are grateful for the encouragement of the series editors, Irena Grugulis, Caroline Lloyd, Chris Smith and Chris Warhurst, and from Palgrave Macmillan, especially Ceri Griffiths.

We are grateful to the University of California Press for permission to reproduce short sections of Miliann Kang's *The Managed Hand: Race, Gender and the Body in Beauty Service Work*, 2010.

Notes on Contributors

Barbara G. Brents is Professor in the Department of Sociology and a faculty affiliate in Women's Studies at the University of Nevada, Las Vegas. She is the co-author, with Crystal Jackson and Kathryn Hausbeck Korgan, of *The State of Sex: Tourism, Sex and Sin in the New American Heartland* (2010). Brents' research uses a political economy lens to study sex and gender in market culture. Her recent work uses the sex industry as a site to understand the intersections of culture and economics, including the construction of 'market morality' in political debates around sexuality; the relation between tourism, consumption and sexuality; and the emotional and bodily labour of selling sex.

Rachel Lara Cohen is Senior Lecturer in Sociology at City University, London. Her interests are in the sociology of work and employment, especially 'non-standard work', including mobile work, self-employment and homeworking. She has published from her PhD research on the working lives of hairdressers in a range of peer-reviewed journals, as well as contributing a chapter to a previous volume in this series titled *Work Less, Live More*. Her current research explores the working lives of car mechanics and accountants. She co-edited a special issue of *The Sociology of Health and Illness* on 'body work' and contributed an article that explored the labour process consequences of body work. She also co-edited an issue of *The International Journal of Social Research Methodology* on feminism and quantitative methods. Cohen was co-organizer of an ESRC Seminar Series on Body Work and a 2011 conference on this theme.

Olive Cheung is currently based at the Centre for Interdisciplinary Gender Studies, University of Leeds, and is Postdoctoral Research Assistant on the ESRC-funded project 'Sun, Sea, Sand and Silicone: Aesthetic Surgery

Tourism'. She received her doctorate in Sociology from Royal Holloway, University of London. Her PhD project explores the risks of disease, violence and emotional consequences in the context of sex work, analysing women's own accounts of these risks. Her research interests include everyday politics, emotions, identity, gender, sexuality, body and cultures.

Kate Hardy is Lecturer in Work and Employment at LUBS, University of Leeds. Her work is strongly interdisciplinary, spanning geography, gender studies, sociology and labour studies. Her main substantive research topics are sex work and cosmetic surgery, although she has interests in feminism, radical education, informal organizing, gender and work and the relationship between paid and unpaid labour. She is involved in activism within and outside the academy around these issues. In addition to a number of journal articles, she has published edited collections, including *Sociologies of Sex Work* (2010), and is working on a monograph entitled *Flexible Workers: Labour, Mobility and Regulation in the Lap Dancing Industry.*

Lori L. Fazzino is a doctoral student in the Department of Sociology at the University of Nevada, Las Vegas (UNLV) and president of the UNLV chapter of Alpha Kappa Delta. She received her BA in sociology with a minor in philosophy from Pacific Lutheran University in Tacoma, Washington and an MA in sociology at UNLV. Lori's research interests span several sub-fields of sociology, including culture, sexualities, religion, social movements and mental health.

Joe Greener is Lecturer in Social Policy at the Liverpool Hope University in the Department of Social Work, Care and Justice. His recently finished PhD project was a participant covert observation of working practices in a Southern Cross-owned care home for the elderly. This current research agenda investigates the role of profit motives in shaping the organization of care labour processes. He is interested in providing sociological accounts of the neglect and mistreatment of care recipients but especially with reference to the political and economic contexts which frame caring relations.

Crystal A. Jackson is a PhD candidate in the Department of Sociology, University of Nevada, Las Vegas studying the political economy of commercial sex. Jackson's co-authored *The State of Sex: Tourism, Sex and Sin in the New American Heartland* (2010), with Barbara Brents and Kathryn Hausbeck Korgan, situates Nevada's rural, legal brothel industry within today's growing service and leisure economies. Her dissertation explores how sex worker rights organizing in the US contests the legal and cultural meanings of 'sex' and 'work' and, on a larger scale, how this represents a reshaping of labour movement in late capitalist society.

Miliann Kang is Associate Professor in Women, Gender, Sexuality Studies at the University of Massachusetts, Amherst where she is also affiliated faculty in Sociology and Asian/Asian American Studies. Her book *The Managed Hand: Race, Gender and the Body in Beauty Service Work* (2010) addresses gendered processes and relations in immigrant women's work, focusing on Asian-owned nail salons in New York City. It won four awards from the American Sociological Association (sections on Racial and Ethnic Minorities; Sex and Gender; Race, Gender, and Class; and Asia/Asian America) and the Sara Whaley book prize from the National Women's Studies Association. She is currently researching work–family issues for Asian American women, and the racial politics of mothering. Her research has been supported by the American Association of University Women, the Ford Foundation, the Institute for Asian American Studies at UMass Boston, the Labor Relations and Research Center at Umass, Amherst and the Social Science Research Council.

Marek Korczynski is Professor of Sociology of Work at the University of Nottingham Business School. His main research focuses upon the service sector working class in the contemporary service-dominated economy. Service workers face important structures embedded in both production and consumption. He has argued that service production tends to be structured as a customer-oriented bureaucracy and that service consumption is structured around promoting an enchanting myth of customer sovereignty. He uses these concepts as his analytical points of departure in the analysis of body work within his chapter in this book. He believes books continue to serve as a vital forum for the creation of sociological knowledge. In the service area, he has written *Service Work: Critical Perspectives* (co-edited, 2009), *Human Resource Management in Service Work* (2002) and *On the Front Line* (co-authored, 1999).

Janet Miller is Senior Lecturer in HRM at the University of the West of England. She has been engaged with the labour process in the horse racing industry, specifically racing stables, since 2000. During this time she has undertaken projects for the British Horseracing Board, the Low Pay Commission and the International Labour Office, all concerned with aspects of work in racing stables. Currently, she is focusing on worker mobilization in the small firm, with stable staff and veterinary nurses as her respondents.

Carrie Purcell teaches in the Sociology department at the University of Edinburgh, where she was recently awarded a PhD. Her research interests span embodiment, gender, sexualities, health and well-being, work, and narrative inquiry. Purcell's doctoral research examined the way massage practitioners constitute a professional stock of knowledge, and the ways in which massage is 'unbounded'. She is also interested in interrogating methodological questions raised by combining narrative inquiry and phenomenological sociology, and in examining the interplay between big and small sociological concerns. Her next research project will undertake a nationwide study of lay and professional perspectives on women's sexual problems.

Giulia Rodeschini is a PhD student in Sociology and Social Research at the University of Trento, Italy. Her fields of study concern care work, gender studies and sociology of ageing. She has worked as researcher on several different European projects focusing on the process of ageing, health care systems and information and communication technologies.

Teela Sanders is Reader in Sociology at the School of Sociology and Social Policy, University of Leeds. Her research focuses on the intersections between gender, regulation and the sex industry, with special attention to exploring hidden economies. Her monographs include *Sex Work: A Risky Business* (2005) and *Paying for Pleasure: Men Who Buy Sex* (2008). She has co-written *Prostitution: Sex Work, Policy and Politics* (2009) with Jane Pitcher and Maggie O'Neill. With Kate Hardy, Sanders recently completed a large-scale, ESRC-funded project on the lap dancing industry and the working conditions of dancers. The findings of this project will be published in *Flexible Workers: Labour, Regulation and Mobility in Lap Dancing* (forthcoming). Working with Rosie Campbell, Sanders' ESRC Follow-on award for further dissemination and impact aims to influence licensing policy on Sex Entertainment Venues and to create an iPhone App for dancers with safety, self-employment rights and tax awareness information.

Giulia Selmi holds a PhD in Sociology and Social Research at the University of Trento, Italy, where she is a member of the steering committee of the Center of Interdisciplinary Gender Studies. She is currently *Erasmus Mundus* post-doctoral fellow at the University Mohammed V of Rabat, Morocco, and conducting research on the transformation of the intimate biographies of second-generation Moroccan youth living in Italy. Among her latest publications is 'Dirty Talks and Gender Cleanliness: An Account of Identity Management Practices in Phone Sex Work', in *Doing Dirty Work: Concepts and Identities* (2012).

Ann Stewart is Reader in Law, Associate Professor, at the Law School at University of Warwick, UK. She specializes in the area of gender and the law, particularly in the context of international development. Her work involves understanding the ways in which gender relations are shaped by global social, economic and political processes and specifically the growth and impact of the commercialization of care and body work relationships. She is the author of *Gender, Law and Justice in a Global Market* (2011).

Gemma Wibberley is Senior Research Assistant in iROWE (Institute for Research into Organisations, Work and Employment), at the University of Central Lancashire (UCLAN). She completed her PhD at Lancaster University on the complex and invisible work of domiciliary care workers in 2011. She previously worked as a research assistant at The Scottish Government, Strathclyde University, Lancaster University and Datamonitor. Her research interests include employees' experiences in the contemporary workplace and employment practices and policies. She is currently examining conflict at work from the perspective of managers, employee representatives and HR practitioners in both the public and private sectors, and evaluating Trade Union organizing campaigns.

Carol Wolkowitz is Reader in the Department of Sociology, University of Warwick. She has published extensively on different aspects of the relation between the body, work and employment, including *Bodies at Work* (2006) and articles in a previous volume in this series, *Working Life: Renewing Labour Process Analysis* (2010), the *Sage Handbook on Gender, Work and Organization* (2011) and *Dirt: New Geographies of Cleanliness and Contamination* (2007). She was Principal Investigator on an ESRC-funded research seminar series on body work and co-editor of a special issue of *Sociology of Health and Illness*. Her more recent research on the growth of body work markets in south Florida has been published in a special issue of *Sociological Research Online* (2012), which she edited with Phillip Mizen. It seeks to advance the use of visual methods to study changing landscapes of work and labour.

Theorizing Body/Sex Work

The Body/Sex/Work Nexus: A Critical Perspective on Body Work and Sex Work

Rachel Lara Cohen, Kate Hardy, Teela Sanders and Carol Wolkowitz

Introduction

This book focuses on intimate, embodied and sexualized labour in body work and sex work, exploring empirically and theoretically the labour process, workplace relations, regulation and resistance in some of the many work sites that together make up these types of work. It seeks to tease out similarities and differences in the ways that sexual and physical intimacy are organized, managed and experienced across different employment contexts, and in doing so provides ways of reframing key questions in critical studies of work and employment.

Many of the authors in this volume are interested in a particular relation between bodies and labour, conceptualized as paid 'body work' (Twigg, 2006, 2000; Wolkowitz, 2006, 2002), or sometimes 'body labour' (Cohen, 2011; Kang, 2003, 2010), which involves 'assessing, diagnosing, handling, and manipulating bodies that become the object of the worker's labour' (Twigg et al., 2011: 1). Conceptualizing 'body work' as work on others' bodies, and not simply physical and cultural work on one's own body, which was its earlier usage (Gimlin, 2007; Shilling, 2005), recognizes the incorporation of body work (and sex work) within market relationships, and emphasizes the role of paid workers in social reproduction. Concretely, body work is typically found in health and social care jobs such as nursing; in aesthetic services such as beauty work; in sex work; and in protective and security services, for example nightclub bouncers or airport security personnel who police and control bodies. Interactions in body work may take various forms: touch, caress, manipulation, transformation, arousal or even incision. Cohen (2011) estimates that, according to this definition, at least 10 per cent of UK jobs involve body work (this does not include sex work, which is rarely measured by labour market data).

Sex work spans a range of activities in which sexuality is explicitly being sold. These are largely coterminous with customer-facing work within the 'sex industry' and include direct sexual services (prostitution in the form of flat, brothel or street work) (Brents and Hausbeck, 2010); erotic dance (stripping, lap dancing and peepshows) (Sanders et al., this volume); pornography (Fazzino, this volume); webcam work; and phone sex lines (Selmi, this volume), amongst others. Much, but not all, sex work involves work on or with another's body (and so comprises a form of body work). Therefore, in this introduction we employ the shorthand body/sex work to indicate work across these broad and overlapping categories, reserving 'body work' or 'sex work' for instances where we want to particularly specify either work on the body of another or work in the sex industry.

The focus on the intimate, embodied and sexualized labour that occurs within body/sex work is part of a new trend toward recognizing the embodiment of labour and that the body, emotions and sexuality are sites of commodification (Gimlin, 2007; Hardy et al., 2011; Hassard et al., 2000; Hochschild, 1983, 2003; Otis, 2011; Witz et al., 2003; Wolkowitz, 2006). The embodiment of occupational cultures and organizational practices has probably been documented most thoroughly by research on medical, nursing and social care (Lawler, 1991; Twigg, 2006; Twigg et al., 2011). Meanwhile, Boris and Parreñas (2010) and McDowell (2009) have carried an interest in embodied labour and interactions between bodies into our understanding of economic relations and the geography of employment in private services, including sex work.

Little previous research on body/sex work, however, has employment relations or the labour process at its heart. In contrast, we focus on what we can learn about the social organization of labour by considering paid work that takes other people's bodies as its focus or 'material of production'; the inter-subjective relations involved, for example the sexualization and desexualization of work involving, or intimating, touch; and the conflicts and organizational problems that arise when work involves bodies working on bodies and/or sexuality.

Workers' bodies and sexuality are implicated in all labour, but bodies and/or sexuality are the *object* of labour in a smaller number of instances. As described in this chapter, bodies and sexuality are peculiar objects of labour because of the social meaning of human bodies and the social, spatial and organizational contexts and constraints of the situations in which they receive attention. The empirical recognition of the peculiarity of bodies as materials of production has as its corollary the conceptual recognition that labour processes are always concrete, located and material, in ways that are consequential for the forms of managerial organization possible. Additionally, in engaging with types and places of work that differ from those usually considered in research on the labour process (Thompson, 1989; Thompson and Smith, 2009) or on the institutional and social organization of labour, consideration of body/sex work may provide new avenues for developing labour process analysis.

Conversely, it is essential that sex work and body work are explored as work – for instance within a labour process framework – rather than viewing these activities as fundamentally different from other forms of work, whether as simply extra-economic oppression (sex work) or 'natural' nurturing (other forms of body work). One reason for the timeliness of this book is the apparent increase in the quantity and visibility of sexual labour and its consumption (Brents and Sanders, 2010), as well as increases in other forms of body work (especially care work), which have also become increasingly commodified as paid labour. This book elucidates the lived experiences of those whose work implies or necessitates sex, sexuality and interpersonal touch, and the implications of this for their experiences of work, temporality, and their ability to organize to transform their working conditions. We explore the managerial constraints and organizational pressures of this work and the emotional and aesthetic implications of intimate embodied interactions for those being worked-upon.

In this introductory chapter, we highlight continuities and differences across a range of work that has tactile, often intimate or sexualized interaction between bodies at its heart. These bodies are mostly, but not always, human and mostly, but not always, co-present. We begin by providing an overview of the changing socio-economic and historical structures of body/sex work. We then conceptualize body/sex work, exploring the embodiment of service sector encounters and how this contributes to wider understandings of embodiment at work, as well as detailing specific issues that arise when workers are engaged in body work. Next, we consider the ways that workers, located within different occupations and managerial regimes, adopt strategies for sexualizing or desexualizing interactions. We then focus in more detail on the social organization of 'body work' as 'body labour' and the ways commodification affects the labour process of body/sex work. The next section considers the consequences of commodification for relationships between workers and those whose bodies they work on. Finally, we explore the impediments that both body work and sex work present for workers' capacities to resist exploitation, via appeal to institutional (especially legal) structures, but also through collective and individual forms of resistance.

The changing socio-economic structures of body/sex work

People, largely women, have worked on the bodies of others, as well as on their own bodies, from time immemorial. Much of this work (for instance, care or aesthetic work as well as sex work) occurred within the home. Yet, with the radical separation of home and work wrought by industrialization and capitalism, and the erosion of extended familial care networks, new institutions dedicated to the provision of health and social care (hospitals, asylums, care homes and nurseries) were established, both by private providers and by emerging welfare states.

In contemporary capitalism, body work is increasingly not simply commodified as body labour, but located within private, profit-making organizations. This movement has its roots in several intersecting processes. First, the entry of increasing numbers of women into paid labour has further reduced the capacity for body work to be provided domestically. Second, the triumph of neo-liberal politics has meant that many states have withdrawn from direct provision of health and social care, while the ongoing responsibility of the state as funder-of-last-resort (for at least a large proportion of health and care provision) is precisely what makes this a viable market for capital (Diamond, 1992).

Third, the growth of the cosmetic, beauty and 'pampering' industries has promoted the development of ever-new aestheticizing techniques and 'specialist' skills. These have moved services like hairdressing from kitchens and bathrooms to dedicated salons (Willett, 2000), and increasingly marketed services towards 'bodies of value' (Anagnost, 2004).

Fourth, a growing cultural acceptance of the commodification of 'intimacy' (Hochschild, 2003; Zelizer, 2005), has opened up new spaces for capital (especially, as discussed later in this chapter, small-scale capital). Consequently, forms of work previously performed for love are increasingly performed for a wage (McDowell, 2009).

Fifth, socio-demographic shifts as well as cultural expectations have meant that ageing bodies in particular represent an increasing market for goods, services and labour (Wolkowitz, 2012). Partly this involves provision of care, but the market has diversified, and now involves selling products and body services to reduce visible signifiers of ageing (such as anti-ageing beauty regimes of Botox and fillers, or, more drastically, facelifts and other cosmetic surgeries).

Sixth, there has been an apparent growth and 'mainstreaming' of the sex industry. The internet has made pornography instantly accessible, often for free, meanwhile table dancing and gentlemen's clubs have etched their way onto high streets. In the context of neo-liberal retrenchment, recession and austerity, more men, women and children may be turning to unregulated and casual jobs in the sex industry for income and survival.

Conceptualizing body/sex work

Work that focuses on the bodily desires and needs of customers, clients and patients, or that involves the manipulation or movement of other people, may involve differing relations to, and social and tactile understandings of, their bodies. Even sex work stretches from the most intimate sexual exchanges to the apparently disembodied communications of the telephone sex line. Other kinds of work also involve varying degrees of touch and direct intervention in the body, ranging from the security guard's pat down to the care-worker's adjustments and from the surgeon's incision to the manicurist's filing.

Exploration of the labour process of body work/labour (including sex work) places centre stage the role of bodies and sexuality within service sector interactions. However, as Twigg et al. (2011) stress, the concept was never intended to displace the concept of 'emotional work/labour' (Hochschild, 1983). Rather, as Kang (2010) and Cohen (2011) make explicit, body work/labour is conceived as analytically complementary to emotional work/labour. Moreover, the recognition that all body/sex work necessitates negotiating powerful social meanings attached to the body, touch, physical intimacy and sexuality highlights the intense emotional labour required to manage the bodies and emotions of patients, clients and customers, as well as workers' own responses. Because bodies are volitional subjects (except when unconscious) body/sex work necessarily involves communicative as well as bodily interaction with clients, customers and patients to get the work done, even when forming a relationship is not the aim (Toerien and Kitzinger, 2007). It can also involve a variety of ways of conceptualizing the body-worked-upon, for instance the mindful body of alternative and complementary therapies or the more objectified body typical of modern medicine.

The lack of attention hitherto paid to the extent of service sector employment now focusing directly on the human body is surprising. One reason for this inattention may be the apparent continuity of this work with women's unpaid labour, which means this work is not consistently recognized as labour. Indeed, as Stewart (this volume) shows, neither care work nor sex work is fully recognized in UK law as employment. The concentration of workers seen as outside the 'mainstream' labour force (women and racialized, often migrant minorities) in body work occupations contributes to the marginalization of this work and increases workers' vulnerability. Even where body work, such as hairstyling, requires dedicated training and skill acquisition, the line between domestic and workplace social relations may remain fuzzy (Cohen, 2008), again undermining recognition of this work as labour. Furthermore, workers themselves, in discussing their work, may obscure its bodily content in an attempt to professionalize their image by privileging the intellectual and affective aspects of their work over what is frequently seen as the stigmatizing 'dirty work' of physical intimacy (Bolton, 2005; Simpson et al., 2012; Twigg et al., 2011).

Body work is also relatively invisible because the places where it is performed are frequently out of view, in the informal sector and/or outside our understanding of 'the workplace', for instance in workers' or recipients' homes, 'behind the screen' in hospital (Lawler, 1991), or in the case of sex work within criminalized locales. Finally, the difficulty in standardizing work on the human body and the labour-intensive nature of the work mean that much body work is incompletely subsumed under capitalist labour processes, and, with the exception of conventional health care, tends to be located in relatively small-scale enterprises in which self-employed workers bear the costs of the 'flexibility' it requires (Cohen, 2011; Sanders et al., this volume).

Because frontline body/sex work is centrally concerned with touch skills, it is in large part haptic (Brents and Jackson, Chapter 5; Harris, 2011; Miller, Chapter 12; Tarr, 2011). As such, much training is (literally) hands-on, with on-the-job training the norm in fields as varied as medicine and hairstyling. The level of skill assigned to particular parts of the labour process is of course not static but shifts with technological development or the development of new disciplines and associated values, such as the shift from feeding to nutrition (Rodeschini, Chapter 13). In addition, whereas we have focused on body work on human bodies, as Miller (Chapter 12) shows, there may be important parallels in work that involves working with and on non-human or animal bodies, specifically in terms of the haptic learning involved.

Investigating the social organization of body/sex work builds on recent concerns with 'embodying labour' (Wolkowitz and Warhurst, 2010), explicitly recognizing the bodily basis of human effort and consciousness. Despite the centrality of embodiment to the labour process – and the incorporation of embodied experience in many ethnographies of work – the dominant tendency hitherto has been to understand the body as a biological constant, which can be bracketed away. Conversely, work was understood as impersonal activity, with bodies, emotion, sexuality and even one's physical attractiveness restricted to the province of private, family life and associated with women rather than men (Gimlin, 2007).

Yet understandings of the body have long been embedded within critical understandings of work. For Marx, the body constitutes both the source of labour and, as an artefact of labour, its product (Scarry, 1985), while, for Foucault (1977), the operation of power *requires* bodies, operating in modern societies through positive forms, especially self-discipline. Others have suggested that flexible, self-regulating bodies lie at the heart of post-industrial society, supplanting the defensive, unbending body of industrial society (Martin, 1994). Research into work and employment is now increasingly engaging with 'body studies' and the debates around modernist, postmodernist and feminist conceptualizations of bodies and embodiment (Butler, 1993; Crossley, 2001; Shilling, 2005), and usually see bodies as both material and constructed through multifarious discourses, inscribed upon and inscribing, and, therefore, culturally and historically contingent (Evans, 2002).

Theorization of the body in the literature on sex work has been somewhat more overt, because representations of the sex worker appear to be wrapped up more closely with her body than is the case for other workers (Hardy, this volume; O'Neill, 2001; Wolkowitz, 2006). Wolkowitz (2006) argues that different approaches to sex work explicitly or implicitly deploy different concepts of the body, which underpin different understandings of the meaning of sex work in contemporary societies and sex workers' agency (something elaborated on by Hardy , this volume). The role of the body in sex work is highlighted in Brents et al.'s (2010) account of working in the Nevada brothels, a topic extended by Chapters 3, 5, 7, 8, 9 15 of this book.

It does not help that analysis of sex work continues to be stuck in the 'sex wars' (as noted by Hardy in Chapter 3). Therefore, notwithstanding research that highlights the complexities of voluntary adult sex worker–client relationships, media and social and criminal justice policy continue to construct the customer or 'punter' as an untrustworthy, dangerous and potentially violent offender (Kingston, 2010).

However, most theoretical writings and empirical research on the body, sex and work are primarily concerned with the body of the worker, for instance the worker's body as the bearer of labour power (Marx), the target of power (Foucault), or the embodiment of 'distinction' or other forms of social hierarchy (Bourdieu). The attempt to 'embody' labour has not, however, yet told us as much about the relation between bodies in the workplace. While there is research on the embodied relations between workmates or members of organizations (which features in Halford et al. [1997] and other research on gendered organizations), this is rarely extended to explore embodied relations between workers and the customers, clients and patients with whom, and on whom, they work. In looking at the interaction between workers and these bodies-worked-upon, including the ways in which this interaction is sexualized or desexualized, we need to consider the role of customers, clients and patients as embodied, wilful subjects, and at how their bodily vulnerability, variability, and unpredictability affects the organization of the work and workers' relation to the labour process, along with the sensory nature of this relationship, which (as evocatively evidenced by Cheung in Chapter 15) involves touch, taste and smell as well as visual and aural interaction.

Sexualizing bodies, desexualizing bodies

Critical investigations of the role of sexuality in labour, within and beyond the sex industry, have demonstrated the ways in which sex is increasingly central to multifarious forms of work (Adkins, 1996; Boris et al., 2010; Brewis and Linstead, 2000; Wolkowitz, 2006), not least sex work (Bernstein, 1999; Charusheela, 2009; Day, 2007; Hardy et al., 2010). Body work involves confronting the sexual meanings of the body and, therefore, always involves sexualization/desexualization. As such, it requires the management not only of the bodies that comprise the material of labour, but also workers' own bodies. As an important component of work that cuts across different forms of body work, within and outside the sex industry, processes of sexualization and desexualization in body/sex work are discussed in this section.

In sex work, workers construct a sexualized body/self through aesthetic labour, both to produce a particular body image and form and also to dress it 'appropriately' (Brents and Jackson; Hardy; and Fazzino, all in this volume; Pilcher, 2012). Depending on the specific labour process, this sexualized presentation often, however, goes much further to develop a complex 'manufactured identity' (Sanders, 2005), providing, for example, a 'girlfriend experience' (Bernstein, 2007; Sanders, 2008). The importance of the sexualized persona becomes particularly evident amongst sex workers who are unable to utilize aesthetic cues, for instance those engaged in phone sex work (Selmi, this volume). Also, while the sexualization that occurs in instances such as phone sex could be understood as disembodied, in order to 'sell' the illusion it is critical that a sexualized body is verbally constructed and narrated.

Beyond the sex industry, as workers' bodily presentation and aesthetic representation are systematically incorporated into consumer landscapes, sexualization becomes increasingly common across the service sector (Warhurst and Nickson, 2009). Although workers' sexualization may be part of a resistant or informal worker strategy (Warhurst and Nickson, 2009), it is also harnessed and organized by management across retail, hospitality and leisure environments, with services marketed on the 'sexi-ness' of staff (for example, Hooters or Abercrombie & Fitch). Management control operates via the recruitment of 'certain personalities'. Notably these 'personalities' are then most frequently employed within relationships in which their income is dependent on tips (restaurants and bars) or commis-sion (sales), providing workers with a material incentive to sexualize their workplace interactions. Such employment relations shift risk and respon-sibility for pleasing clients to the worker, thereby facilitating a highly sexualized working environment, while enabling employers to avoid the punitive constraints of equalities legislation. In this sense, there is a paral-lel between these sexualized leisure services and workers in the sex indus-try, who are largely employed as either self-employed, own-account workers or are dependent on commission/tips (see Sanders, Cohen and Hardy, this volume).

The sexualization of some service interactions has a knock-on effect on other intimate service interactions, especially where these involve body work. When it is a female body being touched by a male body worker, the 'need' to desexualize the encounter is exacerbated by dominant socio-cultural gender understandings of the passive yet sexual female and the predatory, sexually demanding male (Simpson, 2009). Conversely, in the more common case (given the gender distribution of body work), when a young woman works upon often older men (such as care work), desexualiza-tion requires workers to use their relative physical power and professional identity as a mechanism to overcome or neutralize extra-work social rela-tions of feminine disempowerment/sexuality. The frequent failure of such desexualization is evidenced by incidents of sexual harassment of care workers (Wolkowitz, 2012). The sexualization of women service workers may be exacerbated where workers' sexuality is constructed through customers' racialized stereotypes (see Kang, this volume).

In all these cases, workers conducting relatively mundane tasks are required to desexualize touch to avoid 'misinterpretation'. Strategies of desexualization may involve aesthetic clues, such as the white 'medical' gown of the beautician that marks beauty therapy as a treatment, not a sexual service (Oerton, 2004), or relocating the work, for instance the movement of therapeutic massage into complementary and alterna-tive therapy centres (Purcell, this volume). Desexualization also may be achieved verbally: by making rules explicit, through implicit clues, by preceding touch with a verbal description of an upcoming procedure, by establishing a relationship or through the strategic use of humour (Brown et al., 2011; Giuffre and Williams, 2000; Purcell, this volume). As Kang and Purcell show, however, it is difficult to verbally desexual-ize an encounter without undermining what Korczynski and Ott (2004) and Korczynski (this volume) term the 'enchanting myth of customer sovereignty'.

In various forms of sex work, a key part of the worker's emotional and physical labour is related to sexualizing the client's body. This might involve discursive framing: highlighting how 'good' the customer is at sexual activities, especially in sexually pleasing the worker, the praising of specific bodily attributes, how 'big' he is, or (in phone sex) his capacity to fulfil needs/desires (if worker and client were ever to be co-located). But in interactive sex work, this might also entail physical or embodied framing, with forms of touch deployed specifically to symbolically designate the worker's lust, even lack of control. This may simply be the light and suggestive touch employed by dancers/hostesses in sex work venues (Parreñas, 2010; Sanders, Cohen and Hardy, this volume). Alternatively, the embodiment of desire may be more complex, with prolonged and reciprocal worker–client sexual engagement (see Brents and Jackson, this volume). As such, production of a sexualized body-worked-upon is in stark contrast to most body work, in which workers work hard to desexualize the client's or patient's body.

The social organization of body/sex work labour processes

Commodification continually alters the social organization of body/sex work. This is because the commodification of body work (including sex work) transforms it into body labour, and produces two contradictory impulses: commoditization and individualization. Commoditization involves standardizing the service offered and, therefore, the labour processes. This necessitates standardization of the bodies-worked-upon so that they can be treated in standardized, labour-saving and cost-saving ways. Several chapters in this book highlight the process whereby commodification of bodily care work alters the ways in which workers work with patients and clients. The work activity itself is speeded up and fragmented (Diamond, 1992; James, 1992) and reorganized around conformity to written rules and rotas, which Campbell (2008) calls 'textualization'. In her study of Italian care homes, Rodeschini (this volume) demonstrates the ways in which the use of artificial nutrition removes the need for copresence during feeding. Commodified care work seems to seek to tame the unruly nature of variable and unpredictable bodily needs; for instance, through sophisticated technology (Rodeschini); by dealing with incontinence by putting adult care-home residents in diapers (Greener); or by establishing standardized rotas, which ignore individual needs and variations in these (Wibberley).

However, bodies are diverse and as Cohen (2011) points out there are constraints on labour process (re)organization where the body is the object of labour, which make it difficult to rationalize without leading to neglect. These constraints include a stickiness in the ratio of workers to bodies worked-upon, the need for co-presence combined with temporal unpredictability and bodily inviolability (the difficulty of dividing up the body-worked-upon) and that bodies comprise a highly varied and changeable material of production. As such, discussions in this book highlight both the perennial desire of capital, embodied in management, to standardize and rationalize labour for the greatest possible profit and the consequent contradictions and tensions for workers and for those worked-upon.

Those things that make bodies peculiarly difficult to standardize are the reason that in many forms of body work (outside of state subsidized sectors), there has been relatively little capital entry. Instead, small firms and self-employed workers seek to attract higher-end niche markets (in beauty services, sex work, aesthetic and holistic medicine) by responding to the individual needs of specific people and their bodies. The ways in which such individuation and personalization occur are discussed in greater detail in the following section. Notably, however, where strategies for attracting high-end consumers are unsuccessful, body work remains labour intensive and, as such, is also synonymous with low wages. For instance, hairstylists frequently rank at the bottom of wage scales in the United Kingdom.

In most labour processes, standardization and commoditization are facilitated by the introduction of technologies. In body work and sex work, technological change has had differing and somewhat bifurcating effects. Some types of body work are near impossible to perform remotely or with non-human machinery (Cohen, 2011); for example, a dental extraction or even the mundane activities of painting a fingernail. Moreover, as Greener highlights, even simple technologies like body hoists may actually slow down the labour process, and are unlikely to perfectly 'fit' all bodies, so their use in body work settings is inconsistent.

Absent the substitution of non-human for human labour, and despite continual attempts to divide the labour process (for example, reconfiguring the division between high-status doctors who diagnose, nurses who medically treat, care assistants who clean, and orderlies who move bodies), the ongoing requirement for co-presence has made concentrating body work in particular geographic locations difficult. Indeed, although it has been suggested that 'body work without bodies' is developing in medicine, where doctors examining laboratory results and scans may never see patients and instead (re)construct their bodies technologically in order to make a diagnosis (Atkinson, 1995), thus far only some kinds of body work have been moved to remote locations: largely diagnostic work (such as that involving scans) and advice work (May et al., 2005). In contrast, care work, or even the work involved in testing the body in order to conduct diagnosis (inserting a thermometer, drawing blood, scanning the body), as well as most aestheticizing services, continue to require co-presence. This requirement has implications for the geographies of body work as it means that body work requiring the most extended physically intimate contact is unlikely to be off-shored. This is notwithstanding the development of certain hubs and enclaves, often in the majority world, to which customers travel to receive body work, with sex and cosmetic surgery tourism being the most obvious examples (Holliday et al., forthcoming; Sanchez-Taylor, 2000). We also see increasing migratory flows of, largely but not exclusively, women from the majority world to minority world cities to perform body/sex work for those with more access to capital (McDowell, 2009).

In the sex industry, the transformative impact of new technologies has been more striking. Thus, as Fazzino documents (this volume), the dramatic cheapening and pervasive distribution of recording and broadcasting technologies (namely, the internet) have contributed to the widespread production and dissemination of 'amateur' pornography. This raises questions about whether this amounts to decommodification of sex and sexuality. Full discussion of this requires more space than is available here, but it is worth noting that the forms taken by amateur porn remain highly interwoven with the commodification of sex (for instance, pay-to-view websites). The centrality of the internet to these forms of sex work, and the extent to which the work has become truly 'mobile', dissociated from space/place, is in stark distinction to forms of interactive sex work (for instance, involving escorts). The latter, despite being increasingly marketed online, retain a strong connection to place, both because of the co-presence required for intercorporeality, but also because such work occurs within particular worksites (brothels, flats, streets) and particular regulatory constraints and boundaries.

Organization of the body/sex work labour process is also affected by status differentials between workers and bodies-worked-upon (Abel and Nelson, 1990; Wolkowitz, 2002), in relation to both their positioning within the body work interaction (patients queue to see doctors, not vice versa) as well as their relative status in the wider society. As Twigg et al. (2011: 178) note, the relationship between body status and labour process is profound. Class and other distinctions play out in embodied ways, with, for example, poor, ethnically 'other' or ageing bodies likely to smell, touch, and feel different. Therefore, the desirability of bodies-worked-upon varies in socially meaningful ways. Where body work is funded by the public sector, or where it is organized to serve more disadvantaged groups, workers encounter the most socially 'undesirable' and unappealing bodies. As Raghuram et al.'s (2011) study of geriatric medicine shows, where body work, even high-skill, highly paid body work, takes socially undesirable bodies as its object, it is often also performed by more socially disadvantaged groups.

The relations between workers and client, customers and patients

The ways in which the labour processes of body work and sex work are organized shape the relations between workers, clients and customers, as does the type of work and the consumer market. Body work interactions are structured very differently where workers are in direct economic relationships with their clients/patients/customers (for example, self-employment, own-account work, and even commission or tipping) than where body work is wholly funded by a third party (for example, the state); or where it is ultimately funded by the recipient, but the economic relationship between recipient and worker is indirect (for example, in private care homes where workers are employed by the home or in nightclubs where bouncers are employees of the venue). In all these cases, the incentive for employers to rationalize structures of employment, and the tensions of the rationaliztion process, are felt more strongly. On the other hand, when workers are independent contractors or otherwise dependent on customer/client repeat or prolonged interactions, there may be strong structural incentives to facilitate greater physical and emotional intimacy (Cohen, 2010; Sanders, Cohen and Hardy, this volume; Sanders and Hardy, 2012).

An advantage of exploring the three-way relationships (employer, worker, consumer) typical of service work (Macdonald and Sirianni, 1996) through a body work lens is that it highlights the ways in which the organization of work and workers' strategies affect and are affected by the embodiment of the encounter. In Chapter 2, Korczynski argues that the key social dilemmas (between worker and customer) are different where workers navigate different kinds of body work. Care workers, he suggests, face severe difficulties in maintaining the patient's or client's sense of autonomy, never mind 'sovereignty'. In contrast, work in aestheticizing services, involving adorning consumers' bodies, flattering and following consumers' wishes, poses potential threats to workers' dignity because the superiority of the service recipient is so accentuated. Korczynski does not, however, consider sex work, in which interactions within the upscale sex markets being produced by diversification take a variety of forms. In particular, threats to workers' dignity may be reduced where worker–client relations are more equal and extra-work sociability, even sensuality, overlap somewhat with work-based relations, something found both in sex work (Brents and Jackson, this volume; Sanders,

2005) and aestheticizing body labour in small firms (Furman, 1997; Van Leuven, 2002).

Where work is intimate obtaining and maintaining the participation or compliance of the client, customer or patient is necessary. Compliance may be secured with both verbal and tactile instruction (Toerien and Kitzinger, 2007). It may also involve the use of chairs, beds, straps or other equipment that moves the body-worked-upon into a suitable state to be worked-upon, often temporarily leaving the body prone or otherwise vulnerable (Wolkowitz, 2002). In this process, establishing and retaining trust is essential (Brown et al., 2011; Eayrs, 1993; Soulliere, 1997). In body/sex work, trust is facilitated by long-term worker–client relations (Cohen, 2010). For instance, Sanders (2008a) notes that a significant number of men who buy sex do not want to purchase what they consider an intimate interaction from 'a stranger', so therefore seek out a commercial partner with whom they can become physically, socially and perhaps emotionally familiar. Therefore, in the indoor sex markets (escorting, brothels, or working flats, for example) research has found that a third of customers become 'regulars' to the same sex worker over a period of time. These regulars engage in 'normalized' male sexual scripts such as romancing, flirting, social support and emotional interactions and the possibility of creating mutual sexual pleasures (Atchison et al., 2006; Monto, 2000; Sanders, 2008b).

The possibility of 'mutual intimacy' in any commercial marketplace is a huge topic and beyond the remit of this introduction. Yet, we note that it may both be true that sex workers do not have to experience intimacy to provide it (Zeilzer, 2005) and can, and sometimes do, gain intimacy and sexual pleasure from their work (Kontula, 2008). Not dissimilarly, workers involved in other body work may experience emotional engagement (Cohen, 2010) and more limited forms of pleasurable touch (Miller, this volume). One example of how important intimacy within sex work is to customers is provided by men with physical impairments. They describe how physical non-sexual interactions around touch, caressing and caring purchased through sex work are part of their 'human needs' that can be met in the marketplace (albeit illegally in most places), especially where few other intimate relationships are present (Sanders, 2007). These men seek romance and caressing, and in doing so upturn stereotypes of male purchasers of sex as driven purely by biological sex urges to seek rampant sexual encounters with as many women as possible.

While all forms of body work involve the worker in initiating touch and intimacy, in many examples of commercial sex work interactions, especially between escorts and customers, the customer is not a passive actor but rather is encouraged and expected to *interact* sexually and at times emotionally

(Hardy and Brents and Jackson, this volume). Brents and Jackson argue that some of the sex workers in their study represent these interactions as 'holistic' (relatively equal interactions involving mind and body), which echoes the understandings of holistic masseurs in Purcell's study (this volume). Nonetheless, most body/sex workers clearly bound their working lives from their non-working. For instance, sex workers in Cheung's study (this volume) set clear boundaries around touch and also taste.

In sex work, there are economic incentives for reciprocal bodily interactions and for allowing customers some control over touch; often as the price of the service increases, the more sexual touching is incorporated, especially where customers can touch intimately as well as being touched. For example, self-employed erotic dancers regularly allow, even encourage, customers to touch and interact with their body in the build up to (hustle) a performance of striptease as a way of drawing customers in to spend more (see Sanders, Cohen and Hardy, this volume). Even where the body is not present in telephone sex work (Selmi, this volume), sex workers employ narrative strategies to allow the customer to feel in control of the conversation. In this context, the standardized 'scripts' seen in call centres elsewhere in the service sector (Bain and Taylor, 2000) are notable by their absence. Here prolonged, and necessarily individualized, interactions are more profitable than efficient ones, and intimacy is the key to repeat custom.

In Chapter 2, Korczynski demonstrates that in sectors such as healthcare mutual interactions between the customer and the worker are less typical, particularly where customers are patients and are made passive by their health status and/or (social or physical) vulnerability. Interactions in these settings increasingly rely on routinized and standardized 'care' and treatment provided by a practitioner who ultimately is conditioned by institutional and organizational power relations (condensed, for instance, in 'the rota' governing domiciliary care, as Wibberley shows in Chapter 14). The division of labour within health and social care also means that patients commonly interact with multiple different workers, each of whom is required to produce a record of their interaction for each other (Greener, this volume). These records disembody and disaggregate the body-worked-upon; their insufficiency highlighted by repeated public calls for 'joined up care' (Cohen, 2011). In contrast to science-led medicalized care, therapeutic-led care and holistic interventions (Purcell, this volume) contain 'a more equalitarian view of practitioner-patient relations' (Twigg et al., 2011: 179) and seek to recombine body and mind, but such interventions comprise a small part of all body labour.

Where the patient's embodied integrity as a person is denied, and the organization of body work means that workers struggle to relate to the embodied patient as another subject, the contradictions of commodified body labour become particularly apparent. It is in these contradictions, Korczynski argues, that 'workers skilfully reclaim dignity, sometimes for themselves, sometimes for the service-recipient'. What is perhaps a bleaker alternative is depicted by Greener and Wibberley in their studies of care home and domiciliary work, in which workers 'responsible' for bodies cannot even complete the work required for bodily reproduction within the time allotted. In these circumstances, workers may provide additional unpaid labour and still not complete tasks adequately, yet they, as the human face of the institutions for which they work, shoulder the blame (from recipients, relatives or even the media) for the inhumanity of commodified care.

Resistance and consent

Identifying the characteristics of body/sex work sheds light on specific difficulties workers have in mitigating the negative consequences of the work and the possibilities for organized resistance. The first obstacle is that their work is often not recognized as work, with sex workers derided as either vulnerable or deviant, and care work naturalized as women's traditional role. As Stewart (this volume) shows, at present neither sex workers nor many care workers are able to access employment law protections that are supposed to protect the weaker party in employment contracts; rather, British public policy intends to impede the functioning of sex markets while protection in the field of social care is extended mainly to the elderly recipients of care, rather than workers. Similarly, Kang (2010) shows that health and safety controls in United States primarily protect customers, not workers. Moreover, bearing the stigma of 'dirty work', physical or moral, body work and sex work challenge the rhetoric of contemporary high-skill, high tech production – this work is not 'the future'. On the other hand, the intensity of this stigma may, as Cheung shows, be an incentive to delimit what labour workers are willing to perform and thereby facilitate small acts of resistance.

An additional obstacle for body work is that the sector remains labour intensive and funded largely by states with pathological commitments to austerity, or private consumers, often women, limited in the amount they can pay by their own, relatively modest earnings (Himmelweit, 2005). As such the viability of body/sex work is increasingly dependent upon the availability of unorganized, racialized, female labour unable to command high wages. In this context, improvements in earnings are particularly difficult to achieve.

There is nonetheless worker resistance, especially in large-scale care and medical settings (Armstrong and Armstrong, 2008; Diamond, 1992). Yet, as documented in the care sector (Lee-Treweek, 1997), informal resistance is hard to deploy without harm to care recipients. Wibberley (Chapter 14) shows that the unwillingness of workers to commit harm acts as a powerful motivation for quiescence (and extending working hours). Moreover, whereas other research has demonstrated the ways workers work with patients to ignore managers' standardized procedures and achieve a least worst outcome (Lopez, 2007), Greener's study in Chapter 6 suggests that sometimes the only outcome workers can achieve is one that harms at least some of those bodies they work upon and yet, it is workers who will be, and are regularly, judged to be 'callous' or 'uncaring'. Workers' personal sense of responsibility for others' bodies and fear of being represented as uncaring can easily undermine industrial possibilities. This is exemplified by the June 2012 industrial action by the British Medical Association (BMA) over pension reductions. Notwithstanding 'overwhelming' support for industrial action (for example, 84 per cent support from consultants; 92 percent from junior doctors [BMA.org.uk]), the BMA advised frontline services to 'remain open and fully staffed' and patients 'considering themselves in need of urgent attention' to be seen. Although the consideration of patient needs is admirable, unsurprisingly the action ended up as a damp squib, with the minority of doctors who formally took industrial action nonetheless at work and performing unpaid work.

First, the vulnerability of many recipients of body work highlights the need to incorporate physical as well as social vulnerability, power and control in analysis of the social relations of the labour process. More critically, in the context of resistance, the common dependence of some workers and bodies-worked-upon on the willingness of governments to fund services have led to suggestions that care workers' interests lie in making common cause and collective action with care recipients and their relatives (Boris and Klein, 2006; Razavi, 2007). This may be a necessary strategy across body/sex work.

Cheung (this volume) concentrates on the individual resilience that sex workers develop to mitigate and manage the negative consequences of working in sex work. This builds on existing research which charts sex workers' coping mechanisms, including the use of humour (Downe, 1999; Sanders, 2004), client screening (Kong, 2006; Sanders, 2005) and 'doubling' (Hubbard, 1999). Although resilience may differ from resistance (Katz, 2004), this contributes to the growing literature that seeks to outline the way in which sex workers resist repression or control through forms of micro-resistance. In contrast, Hardy (this volume; see also 2010) has shown that recognizing sex work as work and the possibilities for larger scale resistance, such as labour organizing, go hand in hand (see also Jenness, 1998; Kempadoo and Doezema, 1998). In arguing for recognition of the complexity of bodies in the production of sex work encounters, Hardy argues for nuanced strategies for challenging sex workers' conditions in work and the production of those conditions themselves by recognizing the ways in which class, gender, race, history and geography, amongst other factors, shape the intercorporeal nature of sex work and social life itself.

Conclusion

Contemporary labour processes oscillate around particular interactions with the body, shaped by the problems bodies present for the organization of the labour process. In this chapter, we have highlighted the variable ways in which bodies are worked with and on, and tried to show that assumptions about these bodies, including those about sexuality, are consequential. We have also highlighted variations around common constraints and possibilities, which exist insofar as the human body (and to some extent the animal body) is a unique and indivisible social and biological phenomenon, both subject and object, experiencing intractable needs and malleable pleasures, open to both gratification and abuse, care and discipline, and power and resistance. We have tried to show that differences in how body work and sex work are organized and experienced are part and parcel of increasing global inequality and the political economy of labour and life itself. Many workers described in this book are engaged in processes which enable bodies to survive, both in a literal sense, by feeding them and watering them, but also in a social sense through providing recognition and attention. As such, the shifting boundaries of body and sex work – between public and private spaces, between commodified and uncommodified and between paid and unpaid labour – has wide-ranging social implications.

In the chapters that follow, authors explore the different contexts in which body work and sex work occur, the constructions of the bodies of workers and clients, customers and patients, and the experiences of workers involved in those labour processes previously outlined. In Part I, which is entitled *Theorising Body/Sex Work*, the chapter following this Introduction is Marek Korczynski's *Touching Moments: An Analysis of the Skillful Search for Dignity within Body Work Interactions*. Korczynski locates his analysis of different types of body work (body care/maintenance, controlling body work and body aestheticizing work) within the wider literature on consumption in service work, especially the potential conflict between efficient production and customer enchantment, and indicates key tensions in body work.

In Chapter 3, *Equal to Any Other, but Not the Same as Any Other: the Politics of Sexual Labour, the Body and Intercorporeality*, Kate Hardy builds on existing understandings of the body in sex work and proposes that understanding sex work as 'intercorporeal' enables us to account for the complexity and diversity of the structures and experiences of sex work. Central to her argument is a concern with understanding existing sex worker politics and developing a terrain on which struggles over sex work – and work more generally – may be fought in the future.

In Part II, which is entitled *The Legal and Socio-Economic Contexts of Body Work/Sex Work*, the authors concentrate on how these contexts shape the position of workers and the labour process. In Chapter 4, Ann Stewart uses the example of the provision of commercial sex and caring for the vulnerable to consider the ways in which intimate, embodied and sexualized labour is regulated within UK law, how the relationships involved are understood within law, and the limitations of the existing regulatory norms and frameworks.

Next, in Chapter 5, Barb Brents' and Crystal Jackson's *Gender, Emotional Labour and Interactive Body Work* uses the context of Nevada's legal brothels as a case study to examine the ways that sex workers talk about their bodies and their labour. They argue that the body/work nexus must be understood as a body/emotion/work nexus involving a variety of dimensions assembled in different ways, even within similar jobs.

In Chapter 6, Joe Greener's focus is the consequences of the extensive privatization of the ownership and management of nursing homes on work and on care standards for the elderly residents. He examines some of the frontline effects for workers and residents of the struggling profit margins of Southern Cross, a British firm that acquired a large number of nursing homes before its financial collapse in 2011.

Finally, in Chapter 7, Teela Sanders, Rachel Cohen, and Kate Hardy's *Hairdressing/Undressing: Comparing Labour Relations in Self-Employed Body Work* provides a comparative analysis of body labour in two settings. Drawing on empirical studies, the authors explore how interactive service work is undertaken by both hairdressers and strippers to perform aesthetic, emotional and body labour for their customers.

Part III of the book, which is entitled *Sexualizing and Desexualizing Bodies in the Labour Process*, compares and contrasts the strategies of workers whose earnings depend on sexualizing their engagements with male clients with those working in mundane forms of body work, such as in nail salons or therapeutic massage, who struggle to desexualize their interactions. In Chapter 8, American researcher Lori Fazzino explores the body work women performers do to sexualize their own bodies. Fazzino's chapter, titled *Altered Bodies, Engineered Careers: The Effect of Body Technologies on Pornographic Performance*, compares professional and amateur women performers who appear in corporate as against do-it-yourself pornography.

In Chapter 9, *From Erotic Capital to Erotic Knowledge: Body, Gender and Sexuality as Symbolic Skills in Phone Sex Work*, Guilia Selmi discusses erotic capital and sexualized performance by sex workers through the medium of technology and voice. Absent the physical body or any corporeal engagement with the male customer, Italian phone sex workers translate sexual and emotional intercourse through voice, language, tone and narrative by drawing on a range of corporeal, sexual and gender resources.

Chapters 10 and 11 by Miliann Kang and Carrie Purcell each explore ways that women who undertake body work attempt to deflect sexualization that leads to sexual harassment. Kang, however, stresses that the sexualization of body work takes specifically racialized forms. Drawing on *The Managed Hand* (2010), her wider study of mainly Korean-owned nail salons in the United States, she argues that the manicurists she came to know were subject to sexualization not only because of the connotations of 'body labour' but because of what she calls 'racialized sexualization'. Purcell looks at the practice of Holistic Massage in a Scottish city in the context of what she argues is widespread devaluation of touch, despite its powerful immediacy. She argues that in attempting to deflect the sexualization of their work through recourse to an ideology of maternal care, female practitioners ended up naturalizing their skills.

In Part IV, entitled *Disciplining and Resistant Bodies,* the authors consider the ways in which workers' bodies and the bodies they care for are disciplined, and workers' resilience in the face of social hostility. In Chapter 12, Janet Miller's *Racing Bodies* uses the framework of body work to study stable-yard work in Britain, exploring both workers' interaction with the horses they care for and the work required on their own bodies. In Chapters 13 and 14, Giulia Rodeschini and Gemma Wibberley are both concerned with the ways in which care recipients' individual needs are denied, under conditions of standardization that reduce the need for temporally specific interactive body work. Rodeschini considers a trend in Italian nursing homes towards the adoption of artificial nutrition through a feeding tube inserted into the patient. Wibberley shows how the rota through which domiciliary care is timetabled, paced and curtailed to the bare minimum disciplines both workers themselves and the amount and kind of care they have time to provide.

Finally, in Chapter 15, Olive Cheung considers the resilience Hong Kong sex workers develop to cope with the 'dirty work' their work entails, both in terms of preventing and managing contact with bodily substances. Cheung details the levels and specificity of disgust sex workers experience, resist and develop strategies to control, as intimate bodily interactions with customers jar with cultural codes around physical contact. This contrasts with those sex workers who describe intimate body work as providing 'pleasure', including sexual excitement and satisfaction.

REFERENCES

Abel, E.K. and Nelson, M.K. (1990). *Circles of Care*. Albany: State University of New York Press.

Adkins, L. (1995). *Gendered Work: Sexuality, Family and the Labour Market*. Buckingham: Open University Press.

Anagnost, A. (2004). The Corporeal Politics of Quality. *Public Culture* 16(2): 189–208.

Armstrong, P. and Armstrong, H. (2008). *Critical to Care: The Invisible Women in Health Care*. Toronto: University of Toronto.

Atchison, C., Fraser, L. and Lowman, J. (1998). Men Who Buy Sex: Preliminary Findings of an Exploratory Study. *In* J. Elias, V. Bullough, V. Elias and J. Elders (Eds) *Prostitution: On Whores, Hustlers and Johns*. New York: Prometheus Books. Pp. 172–203.

Atkinson, P.A. *Medical Talk and Medical Work*. London: Sage.

Bain, P. and Taylor, P. (2000). Entrapped by the 'Electronic Panopticon'? Worker Resistance in the Call Centre. *New Technology, Work and Employment* 15(1): 2–18.

Bernstein, E. (2007). *Temporarily Yours: Intimacy, Authenticity and the Commerce of Sex*. Chicago: University of Chicago Press.

Bolton, S.C. (2005). Women's Work, Dirty Work: The Gynaecology Nurse as 'Other'. *Gender, Work & Organization* 12(2): 169–86.

Boris, E. and Klein, J. (2006). Organising Home Care. *Politics and Society* 34(1): 81–108.

Boris, E. and Parreñas, R.S. (Eds) (2010). *Intimate Labors: Cultures, Technologies, and the Politics of Care*. Stanford: Stanford University Press

Brents, B.G., Jackson, C.A. and Hausbeck, K. (2010). *The State of Sex: Tourism, Sex and Sin in the New American Heartland*. New York: Routledge.

Brewis, J. and Linstead, S. (2000). *Sex, Work and Sex Work*. London: Routledge.

Brown, P.R., Alaszewski, A., Swift, T. and Nordin, A. (2011). Actions Speak Louder Than Words: The Embodiment of Trust by Healthcare Professionals in Gynae-oncology. *Sociology of Health & Illness* 33(2): 280–95.

Butler, J. (1994). *Bodies That Matter*. London: Routledge.

Campbell, M. (2008). (Dis)Continuity of Care: Explicating the Ruling Relatons of Home Support. *In* M. DeVault (Ed.) *People at Work: Life, Power and Social Inclusion in the New Economy*. New York: NYU Press.

Cohen, R.L. (2008). Work Relations and the Multiple Dimensions of the Work-Life Boundary: Hairstyling at Home. *In* A. Haunschild, D.R. Eikhof and C. Warhurst (Eds) *Work Less, Live More?* London: Macmillan.

——— (2010). When It Pays to Be Friendly: Employment Relationships and Emotional Labour in Hairstyling. *Sociological Review* 58(2): 197–218.

——— (2011). Time, Space and Touch at Work: Body Work and Labour Process (Re)organisation. *Sociology of Health & Illness* 33(2): 189–205.

Crossley, N. (2001). *The Social Body*. London: Sage.

Diamond, T. (1992). *Making Gray Gold: Narratives of Nursing Home Care*. Chicago: University of Chicago Press.

▶

Downe, P.J. (1999). Laughing When It Hurts: Humour and Violence in the Lives of Costa Rican Prostitutes. *Women's Studies International Forum* 22(1): 63–78.

Eayrs, M.A. (1993). Time, Trust and Hazard: Hairdressers' Symbolic Roles. *Symbolic Interaction* 16(1): 19–37.

Evans, M. (2002). Real Bodies. *In* M. Evans and E. Lee (Eds) *Real Bodies: A Sociological Introduction.* Basingstoke: Palgrave Macmillan.

Feminist Fightback Collective (2011). Cuts Are a Feminist Issue. *Soundings* 49: 73–83.

Foucault, M. (1977). *Discipline and Punish: The Birth of the Prison*, trans. A. Sheridan. London: Allen Lane.

Furman, F.K. (1997). *Facing the Mirror: Older Women and Beauty Shop Culture.* New York: Routledge.

Gimlin, D. (2007). What Is 'Body Work'? A Review of the Literature. *Sociology Compass* 1(1): 353–70.

Giuffre, P.A. and Williams, C.L. (2000). Not Just Bodies. *Gender & Society* 14(3): 457–82.

Halford, S., Savage, M. and Witz, A. (1997). *Gender, Careers and Organization.* Basingstoke: Palgrave Macmillan.

Hardy, K. (2010). (Sex) Working Class Subjects: Integrating Sex Workers in the Argentine Labour Movement. *International Labour and Working Class History* 77(1): 89–108.

Harris, A. (2011). In a Moment of Mismatch: Overseas Doctors' Adjustments in New Hospital Environments. *Sociology of Health & Illness* 33(2): 308–20.

Hassard, J., Hollliday, R. and Willmott, H. (Eds) (2000). *Body and Organization.* London: Sage.

Hochschild, A.R. (1983). *The Managed Heart: Commercialization of Human Feeling.* Berkeley: University of California Press.

——— (2003). *The Commercialization of Intimate Life: Notes from Home and Work.* Berkeley: University of California Press.

Holliday, R., Hardy, K., Bell, D., Jones, M., Probyn, E. and Sanchez, T.J. (forthcoming). Beauty and the Beach. *In* D. Botterill (Ed.) *Medical Tourism and Transnational Health Care.* Basingstoke: Palgrave Macmillan.

Hubbard, P. (1999). *Sex and the City: Geographies of Prostitution in the Urban West.* Aldershot: Ashgate.

James, N. (1992). Care = Organization + Physical Labour + Emotional Labour. *Sociology of Health & Illness* 14(4): 488–509.

Jeffreys, S. (1997). *The Idea of Prostitution.* North Melbourne: Spinifex.

Jenness, V. (1998). *Making It Work: The Prostitutes' Rights Movement in Perspective.* New York: Aldine de Gruyter.

Kang, M. (2003). The Managed Hand: The Commercialization of Bodies and Emotions in Korean-Owned Nail Salons. *Gender and Society* 17(6): 820–39.

——— (2010). *The Managed Hand: Race, Gender, and the Body in Beauty Service Work.* Berkeley: University of California Press.

Katz, C. (2004). *Growing up Global: Economic Restructuring and Children's Everyday Lives.* Minneapolis: University of Minnesota Press.

▶

Kempadoo, K. and Doezema, J. (Eds) (1998). *Global Sex Workers: Rights, Resistance and Redefinition.* London and New York: Routledge.

Kingston, S. (2010). Intent to Criminalize: Men Who Buy Sex and Prostitution Policy in the UK. *In* K. Hardy, S. Kingston and T. Sanders (Eds) *New Sociologies of Sex Work.* Aldershot: Ashgate. Pp. 23–38.

Kong, S.K. (2006). What It Feels Like for a Whore: The Body Politics of Women Performing Erotic Labour in Hong Kong. *Gender, Work & Organization* 13(5): 409–34.

Kontula, A. (2008). The Sex Worker and Her Pleasure. *Current Sociology* 56(4): 605–20.

Korczynski, M. and Ott, U. (2004). When Production and Consumption Meet: Cultural Contradictions and the Enchanting Myth of Customer Sovereignty. *Journal of Management Studies* 41(4): 575–99.

Lawler, S. (1991). *Behind the Screens: Nursing, Somology and the Problem of the Body.* Melbourne: Churchill Livingstone.

Lee-Treweek, G. (1997). Women, Resistance and Care: An Ethnographic Study of Nursing Auxiliary Work. *Work, Employment & Society* 11(1): 47–63.

Lopez, S.H. (2007). Efficiency and the Fix Revisited: Informal Relations and Mock Routinization in a Nonprofit Nursing Home. *Qualitative Sociology* 30(3): 225–47.

Martin, E. (1994). *Flexible Bodies.* Boston: Beacon Press.

May, C., Finch, T., Mair, M. and Mort, M. (2005) Towards a Wireless Patient. *Social Science & Medicine* 61(7): 1485–94.

McDowell, L. (2009). *Working Bodies: Interactive Service Employment and Workplace Identities.* Chichester: Wiley-Blackwell.

Monto, M. (2000). Why Men Seek Out Prostitutes. *In* R. Weitzer (Ed.) *Sex for Sale.* London: Routledge. Pp. 67–83.

Oerton, S. (2004). Bodywork Boundaries: Power, Politics and Professionalism in Therapeutic Massage. *Gender, Work & Organization* 11(5): 544–65.

Otis, E. (2012). *Markets and Bodies: Women, Service Work and the Making of Inequality in China.* Stanford: Stanford University Press.

Parreñas, R.S. (2010). Cultures of Flirtation: Sex and the Moral Boundaries of Filipina Migrant Hostesses in Tokyo. *In* E. Boris and R.S. Parreñas (Eds) *Intimate Labors.* Stanford: Stanford Social Sciences. Pp. 132–47.

Pettinger, L. (2011). 'Knows How to Please a Man': Studying Customers to Understand Service Work. *Sociological Review* 59(2): 225–41.

Pilcher, K. (2012). Performing in a Nighttime Leisure Venue. *Sociological Research Online* 17(2): 19.

Raghuram, P., Bornat, J. and Henry, L. (2011). The Co-marking of Aged Bodies and Migrant Bodies: Migrant Workers' Contribution to Geriatric Medicine in the UK. *Sociology of Health & Illness* 33(2): 321–35.

Razavi, S. (2007). *The Political Economy of Care in a Developing Context.* UNRISD Research Institute for Social Development, Gender and Development Programme, Paper 1.

▶

Rivers-Moore, M. (2011). Imagining Others: Sex, Race and Power in Transnational Sex Tourism. *ACME: International E-Journal for Critical Geographies* 10(3): 392–411.

Sanchez-Taylor, J. (2001). 'Dollars Are a Girl's Best Friend?' Female Tourists' Sexual Behaviour in the Caribbean. *Sociology* 83(1): 42–59.

Sanders, T. (2007). The Politics of Sexual Citizenship: Commercial Sex and Disability. *Disability & Society* 22(5): 439–55.

—— (2008a). *Paying for Pleasure: Men Who Buy Sex.* Cullompton: Willan.

—— (2008b). Male Sexual Scripts: Intimacy, Sexuality and Pleasure in the Purchase of Commercial Sex. *Sociology* 42(1): 400–17.

—— (2005). *Sex Work: A Risky Business.* Cullompton: Willan.

—— (2004). The Risks of Street Prostitution: Punters, Police and Protesters. *Urban Studies* 41(8): 1703–17.

Sanders, T. and Hardy, K. (2012). Devalued, Deskilled and Diversified: Explaining the Proliferation of Strip Clubs in the UK. *British Journal of Sociology* 63(3): 513–32.

Scarry, E. (1985). *The Body in Pain.* Oxford: Oxford University Press.

Shilling, C. (2005). *The Body in Culture, Technology and Society.* London: Sage.

Simpson, R. (2009). *Men in Caring Occupations: Doing Gender Differently.* Basingstoke: Palgrave Macmillan.

Simpson, S., Slutskaya, N., Lewis, P. and Höpfl, H. (Eds) (2012). *Dirty Work: Concepts and Identities.* Basingstoke: Palgrave Macmillan.

Soulliere, D. (1997). How Hairstyling Gets Done in the Hair Salon. *Michigan Sociological Review* 11: 41–63.

Tarr, J. (2011). Educating with the Hands: Working on the Body/Self in Alexander Technique. *Sociology of Health & Illness* 33(2): 252–65.

Thompson, P. (1989). *The Nature of Work.* Basingstoke: Palgrave Macmillan.

Thompson, P. and Smith, C. (Eds) (2009). *Working Life: Renewing Labour Process Analysis.* Basingstoke: Palgrave Macmillan.

Toerien, M. and Kitzinger, C. (2007). Emotional Labour in Action: Navigating Multiple Involvements in the Beauty Salon. *Sociology* 41(4): 645–62.

Twigg, J. (2000). Carework as a Form of Bodywork. *Ageing and Society* 204: 389–41.

—— (2006). *The Body in Health and Social Care.* Basingstoke: Palgrave Macmillan.

Twigg, J., Wolkowitz, C., Cohen, R.L. and Nettleton, S. (2011). Conceptualising Body Work in Health and Social Care. *Sociology of Health & Illness* 33(2): 171–88.

—— (Eds) (2011). *Body Work in Health and Social Care: Critical Themes, New Agendas.* Chichester: Wiley-Blackwell. Originally published as Issue 33(2) of *Sociology of Health & Illness.*

Van Leuven, L.C. (2002). *When Frames Collide: Personalized Service Work and the Negotiation of Relational Boundaries.* Unpublished doctoral dissertation, UCLA, Los Angeles.

Wainwright, E., Marandet, E. and Rizvi, S. (2011). The Means of Correct Training: Embodied Regulation in Training for Body Work among Mothers. *Sociology of Health & Illness* 33(2): 220–36.

▶

Warhurst, C. and Nickson, D. (2009). 'Who's Got the Look?': Emotional, Aesthetic and Sexualized Labour in Interactive Services. *Gender, Work & Organization* 16(3): 385–404.

Witz, A., Warhurst, C. and Nickson, D. (2003). The Labour of Aesthetics and the Aesthetics of Organization. *Organization* 10(1): 33–54.

Wolkowitz, C. (2002). The Social Relations of Body Work. *Work, Employment & Society* 16(3): 497–510.

——— (2006). *Bodies at Work*. London: Sage.

——— (2012). '*Flesh and Stone*' Revisited: The Body Work Landscape of South Florida. *Sociological Research Online*, Special Issue on 'Visualising Landscapes of Work and Labour', 17(2): 26. Available at http://www.socresonline.org.uk/17/2/26.html.

Wolkowitz, C. and Warhurst, C. (2010). Embodying Labour. *In* P. Thompson and C. Smith (Eds) *Working Life*. Basingstoke: Palgrave Macmillan. Pp. 223–43.

Zelizer, V. (2005). *The Purchase of Intimacy*. Princeton: Princeton University Press.

Touching Moments: An Analysis of the Skilful Search for Dignity within Body Work Interactions

Marek Korczynski

In this chapter, I theorize some important elements of that which is beautiful in the enactment of body work by workers. There are various forms of behaviour that deserve to be both celebrated and analysed in the processes of body work interactions, but underlying these various forms is often a common social structure. Beauty lies primarily in the way workers skilfully reclaim dignity, sometimes for themselves and sometimes for the service-recipient, just where the tensions and contradictions of body work interactions are at their most intense. I label these points *touching moments*.

The argument in this chapter is structured as follows. I begin by noting that body work is a subset of service work. This means that we can usefully look to analytical tools that have aided the analysis of service work to also potentially aid the analysis of body work. In particular, seeing consumption in body work interactions as framed by the enchanting myth of customer sovereignty can be useful. This points to the way in which the social meaning of the body may relate to sovereignty in terms of autonomous choice and sovereignty in terms of relational superiority. Key forms of tension in body work interactions emerge from differences between these social meanings, relating to sovereignty, and the contextual social meanings of the body within three distinct types of body work interactions – body care/maintenance work, controlling body work and body aestheticizing work. I explore distinct types of tensions within these three types of interaction and show with the aid of ethnographic studies how body workers can and often do mediate these tensions through touching moments. In the conclusion, I call for the sociology of body work to develop an analysis of the factors that promote and obstruct the playing out of these touching moments.

Body work, service work and the enchanting myth of customer sovereignty

Within the sociology of work, categorizations of types of work are often constructed according to specific forms of the labour process. The labour process constitutes the material base around which other forms of social relations come to be configured. Using definitions of service work and body work based on the labour process, we can understand the relationship between these two categories of work. Service work is usefully defined as work in which interaction with a service-recipient is a central part of the labour process (Korczynski, 2009). Twigg et al. (2011) define body work as work involving a direct focus on the body of a service-recipient. Therefore, it is clear that body work is a particular form of service work. Body work is a subset of service work in which the form of the interaction with the service-recipient centres on the service-recipient's body. Korczynski (2009) estimates that 28 per cent of the UK labour force are employed as service workers and Cohen (2011) has estimated that 10 per cent of the UK labour force are employed in body work occupations. Although these figures are not directly comparable, these estimates point to body work being an important type of service work.[1]

It is useful to think of body work as a type of service work, because it points to the importance of using ways of conceptualizing service work interactions to facilitate the analysis of body work interactions. So far, the literature on body work understandably has tended to emphasize the specificities of body work and concentrates on developing its separate analysis. There is a relative lack of engagement among many body work writers with the wider literature on service work. A wider aim of this chapter is to show that the analysis of body work can be aided by engaging with the wider literature on service work and that such an approach can still take into account important specific characteristics of body work.

Service work, as defined above, involves simultaneous production and consumption. What the worker does is part of what the service-recipient consumes. Therefore, in analysing social relations of service work interactions (and, thus, body work interactions), we need to consider the frames set not only by the organization of production, but also by the *organization of consumption*. In this chapter, given the constraints of space, I focus mainly on analysing the frame of consumption. In Korczynski and Ott (2004), I argue that the *enchanting myth of customer sovereignty* tends to be promoted across service settings. Although norms of customer sovereignty are more strongly culturally and historically associated with some sectors than others (e.g. restaurants in comparison to state welfare services), it is argued that these norms have now come to resonate across all sectors to a significant degree. I lay out the key elements in the concept of the enchanting myth of customer sovereignty before bringing out its relevance to the analysis of body work interactions.

Before examining this concept in detail, it is necessary to step back and consider why service organizations promote this myth. As a number of authors have pointed out, the point of interaction between service workers and consumers is tension-laden in that it brings together two arenas, production and consumption, which are often culturally and spatially dislocated. Production arenas tend to be structured by logics of rationalization in the pursuit of efficiency and are arenas in which motifs of discipline and control are written large. By contrast, consumption is an arena in which motifs of freedom, absence of constraint, pleasure and desire tend to dominate (Gabriel and Lang, 2006). Korczynski and Ott's (2004) key thesis is that at the point of service consumption, where customers interact with front line service workers, management seek to manage the underlying contradiction between the realms of production and consumption by promoting the consumption *of the enchanting myth of customer sovereignty* during the service interaction. This form of enchantment is promoted such that within the interaction it appears to the customer that s/he is sovereign, while space is also created for the worker to guide the customer through the constraints of production.

The intellectual origins of the concept of enchantment are in Weber's argument that the processes of rationalization enveloping the modern world lead to disenchantment. Campbell (1987) aptly argues against the death of enchantment thesis in his key book with the deliberately iconoclastic title: *The Romantic Ethic and the Spirit of Modern Consumerism*. Ritzer (1999), Jenkins (2000) and Baerenholdt (2010) take this further by arguing that processes of enchantment are actually fundamental to contemporary 'Disneyized' (Bryman, 2003) and 'experience' economies (Pine and Gilmore, 1999). The concept of enchantment is a useful one because it implies active agency on the part of the enchanted. A storyteller cannot enchant a passive audience. There are two levels of knowing operating while the process of enchantment unfolds. The process of enchantment suspends disbelief – a process that a number of writers see as central to consumer behaviour. Although individual customers, at some level, may know that notions of their sovereignty are mythical, the fact they may still go along with this myth reflects the 'distinctively modern faculty, the ability to create a illusion which is known to be false but felt to be true' (Campbell, 1987: 78). Consumers may feel that they are sovereign and at the same time, know that they are not. The enchantment that service firms promote to individual consumers at the point of interaction with service workers is that of a sense of their sovereignty. Korczynski and Ott (2004) discuss sovereignty in a modern and pre-modern sense. In the modern sense, it relates to the neoclassical economics figure of the sovereign consumer. Central to this sense of sovereignty is the status of the customer as an autonomous choice maker. In the pre-modern sense, it relates to the relational superiority and status of importance of the sovereign who reigns over his/her subjects.

For an everyday illustration of how the enchanting myth of customer sovereignty is promoted, consider this scene in a restaurant: a waiter approaches the customer who just entered and asks, 'Would you like to follow me this way, Sir/Madam?' Here, we have the customer positioned as a relational superior (s/he is addressed as 'Sir/Madam') and as an autonomous choice maker (s/he is given the choice of whether to follow the waiter). Further, even as the phrase enchants the customer, it also allows the worker to guide the customer through the rationalized constraints of production (the customer has to go to table 43 because of the organization of staff that evening). Service organizations promote the enchanting myth of customer sovereignty in three clear ways. First, there is the key role for the 'menu' (Korczynski and Ott, 2006). 'Menu' here refers to ritualized presentation to the customer of a range of choices. The menu is created to enchant and appeal to the customer, and it does this not only substantively through the descriptions of the available choices, but also formally through the placing of the customer as the autonomous figure who chooses between available alternatives. In a restaurant, the ritualized emphasis on autonomous choice can make the act of choosing as delicious as the actual food consumed. Second, the enchanting myth of sovereignty is promoted by the deployment of empathetic emotional labour. Service workers are directed to empathize with customers; they are expected to treat customers as if they are 'personal guests' in their own homes (Hochschild, 1983). Therefore, customers are presented with statements such as, 'I know how you feel, but I'm afraid that this is the policy', which create feelings of importance for the customers while also directing customers to follow the rationalized constraints of production. Aesthetic labour (Nickson et al., 2001) also promotes the enchanting myth of sovereignty. Paules (1991) convincingly argues that the managerially defined dress codes and uniforms common in many forms of service work serve the symbolic role of casting the front line worker as a subordinate to the customer, who is left to dress as he or she pleases. Uniforms and appearances here create the *dressings* of customer sovereignty. The promotion of the enchanting myth of customer sovereignty has become so entrenched within the service economy that it sets an overall normative frame for all service interactions.

The body and sovereignty

For the analysis of body work interactions, we need to consider how the enchanting myth of sovereignty relates to the body of the service-recipient.

The body is intimately connected with the sense of autonomy in the autonomous choice maker aspect of sovereignty. It is widely acknowledged in the considerable literature that the body in Western modernity is a highly individualized and demarcated one (Shilling, 2003: 131). For instance, Falk (1994) writes that in modernity the body has become an increasingly closed, demarcated one, compared to the more open and connected body of pre-modernity, and Foucault's (1997) explorations of the technologies of the self have given rise to a whole field of research examining self-building projects of the modern individual which focuses on the body. In modern societies, 'keep your hands off me' has replaced John Donne's 'no man is an island unto himself' as the touchstone of the relationship between the body and autonomy. One way in which this has become manifest has been in the rise of the concept of 'personal space'. Personal space is a socially defined space in which the demarcated body has the comfort of separation from others. Widding Isaksen (2002) argues that this closed, separated conception of the body is primarily tied to masculinity, but it must also be acknowledged that a central part of feminist political agendas has been the establishment of the woman as the sovereign of her own body. Overall, the individualizing processes within Western modernity have been deeply connected with the body such that one of the key social meanings of the body has become that of a carrier of the autonomous self, as the site for self-directed choice.

The body can also be intimately tied to sovereignty in terms of relational superiority and a sense of importance. The body of the sovereign had servants waiting upon, washing, massaging, dressing, and adorning it. Such body work interactions featured not only functional task completion but also the playing of clear social meanings of the superior body attended to by the social inferior. Contemporary body work interactions featuring similar functional task completion may be overlain by these social meanings of superiority of the body attended to and the inferiority of those who do the attending.

These social meanings of the body of the service-recipient – linked to the autonomous choice maker and relational superiority aspect of sovereignty – are accentuated within the promotion of the enchanting myth of customer sovereignty in body work interactions. It is how these meanings are strengthened or come to clash with other contextual social meanings within body work that underpins key tensions within body work interactions.

Social meanings of the body and types of body work

The framing of consumption set by the promotion of the enchanting myth of customer sovereignty has important implications for the analysis of the key points of tension within body work interactions. There are important *contextual* differences across types of body work in the competing social meanings of the service-recipient's body. In this analysis, I concentrate exclusively on the body work interactions that do not include sex work.[2] The analysis proceeds by disaggregating (non-sex work) body work into three main types – body care/maintenance work, body controlling work and body aestheticizing work. In each, there are distinctive contextual social meanings attached to the body of the service-recipient which is worked upon. It is accepted that in the empirical reality of body work occupations, there may be considerable grey areas, with some occupations straddling across types, and there will be cases where even within a specific body work interaction such clear distinctions are not easy to discern. Nevertheless, the creation of categories and typologies are often crucial in aiding analysis. Therefore, these categories are put forward as ideal-types, theoretical constructions as heuristic devices to aid analysis (Eliaeson, 2000).

The central argument advanced is that by examining the relationship between the contextual social meanings in these three areas and the meanings of the body as an arena for sovereignty (prioritized within the enchanting myth of customer sovereignty), we can see key points of

Table 2.1 Three types of body work interaction and tensions in the social meaning of the body of the service-recipient

Type of Body Work	Occupational Examples	Key Contextual Social Meaning of Service-Recipient's Body	Key Point of Tension in Relation to Enchanting Myth of Sovereignty
Body Care/ Maintenance Work	Nurse, care home assistant	Body parts as objects of medical rationality	Body as holder of autonomy intruded upon
Controlling Body Work	Bouncers, prison guards	Emphasis on body as immanent holder of potential violence and deviancy	Body as holder of autonomy intruded upon
Aestheticizing Body Work	Hairdressers; manicurists	Emphasis on body as site of adornment	Potential threat to dignity of worker from adornment accentuating superiority of service-recipient

tension within body work interactions. The discussions of the tensions within the three types of body work interactions draw on key ethnographic studies in relevant occupations. As Twigg et al. (2011) note, ethnography, in which observation of the body work interactions takes place, is important to properly understand the texture of body work interactions. Each type of body work interaction is examined in turn, and the ways in which touching moments may be enacted to mediate the highlighted tensions are discussed.

Body care/maintenance work involves work where the worker attends to the physical functioning of the service-recipient's body. An important social meaning of the body in such interactions derives from the primacy of Western medical rational knowledge, which prioritizes scientific, objective and impersonal knowledge that is applied to the service-recipient's body as object. At its most extreme, this approach focuses upon specific body parts as objects to be acted upon. As Twigg et al. (2011) note, there is a strong division of labour within the playing out of this medical rationality to service-recipients' bodies. Senior professionals tend to enact the mental conception of diagnosis and have relatively little direct contact with the patient's body, whereas the physical execution of tasks, involving much higher levels of direct contact with the patient's body, are central to job roles of lower status occupations such as nurses and home care aides. Given that these lower status occupations have the most intense forms of body work, I concentrate the analysis here. There is clearly considerable tension between the body as an object of medical knowledge and the body as a carrier of autonomy. This tension becomes manifest at the points where the worker touches the patient's body. The touch of the worker exposes the myth of the body as the carrier of autonomy. Given the deep embedding of the body as a carrier of autonomy within modern societies, such a touch can, therefore, be deeply destabilizing and troubling for the patient, with patients experiencing a loss of self and dignity through the application of this touch.

It is the reaction of the body worker to these points that has a profound influence on how the patient experiences the body work interaction. A number of studies have shown how some body care/maintenance occupations inhabit powerful organizational structures, which structure their response to be that of the cold, unfeeling hand of bureaucracy (Foner, 1994). The application of the touch simply becomes part of the necessary task completion, with a focus on efficient throughput of bodies worked upon. In such settings, service-recipients are left alone to cope with or suffer the effects of the unmediated intrusion upon their body as a carrier of autonomy.[3]

However, there have also been some studies which show that deep humanity can be enacted by body workers at these points. These are the first and most profound example of touching moments within body work interactions that I seek to elucidate. They are the points where the tensions heightened by the physical touch on the patient's body are mediated by the skilful enactment of emotional labour. In Huebner's (2007) careful study of nursing, this pattern of behaviour is labelled as the enactment of 'professional intimacy'. A sample of quotes shows the texture of these touching moments. Huebner quotes Carey, a new nurse, who describes her thoughts regarding intimacy and patient care, and argues for the importance of touching patients in a way that involves intimacy:

> You are here in a bed. I'm here. You have to touch them. It's what you do. It's part of the healing. And you don't want to touch people like, 'Ooh icky. I can't touch you'. If they feel that way, how are they going to get better, heal? The bottom line is you have to touch them; you have to put your hands on them. It can be intimate, I think it should be. I don't think it should be so strict and rigid.

Huebner also quotes Tonia, another nurse, on the need for intimacy:

> Most of it is intimate. I mean you're touching other people's body parts. It's intimate. You've got to touch the person. You know how uncomfortable is it for a stranger to touch you?

Here, Tonia is connecting the need for intimacy in the periods of touching the patient's body with an understanding that something potentially profoundly destabilizing is occurring for the patient. The nurse comes close to naturalizing the idea that the touch of a stranger is uncomfortable. But the touch of the stranger is not naturally uncomfortable, it is only uncomfortable in relation to the specific contemporary social meanings of the body, accented by the myth of customer sovereignty. My argument is that discomfort primarily arises because the touch intrudes upon the body as carrier of the person's autonomy. Huebner goes on to quote Jill, a new nurse, who relates the enactment of empathetic emotional labour to the intrusion into the 'personal space' of the patient that occurs in body space. As I argued earlier, 'personal space' is one of the key contemporary expressions of the demarcated body as a carrier of autonomy:

> Intimate is a strange word because there are so many different meanings, but I guess it would be a good way to describe patient care. Yes, I do think

it [nursing] is intimate because you are dealing with people's bodies and that's the most – that's personal space.

Touching, in both senses of the word, is palpable in the description given by Anna, another nurse:

When I asked Anna if nursing is intimate, she responded, 'Yes, because you are touching bodies and I know this is private. This is why I reassure them, because caring for them is intimate. I want to make them comfortable'.

There is a very strong correspondence between Huebner's analysis and that of Savage (1995), who also studied nursing. What Huebner labels 'professional intimacy', Savage calls 'nursing intimacy'. They are both describing touching moments. One nurse quoted by Savage echoes the nurses studied by Huebner:

The closer I feel to a patient, if have to do something that's particularly intimate or particularly unpleasant, then I find it much easier because I can say to the patient, 'Look, this is really awful and I'm sorry if it's embarrassing for you' and they say, if we are close and they know me, 'Well, it's OK, it's you. I know you', sort of thing. (p. 63)

Just as both senses of the word touching come into play, so do both senses of 'closeness':

One nurse said she would explain 'closeness' as: 'well, I suppose in terms of physical closeness, and then there's closeness that comes from knowing somebody...so when I say "closeness", I mean both really.' (p. 63)

As Twigg et al. (2011) also note, this skilful and humane mediation of the tensions of body work is often seen as having the instrumental advantage of allowing an easy application of caring body work. Savage (1995) adds another dimension to our understanding of the beauty of these patterns of behaviour when she shows that it is not only the skilful enactment of emotional labour that helps to mediate tensions, it is the use of the expressive or *emotional touch* that can be important. Savage notes that 'this research did not set out to study touch, yet it was found during fieldwork...that nurses use of expressive touch was so remarkable that it became an important focus of the study' (p. 69). One nurse reflected on the importance of emotional touch to mediate the intrusions of cold medical technology upon the body of the patient:

You see lots of people giving IV drugs, and [they are] just sitting there, watching the drugs go in. I feel sure [patients] would want some human contact as well, so I just put my hand on the side of their hand, or just stroke the vein above where the drug is going in. (p. 70)

If we are moved by the descriptions of these touching moments, Savage's book reassures us that we are not alone in this reaction. A senior nurse is quoted:

We had one particular man who was very distressed one day, and we had a student nurse standing next to me – and the patient said something to me, and...I just kind of stroked his cheeks [as if to say], you know, 'Poor fellow'. And this nurse next to me started crying! I said, 'What's wrong with you?' and she said, 'Oh, that was so beautiful!'. I said, 'What?...What have I done?' I thought I had done something wrong! She said, 'The way you touched that person'. (p. 72)

Lawler (1991: 125) coins the term 'somological' to describe the touching moments where the functional touch is complemented by emotional labour and emotional touch. The somological is when 'the nurse must "do for" the body, while simultaneously recognising personhood'.

The key tension within *controlling body work* also involves the actual or potential touch of the body worker upon the other's body, implying an intrusion upon the body as a holder of autonomy. Controlling body work involves the application of touch to restrain the body of the other, which is judged to be potentially violent or deviant in some way. The main example of controlling body work I examine is the work of the 'bouncer', a type of security guard employed at venues such as bars, nightclubs or concerts to provide security, check legal age and oversee customers' behaviour. Outside of the standardized setting of the search, the touch by the body worker upon the customer is often taken by the customer to be an intrusion upon their autonomy.[4] Therefore, the reaction to such a touch is often a physical attempt by the other to reassert such a sense of autonomy. If we add to this abstract pattern the heightened sense of sovereignty that comes from being a customer in a place of hospitality (bar or club, for instance); the tight intermingling of forms of masculinity with autonomy of the body; and the lubrication from restraining social norms that is imbibed with alcohol, then we have exactly the tension-ridden situation that faces bouncers in their work in the bars and clubs of Britain. Bouncers know that a physical attempt by the other party to reassert a sense of autonomy is likely to come in the form of violence directed towards them. It is of little surprise that Hobbs et al.'s rich ethnographic study, *Bouncers* (2003), finds that bouncers lay considerable emphasis on having a dual strategy of 'talking nicely' (p. 138), and if this fails, then of resorting to strong physical force. The tensions of the body work interaction, the social meaning of the touch on the drunken male customer's body, tend to preclude the middle ground of gentle touch symbolizing restraint. There is little space for touching moments in the work of bouncers. Steve North, a bouncer interviewed in the study, had developed a verbal mode of expressing the bouncers' dual strategy:

> 'Excuse me sir can you just behave yourself, we don't tolerate that sort of fucking business in here'. And you always put an F-word in or a strong language word in at the end. You're very polite, very direct and at the end you just throw it in, as if to say 'I'm not a fucking schmuck'. It's a trick of the trade. 'I'm basically being nice to you. Now if you don't want to be fucking nice, I can be fucking nasty, so please yourself'. (p. 140)

Here are nice words that also carry the threat of direct physical restraint. Contradictory words are used to manage the contradictions and tensions of the situation. Also important to the deployment of this dual strategy by bouncers is that they are able to project a bodily image to the customers that the threat of physical restraint is a very real one. Thus, bouncers pay considerable attention to their physique, clothes and comportment to ensure that these are symbolic of this dual strategy. We have the common sight of the male bouncer dressed in a suit, which is used to accentuate the physical power of his body and indicate the readiness to use this power. These are forms of aesthetic labour that carry exactly the same meaning as the verbal strategy of Steve North, the bouncer previously quoted. Hobbs et al.'s study unambiguously shows that if the 'nice' part of the strategy fails, then bouncers readily resort to direct physical restraint to regulate the body of the identified deviant customer. The social structuring of the tensions of controlling body work mean that touching moments are all but absent in such settings.

When we move to consider *aestheticizing body work*, such as that practised by hairdressers and manicurists, then the key form of tension within the body work interaction is of a different kind. Here, the tension centres around the relational superiority aspect of sovereignty. Within these interactions, the body of the service-recipient is situated as a site of adornment. Here the adornment of the service-recipient by the body worker has the strong potential to accentuate the sense of importance and relational superiority that is part of the meta framework of the enchanting myth of customer sovereignty that overlays contemporary service interactions.[5] Further, many organizational symbols within such aestheticizing body work sites serve to accent this sense of sovereignty – not least, the 'thronelike pedicure chairs' observed by Kang (2010: 144). The prime problem facing body workers is to create a framing of this interaction which allows the service-recipient to experience a sense of importance, but which does not position the workers as socially subservient inferiors. Workers act to protect their sense of dignity in terms of equality of recognition and respect. Kang's illuminating ethnography of manicurists, *The Managed Hand*, suggests that one of the key ways that workers protect their dignity is to seek to socially embed the interaction. Thus, manicurists (and hairdressers) engage in extended engaged conversations with service-recipients (p. 134). For hairdressers, Cohen (2010) suggests that a key motivation for such extended conversations is to tie the service-recipient into an ongoing relationship with the hairdressers, so that continued custom is promoted. My argument is that this may be part of the motivation, but another key motivation comes from the way in which 'positive microinteractions take the sting out of subservience', as Kang acutely puts it (p. 159). Kang illustrates this with an example of a manicurist named Charlie:

> As she had with many of her customers, Charlie had developed a special relationship with Pattie, a hospital social worker and chronic nail biter. These two women had forged a relationship as customer and manicurist that was mutually supportive and humanizing, and they attempted to rewrite the dynamics of service as a story of genuine friendship. (p. 158)

Conversations and chats reframe the interaction away from the superior being adorned by the inferior to an interaction between two parties who share forms of interest, whether it is films, books, television programmes, holidays, news stories, cars, clothes and so on. Finding these areas of shared interest implicitly places the body worker as a party receiving equality of recognition and respect. Kang points out that the mutual forms of reciprocity that pertain to social relations outside of economic exchanges do not exist in the structure of the manicurist-customer relationship, but the conversations allow a reframing of this structural relationship. The extended conversation is one of the key ways in which the body worker holds tight to his/her dignity. While some customers may grate against what they perceive as the 'banal' and the 'inane' in the hairdresser's chat, it is perhaps wiser to celebrate the lightness of this reclaiming of dignity within the structure of the body work interaction that is heavy with tension.[6] These are the touching moments of the body aestheticizing occupations.

Conclusion

There are touching moments in many body work occupations – the points where workers skilfully mediate the tensions within body work interactions to reclaim dignity, sometimes for the service-recipient and sometimes for themselves. Touching moments may come in the form of the texture of the touch given by the worker to the service-recipient, be manifest in the emotional labour in workers' expressions of care or even in the light and breezy conversations of the hairdresser or manicurist. In this chapter, I have attempted to highlight and analyse these touching moments. I argued that key points of tensions within body work interactions usually arise from different social meanings of the body that are embedded in the meta framing of the enchanting myth of sovereignty that structures service interactions generally, and those that pertain contextually to specific types of body work interaction. For instance, most starkly, in body care interactions, tensions arise from the simultaneous social meaning of the body as sovereign, as carrier of autonomy and the social meaning of the body as object of medical, rational knowledge.

It appears that touching moments are pivotal elements in the texture of body work interactions. When they are absent, body work interactions tend to leave one of the parties in want of dignity; when they are present, both the body worker and the service-recipient emerge with a greater sense of humanity. In service economies, in which body work occupations continue to grow apace, the relative absence or presence of touching moments tells us much about the texture of our societies. Given this, we need to know much more about the organizational and normative factors that promote and obstruct the enactment of touching moments. We need also to know more about the active role of the service-recipient in the playing out of touching moments. Overall, we need to move to a sociology of body work that can not only highlight touching moments and celebrate them, but which can also analyse them and offer suggestions for interventions that can help such touching moments to flourish.

Notes

1 One factor is that the estimates use different databases relating to the labour force. The other complicating factor is that Korczynski's definition of service excludes senior professionals who interact with service-recipients, whereas Cohen's definition of body work includes relevant professional occupations.
2 Sex work is a distinct subset of body work. In direct sex work, it is not only the service-recipient's body which is worked upon, but crucially it is the worker's body that is worked with. This makes its separate analysis important.
3 A key way in which the service-recipient may cope in such settings is to enact a form of mind-body dualism in which s/he distances himself/herself from his/her body and its social meanings.

4 Within the search by the body worker on the body and clothing of the customer, the tensions of this process are primarily managed by body workers enacting a standardized, bureaucratic form of touch. The standardized signalling of the search, and the standardized process of the search, signals to the service-recipient to temporarily disassociate his/her body from its meaning as a carrier of autonomy. This is most plain within airport security body searches.

5 My analysis of body aestheticizing work concentrates on those interactions where the social position of the customer is above that of the worker. A majority of body work interactions would appear to have this texture. But there are variations in this social positioning, with some body work interactions existing in which this main social positioning is reversed. For instance, where the body worker is tied to clear signals of specialist knowledge, market niches or brands, then the framing of the interaction may position the body worker as the social superior. There is little research to allow us to consider the ways in which touching moments may or may not be played out in such settings.

6 See for instance, a web forum page discussing the discomforts that accompany a visit to the hairdresser (http://www.gransnet.com/forums/chat/a1189958-Does-anyone-enjoy-going-to-the-hairdressers – accessed March 27, 2012). There is even a book (Doycheff, 1993) written for those who worry about the process of visiting the hairdresser.

REFERENCES

Bærenholdt, J. (2010). Enactment and Enchantment in Experience Economies. Working Paper, Roskilde University.

Bryman, A. (2003). *The Disneyization of Society*. London: Routledge.

Campbell, C. (1987). *The Romantic Ethic and the Spirit of Modern Consumerism*. Oxford: Blackwell.

Cohen, R.L. (2010). When It Pays to Be Friendly: Employment Relationships and Emotional Labour in Hairstyling. *Sociological Review* 58: 197–218.

Cohen, R. (2011). Time, Space and Touch at Work. *Sociology of Health & Illness* 33(2): 189–205.

Doycheff, J. (1993). *'Excuse Me, I'm Going to Kill My Hairdresser!': A Humorous Survival Guide for Women Who Visit Hair Salons*. Columbus: Gadoda Adanta.

Eliaeson, S. (2000). Max Weber's Methodology: An Ideal Type. *Journal of the History of the Behavioral Sciences* 36: 241–63.

Falk, P. (1994). *The Consuming Body*. London: Sage.

Foner, N. (1994). *The Caregiving Dilemma*. Berkeley: University of California Press.

Foucault, M. (1997). Technologies of the Self. *In* P. Rabinow (Ed.) *Michel Foucault: Ethics: Subjectivity and Truth*. New York: The New Press.

▶

Fullerton, R. and Punj, G. (1993). Choosing to Misbehave. *Advances in Consumer Research* 20: 570–74.

Gabriel, Y. and Lang, T. (2006). *The Unmanaged Consumer*. London: Sage.

Hobbs, D., Hadfield, P., Lister, S. and Winlow, S. (2005). *Bouncers*. Oxford: Oxford University Press.

Hochschild, A. (1983). *The Managed Heart*. Berkeley: University of California Press.

Huebner, L. (2007). *Professional Intimacy*. PhD thesis, University of Pittsburgh.

Jenkins, D. (2000). Disenchantment, Enchantment and Re-enchantment. *Max Weber Studies* 1: 11–32.

Kang, M. (2010). *The Managed Hand: Race, Class and Gender in Beauty Service Work*. Berkeley: University of California Press.

Korczynski, M. (2009). The Mystery Customer. *Sociology* 43(5): 952–67.

Korczynski, M. and Ott, U. (2004). When Production and Consumption Meet. *Journal of Management Studies* 41(4): 575–99.

——— (2006). The Menu in Society. *Sociology* 40(5): 911–28.

Lawler, J. (1991). *Behind the Screens: Nursing, Somology and the Problem of the Body*. Melbourne: Churchill Livingstone.

Nickson, D., Warhurst, C., Witz, A. and Cullen, A. (2001). The Importance of Being Aesthetic. *In* A. Sturdy, I. Grugulis and H. Willmott (Eds) *Customer Service*. Basingstoke: Palgrave Macmillan. Pp. 170–90.

Paules, G. (1991). *Dishing It Out*. Philadelphia: Temple University Press.

Pine, B. and Gillmore, J. (1999). *The Experience Economy*. Cambridge: Harvard University Press.

Ritzer, G. (1999). *Enchanting a Disenchanted World*. Thousand Oaks: Sage.

Savage, W. (1995). *Nursing Intimacy*. London: Scutari.

Shilling, C. (2003). *The Body and Social Theory*. London: Sage.

Twigg, J., Wolkowitz, C., Cohen, R. and Nettleton, S. (2011). Conceptualising Body Work in Health and Social Care. *Sociology of Health & Illness* 33(2): 171–88.

Widding Isaksen, L. (2002). Toward a Sociology of (Gendered) Disgust: Images of Bodily Decay and the Social Organization of Care Work. *Journal of Family Issues* 23(7): 791–811.

Equal to Any Other, but Not the Same as Any Other: The Politics of Sexual Labour, the Body and Intercorporeality

3

Kate Hardy

Introduction

Sex workers' bodies and their roles within exchanges in prostitution, erotic dance, pornography and other forms of sexual labour have been central to the political and theoretical debates around commercial sex. Indeed, the notion that in prostitution women, men or transgender people 'sell their bodies' has almost cultural ubiquity. Many have argued, however, that this notion misrepresents what is, in fact, sold in the commercial sex encounter. A key claim of the sex workers' rights movement and authors who support their approach has been that commercial sex does not involve selling the body, but instead that 'sex work is *work*' and what is sold is a service (Jenness, 1997) or a form of labour. All of these conceptualizations have implications for the form of politics that can be constructed for transformation and change in the sex industry. In what follows, I explore differing approaches to understanding the labour involved in corporeal sex work encounters and examine the political possibilities they may contain.

In this chapter, I draw on primary data from my own research into sexual labour, research conducted with or on behalf of colleagues (Teela Sanders and Nick Mai), and secondary sources from the rich literature on sex work and sexual labour. I intentionally cut across different labour processes in the industry in order to illustrate nuance and diversity in the deployment of the body within forms of work which explicitly incorporate sex. I first outline the two core ways in which the body has been considered within prostitution and sex work, including (1) the essentialized body, and (2) sexual labour, incorporating aesthetic labour, body work and interactive sexual labour. To these existing approaches, I add a further conceptualization, which stresses the intercorporeal nature of sexual labour. This is not so much a novel approach in and of itself, but a development of the notion of sexual labour and a particular lens through which to understand it. Existing approaches are sketched briefly, as similar arguments have been offered far more comprehensively and forcefully elsewhere (Brents and Hausbeck, this volume; Wolkowitz, 2006). I then use these models to address issues relating to the body politics of sexual labour, both existing politics and potentialities, in the hope of opening up these issues for further debate and praxis. I argue that the notion of intercorporeality offers a multi-scalar way of analysing and understanding sex work as constituted by social relations and processes from the micro to macro. I suggest that this opens up political terrain on which to attempt to transform sex work through challenging the multiple processes which produce and shape it, including racism, sexism and the mandatory nature of labour under capitalism.

Beyond the binaries

In much academic writing, the debate about commercial sex continues to be constructed around the polarization between radical feminists, who see it as violence against women (Barry, 1995; Jeffreys, 2009) and other feminists and theorists who argue that it should be conceptualized and recognized as a form of work (Chapkis, 1997; Oerton and Phoenix, 2002). This is often frustrating, as there has been an effervescence of writings on 'sex work' over the last decade that has produced a significantly more nuanced and subtle debate than that which emerged from the 'sex wars' of the late 1970s (Kotiswaran, 2011; O'Connell Davidson, 1998, forthcoming). Most theorists writing on prostitution and sexual labour now concede that it does constitute a form of work, that is, an exchange of labour for some form of capital or financial gain. That commercial sex constitutes a form of work is not a normative judgement about the value – or otherwise – of sexual labour and its social utility or desirability. That is, to assert that sex work is work is not to assert that it is necessarily good work.

Talking about 'sex work' and 'sexual labour' in the abstract is difficult, as the terms encompass a wide range of labour processes and relations, and because they are produced in particular material circumstances. This is not to state that sexual labour is simply constituted by individualized subjective experience, but that it is heterogeneous and shaped by class, race, geography, history, material conditions of wealth and narratives about gender, sexuality and desire, amongst others. Sexual labour is not only performed by women, nor does it only take place on the street. As such, there is no one, singular, unifying story of the sex industry. In this chapter, I refer to sexual labour in the broadest sense, incorporating all elements of the sex industry including direct sexual services, pornography and erotic dance. Although I recognize the important contributions that demonstrate continuities with the sexualization of work outside the sex industry (Adkins, 1995; Warhurst and Nickson, 2009), and unpaid work (Agustín, 2012), I refer here to those explicitly using sex as part of the commodified exchange.

Two main approaches have characterized understandings of the role of the body in sexual labour encounters. First, the notion that the body, self and sexuality are inextricably linked and, therefore, that it is the person in and of themselves that is for sale. Second, approaches which see the body as selling labour or labour-power. This first section outlines these different approaches and in doing so borrows heavily from work by Carol Wolkowitz and Julia O'Connell-Davidson, to whom I owe an intellectual debt.

Radical feminism and the essentialized body

An influential approach to the understanding of the body in the sexual labour exchanges has been that of radical feminism. This understands sex work – generally referred to as prostitution – as 'being used physically as a sex object' (Jeffreys, 1997: 173). It is this objectification of the body, which has been the core agitator of anti-prostitution commentators and radical feminists. These authors abhor prostitution as an institution borne out of patriarchal oppressive structures in which women's bodies are subjugated and objectified for the purpose of male pleasure and gain. Sex worker bodies are reduced, in these constructions, to little more than a disembodied mouth or vagina, silhouette or pair of breasts, succinctly represented in the title of Sheila Jeffreys' 2009 book, *The Industrial Vagina*. The inextricable connection between body-self in this sense means that the prostitute is stripped of her selfhood and personhood, through the acts performed 'on' her body. Further, as Oerton and Phoenix (2001) and Wolkowitz (2006) point out critically, in this view it is sexuality which lies at the heart of selfhood itself, as a unique embodied and social interaction, distinct from all others. In addition to such authors, sex workers themselves have also challenged this notion, arguing that:

> the claim that sex workers 'sell our bodies' is not only logically absurd (I was a prostitute for years, but my body is still right here with me), but totally sexist because it is based on the notion that a woman's sexuality is her entire worth. The belief behind this expression is that since a woman has nothing of value to offer except her sexuality, if she 'sells' that she has 'sold herself' and there is nothing left. (McNeal, 2012)

In this sense, in the direct connection between body-sexuality-self sex workers are stripped of autonomy and self, and reduced to 'mere bodies' (O'Connell-Davidson, forthcoming) or something akin to Agamben's (1998) concept of 'bare life'. Wolkowitz (2006) has pointed out that in this view, the sex worker body is essentialized, in that there is a direct, clear and static relationship between self and body, which is shared by all women (who also constitute an essentialized category). In this formulation, the bodies interact in a zero-sum game in which one body is active whereas the other is entirely passive, powerless and unmoving.

The labour of sex work: liberal and labour process approaches

A second influential approach is to see the body as selling labour that is detachable from the self and, therefore, that it is labour *as a commodity*, which is sold in the sex work exchange.

For liberal thinkers, a worker 'owns' the labour produced by his body and, therefore, is at liberty to sell it to an employer; this is a fundamental freedom that forms a basis of civil liberties and should be enjoyed by all. Labour in this sense is 'a form of property, a legitimate object of trade, that the subject is, or should be, free to use as he (or she) wishes' (Wolkowitz, 2006: 128). For many of these authors, the self can be made separable from the labour that is sold, as workers use emotional labour or performance to generate a working self in distinction from a 'private' self (Chapkis, 1997; Cheung, this volume).

Similarly, labour process theorists argue that labour-power is exchanged with capital for financial gain. However, they are more critical and do not recognize this as simply an equal exchange between two equal parties. Moreover, they recognize that the body is central to all work, as it is productive of labour-power, and it is this power to labour that is sold in exchange for a wage. For Marx (1970, cited in O'Connell-Davidson, forthcoming), labour-power is 'the aggregate of the mental and physical capabilities in a human being which he exercises whenever he produces a use-value of *any description*'. Marxist analyses assert that, stripped of their ability to live and survive through any other means, 'dull economic compulsion forces the dispossessed to treat themselves as commodities, offering their bodily capacity for sale to the highest bidder' (O'Connell-Davidson, forthcoming). Yet, differing from liberal approaches, it is argued that the detachability of labour from the worker is an illusion, as labour cannot be extracted from the worker in the manner of property. Labour-power exists only as the living self of the worker, who must deliver the labour through their active body and thus experience the act of labouring which concretizes as a commodity to be exchanged with capital (O'Connell-Davidson, forthcoming;

Pateman, 1988). In this sense, all labour is embodied in that it requires a body through which labour-power can be channelled. Within this tradition, it is *sexual labour* which is sold during the exchange and this adopts four key forms of labour process; 'aesthetic labour', 'body work', 'interactive sexual labour' and 'intercorporeality'.

Aesthetic labour

The notion of aesthetic labour has been developed to refer to labour within interactive service industries in which the embodiment of the worker is intended to appeal to the 'senses' of customers (Warhurst and Nickson, 2009). Aesthetic labour is not always sexualized, but does often extend to it, commodifying sexual appeal as part of workers' bodies and 'looks'. Although there is a common concern with employees' appearance or 'looks' and in particular, their sexualized aesthetic across the service industries (McDowell, 2009; Warhurst and Nickson, 2009), this also has particular pertinence in the sex industries.

In sex work, like other service work, the product ('service') is used up at the point of exchange (McDowell, 2009) and the specific physical attributes of the worker are part of the exchange. As in other contexts, certain bodies attract more value; namely the young, the slim and the white, whereas dirtier service work such as cleaning or care of the elderly is the reserve of the dark, migrant and the old (Wills et al., 2009). As such, this labour of 'self-presentation' requires that workers work on their own bodies in order to acquire the 'well-groomed, preferably slim body, produced through exercise, adornment or self-improvement, whether temporary ... or more permanently through radical interventions such as surgery' (McDowell, 2009: 8). This applies as much to lap dancers (Frank, 2002) and escorts (Anderson and O'Connell Davidson, 2002) as to other service workers and increasingly also to professional jobs.

Management perceptions of 'market demands' strategically prescribe the bodies that are deemed to have the correct aesthetic attributes through strict and explicit rules on appearance (Chapkis, 1997; Sanders and Hardy, 2012). In the erotic dance industry in the United Kingdom, this has resulted a narrower of the 'stripper look' inclusive of no short hair (many wear wigs), particular types of clothing, weight rules, removal of body hair and adornments such as piercings and tattoos (Cohen et al., this volume). In direct sexual services, the ideal category tends to be less narrow. Escort websites, for example, as well as some pornography, offer a number of different bodily niches, including particularly raced or aged bodies or preferences for bodies which do not fit the general 'desirable' stereotype. The public consumption of lap dancers' labour often results in consumption of attention from a body that is stereotypically attractive, whereas private consumption of sexual labour tends to concede less to socially acceptable images of desire and may be more diverse, responding to more individualized (albeit still socially constructed) desire.

Body work/body labour

The term 'body work', largely developed by Carol Wolkowitz (2002, 2006), refers to work that 'involves intimately bodily contact' (2006: 147). In contrast to aesthetic labour, the concept brings into view the material and symbolic body not just of the worker, but also of the customer.

Whereas it is frequently sex workers' bodies that sit at the centre of analyses of commercial sex, in all commercial sex encounters there is necessarily another body, which is frequently invisibilized: the body of the client. Yet, the degree of contact and therefore 'body work' in commercial sex differs depending on the type of sex work being performed and the legal and regulatory framework that surrounds it. For example, in the United Kingdom, regulations around stripping work in table dancing clubs and strip pubs dictate that a dancer may not touch a customer and vice versa, and this is enforced in some cases by customers being made to sit on their hands or put cushions on their laps during dances (Sanders and Hardy, 2012). However, as Cohen, Sanders and Hardy (this volume) show, these rules are often contravened and dancers touch customers as part of a repertoire for courting custom.

Interactive sexual labour

In the past, both aesthetic labour and body work approaches have tended to downplay or only implicitly refer to the interactive nature of much sex work. Leidner's (1991: 155) concept of interactive service work was seminal in demonstrating that 'the interaction may itself be part of the service offered' and that 'identities are therefore not incidental to the work but are an integral part of it' and was, in many ways, a forerunner of the concept of aesthetic labour previously outlined.

In many sex work encounters, a key difference from other services is that the encounter involves two bodies *touching each other*. Or, as Brents and Jackson (this volume) put it, the customer 'touches back'. As such, here I differ from Leidner in using the term 'interactive sexual labour' to emphasize the haptic and tactile nature of the interaction, rather than a solely intersubjective encounter and to stress that dual direction of touch is a key component of the labour exchange.

At times, this interaction is formalized in sex work as it is the key point of the encounter, as a client or a part of a client's body 'touches back' through either vaginal, anal or oral sex or manual stimulation. In others, such as lap dancing clubs and other erotic dance venues, rules govern which parts of workers' bodies customers may touch, if at all (Chapkis, 1997). These may be either legal requirements or internal club rules (Sanders and Hardy, 2012). For example, in the United States there is no contact during a peep show between dancers and customers, who are separated by a sheet of glass, while lap dancing offers much more direct contact. In contrast, in independent forms of sex work, it is the worker who defines the terms of the bodily interaction, including what she is willing to do to the customers' body and the ways and parts of her own which he is vindicated in touching. This may include refusals to kiss or perform anal sex, for example.

Control over the interaction of bodies in the sex work encounter is often seen as determined by a power struggle between workers and their clients, as workers attempt to limit clients' access to workers' bodies (Sanders, 2005). However, depending on their labour relations, sex workers, like other workers, also struggle with management over control of the labour process and the rate of exploitation (Chapkis, 1997). Often, aside from wage or remuneration struggles, these conflicts circulate around the role of workers' bodies in the labour process. Independent contractors, such as street workers or non-agency based escorts, for example, have more control over what they wear and which sexual acts they are willing to engage in, as well as over issues such as condom use. This is, of course, mitigated by structuring factors, which determine the degree to which they are able to make such demands.

Intercorporeality

Most sex work, then, does not simply involve either the body of the sex worker or the client as a passive, docile body, but two active bodies infused with personhood, activity and subjectivity. Yet, while understanding sexual labour as interactive helps to develop existing approaches to understanding the role of the body in the sex work labour process, the notion of 'inter-corporeality' (Crossley, 1995) can be more useful still in holding in tension these multiple understandings of the body in sex work, while grounding them in wider structural conditions.

Crossley (1995: 143) suggests that intercorporeality refers to the idea that 'human intersubjectivity and thus society itself, is an intertwining of "flesh"...an overlapping of sentient-sensible beings'. In this understanding, neither body is static, as both body-subjects respond relationally, even if that relation is negative for one or the other. In intercorporeal encounters body-subjects are produced in that moment, as well as over time, materially and structurally through historical processes which inscribe and are inscribed on their bodies (Sanchez-Taylor, 2000). As Crossley (1994: 35) argues, 'bodily action is always orientated to a *present situation* which it will both accommodate and transform'. Within sex work, these follow particular 'scripts' (Sanders, 2008) and the 'present situation' is shaped by antecedents of structures of gender, race, class, amongst others, which are embodied in the intercorporeality of the worker and client (O'Connell Davidson, 1998; Sanchez-Taylor, 2000). Sex work encounters are produced contingently and relationally, as they are shaped by historical and material conditions, which delimit the possibilities and predilections of the bodies involved. Yet these are also subject to change and modification because of both the agency of the worker and client, and wider conditions including new technologies, new forms of gendered and sexualized appeal or formations of sexuality and logics of accumulation.

The use of intercorporeality is not intended to transcend or displace the notion of sexual labour, but to keep labour directly in view, and to locate it alongside bodies, consumption, the specific encounter, as well as the wider structural conditions that produce sex work encounters. Whereas aesthetic labour has highlighted the increasing necessity for workers to work on their own bodies as a precondition for working on the bodies of others (Chugh and Hancock, 2009) and body work has highlighted the ways in which there are specific ways in which sex workers must touch bodies in order to sexualize them, these have each tended to consider each body in isolation, hiding the degree of intercorporeality which is involved. In contrast, inter-corporeality can hold all of these in coterminous view, alongside structuring factors shaping the labour-capital exchange. It posits that while it is sexual labour that is for sale in the sex work encounter, this is not 'something fully separable from the body and person of the sex worker' (O'Connell-Davidson forthcoming), and thus the encounter shapes the body-subjectivity of the worker and has wider social implications over multiple scales. In this sense, it accepts part of the radical feminist structural analysis, while rejecting it simplistic analysis of power and reductivist attitude towards sex worker agency.

By pointing out the ways in which bodies are produced and lived historically and intercorporeally, it also serves to illustrate the ways in which a particular moment of sexual labour and consumption are produced. For example, when a Costa Rican sex worker sells sex (and other body work and caring services) to a white male American citizen (Rivers-Moore, 2011), each body has been socially produced in particular ways, which bestow greater amounts of money-capital on the American, locating one in a position to sell sex and another to buy, while sexualizing, gendering and racing each in distinct ways because of narratives, practices and processes of gender, race, colonialism, desire (and others). Social notions of sexuality and acceptable desire shape the ways in which some bodies are considered valuable and desirable, and are inscribed in classed, raced and gendered bodies through markers, dress, gestures and 'body techniques' (Crossley, 1995). In the sex industry, these vary historically and geographically and particular bodies are deemed suitable for particular types of work. For example, in the United Kingdom, working class female bodies tend to populate street sex work, whereas those with more social, cultural and money-capital are more likely to work indoors. Alternatively, it is the eroticized racial other who becomes the desirable sex worker in contexts of sex tourism (Rivers-Moore, 2011; Sanchez-Taylor, 2000).

In my reading, the notion of intercorporeality does not necessitate mutuality in terms of mutual desire or pleasure, although it may do, and this is noted by some sex workers (see for example, Brents and Jackson, this volume). Nor does it necessarily involve mutual recognition in terms of cognitive or social recognition of each other as active subjects in the terms of Nancy Fraser (1995). 'Misrecognition of the other' (Wolkowitz, 2006: 137) can occur even during intercorporeal encounters. Instead, the notion of intercorporeality can speak to the ways in which gender roles and other social hierarchies produce the sex work encounter and also reproduce it, through the co-construction of particular body-subject positions, in specific material contexts. Bodies recognize and respond to each other, but not always on equal terms. It is the desired body of the customer, with the power of money-capital who can convert into the socially recognized subject.

While Crossley (1995) tends to refer to a specific moment of encounter, I want to emphasize the multi-scalarity (Cox, 2002) of such an encounter and as such, highlight both its material antecedents and effects, and the human agency which shapes it. The material conditions of the encounter are shaped by social relations at the micro, meso and macro scale. These include the historically and geographically produced position of the worker and the client (macro), the labour relations in which takes place (meso), as well as in the circumstances in which the two meet and their experience of it (micro). Within this context, the bodies act intercorporeally, embodying and reproducing or resisting these histories and markings. At the micro-level, the different spatial factors in which the sex work take place – in the street, lap dancing club, internet webcam or brothel – shape the encounter, as much as the embodied histories of social inequality that produce the bodies (macro) and the agential actions of both worker and customer. As such, in contrast to the approaches which essentialize experiences of sex work, intercorporeality can speak to its complexity, diversity and bring nuance to understanding how the specific empirical conditions in which it takes place are shaped by multi-scalar factors.

(Re)producing bodies/the body politics of sex work

Having argued for the value of an intercorporeal analysis of sex work, in the following section I review the main concepts previously outlined in terms of their implications for sex worker politics and then outline the ways in which an intercorporeal and multi-scalar analysis may be productive in informing sex workers politics. I use a number of key examples from the United Kingdom and Argentina to demonstrate the ways in which such an analysis, and the politics around it, is already emergent within sex workers' activism. As such, the formulation of such an analysis has been informed by political praxis by sex workers, rather than vice versa.

The radical feminist approach to the role of the passive and docile sex worker body renders sex worker body-subjects as wholly powerless. Many pressure groups that are organizing or have organized around issues relating to the sex industry adopt this position, including Whisper in the United States (US) and Object in the United Kingdom (UK). These organizations are frequently not populated by sex workers, but by concerned activists and sex workers themselves frequently argue that this position is unhelpful for them. X:talk, a migrant sex workers' organization based in London, United Kingdom, state that the passive constructions of their bodies that radical feminists promote means that sex workers 'are spoken for and about but rarely are we allowed to speak for ourselves'.

In contrast, approaches which understand the body as selling a form of labour-power offer a different politics based on a different understanding of their embodied experience. Sexual labour is a form of body politics in and of itself; it is political even when it is not political. As a source of survival and of social reproduction, it sits at the most basic site of politics, that of the reproduction of life. As Natalia, an Argentinean street sex worker told me:

> My body is one of the things that I had…it gave food to my son when he was in my belly, my body keeps giving food to my children…I always think of it like this and I give it value, my body matters and that's why, I'll say it again. When they were in my belly they were sustained by me, they came out of my belly and they keep being sustained by me…

Yet there are further meanings of body politics within the sex industry. It is necessary, I argue, to recognize prostitution as work, even if that work is deeply exploitative – as many other forms of labour are – in order to create better working conditions and reduce the stigma and violence associated with sexual labour. Recognizing sex work as work does not mean denying that it is performed under conditions of exploitation, physical danger, emotional abuse, health degradation, racism, sexism, poverty and immizeration (Schultz, 2006), but instead provides the conceptual framework necessary for approaching these issues. In recognizing commercial sex as a form of labour, multiple plains open up for a potential politics of sex work, one of which formulates around liberal approaches to the body as property and the other to sex work as a labour process.

On the one hand, liberal approaches have tended to assert that liberation for sex workers should be achieved through the removal of repressive laws which delimit and constrain the ways in which they are able to use their bodies. For example, the International Union of Sex Workers (IUSW), a pressure group based in the United Kingdom, 'believes that everyone should have the freedom to choose how they earn their living and freedom to choose what they do with their own body' (IUSW, 2012). This has led to campaign phrases such as 'My Body, My Business' by activists such as those in the IUSW. The interpretation of laws as controlling people's use of their own bodies has led to fundamentally legalistic claims on the state to remove laws that repress the ways in which workers may use their bodies for financial gains, particularly in campaigns for the decriminalization of prostitution, which forms the basis of much contemporary political campaigning around the sex industry (Wolkowitz, 2006). Such an appeal to the state, in a legislative framework, focuses on 'negative liberty' (Mill, 1859) and freeing sex workers from the repressive wings of the state, namely the police.

There are, however, limitations to these legalistic claims to the state (Cruz, forthcoming). While these are important in challenging the current conditions of sex work (the debates about appropriate regulation have been widely discussed elsewhere), regulation is not a panacea, but simply a plaster or a stop gap, to generate damage limitation or what is often called 'harm reduction'. Although this is important in the immediate term it falls short of any transformative potential and does little to challenge the labour relations in which sex workers must operate under the control of a third party – strip club manager, pornography producer or director, escort agency or brothel owner. As such, by recognizing the parallels between sex work and other forms of labour, labour process theories open up space for sex workers to organize as workers in similar ways to other workers in other industries. There are multiple examples of labour organizing within unions across the world, including De Rode Draad in The Netherlands and the IUSW-GMB (separate from the IUSW) in the United Kingdom. AMMAR-CTA, in Argentina, is a union of sex workers who have organized against the repression they have faced by the state and for better working conditions and access to labour, civil and social rights (Hardy, 2010). In doing so, they challenge working conditions within their workplaces, which in this case, are on the street, by seeking to make them safer and collectively setting prices and standards such as condom use.

While liberal regulatory approaches and labour politics based in the workplace are hopeful and each have their own merits – the latter in particular in fundamentally shifting the balance of power in the here-and-now between labour and capital – they are limited by framing the politics of sex work and the possibilities for sex worker struggle within singular frameworks such as the state or the workplace. In contrast, understanding sexual labour as intercorporeal is more productive in opening up the terrain of struggle in multiple directions.

Through intercorporeality, we can see the specific, grounded ways in which sexuality is converted into a commodity by historical structural processes, both in terms of demand for its consumption and the provision of labour (Truong, 1990). It allows us to move through scales from the interactive body-body encounter to the historical structural scales that produce particular bodies with particular social meanings, attachments and power relations. Much like bodies, capital itself is relational and is produced and reproduced through embodied and grounded interactions (Gibson-Graham, 1996). As such, understanding the interaction corporeally enables a politics of sex work to move between the micro-encounter of the sex worker/client bodies, the meso-level of the labour relations, which shape the exchange and the macro social relations which shape the gendered, classed and raced ways in which the two bodies meet in an exchange of labour for money. This can enable a micro-politics of decriminalization alongside a meso-politics of organizing within the workplace, while challenging the multiple structural relations of inequality that produce the conditions in which sex work is produced and takes place.

Although this offers new potentialities for a radical politics of sex work, sex workers around the world are already engaged in such critical politics, which are sensitive to the multiplicities of oppression and power which shape and produce the bodies engaged in the sex work encounter. For example, x:talk state that in addition to the provision of English classes for migrant sex workers and struggles for decriminalization, they 'support critical interventions around issues of migration, race, gender, sexuality and labour'. Interestingly, x:talk speak through one collective voice, that of Ava Caradonna, who is everyone and no one. Their reasons for doing this are 'not because we think that being a "sex worker" is a fixed identity, but because those who have experienced the material conditions of the sex industry are in the best position to know how to change it'. It is by sharing the embodied, lived, intercorporeal experiences of sex work and talking about them, across languages, that the collective body of Ava is produced.

In doing so, they refute the focus on the individual sex worker body and instead insert a collective body, which is disembodied in that Ava has no body and yet is embodied through each and every worker who speaks in her name.

In Argentina, AMMAR have similarly developed an intercorporeal organizing approach. In adopting a class perspective, they have shifted from seeing their suffering as inflicted on their own individual bodies to instead understanding it as part of a collective, historically injured body, that of the working class. Such an intercorporeal identity has enabled AMMAR to 'scale up' and ally with the broader labour movement in Argentina (Hardy, 2010) and combine struggles within and outside the industry itself. In 'scaling up', AMMAR make a distinction between their activity within AMMAR and in the micro and meso-politics of the sex industry, and a broader transformative politics of the wider umbrella union (Hardy, 2010). This enables them to 'engage instead with a much broader and exigent political project to change the distribution of resources and power' (Hardy, 2010: 98). As such, AMMAR not only have short term demands for improving their material well being, but also an analysis and critique of the present system and the position of sex work within it, as well as a vision and a strategy for changing it. They have located their analysis and struggle over sex work in a much wider political economy and movement for change, which exists over multi-scalar terrains of struggle.

As such, it is pre-existing sex worker struggles such as these that have incorporated notions of intercorporeality and multi-scalarity to their analyses of and organizing strategies around sex work, that have influenced the analysis here. A material feminist approach to the notion of intercorporeality enables us to see the historical and material imprints on bodies and how these produce and reproduce power relations between them. In noting not only the embodied experience of the sex work encounter and what it contains in terms of a labour process, but also analysing the production of the time-space encounter of sex work through gender, classed and raced structurations, it is possible to understand the possibilities for transformation that include, but are not only limited to, change of the labour process and relations. A key component of this challenge is not only to argue for valuing sex work as equal to other forms of work, or for challenging the institution of sex work, but to challenge the institution of paid labour itself (Frase, 2012; Weeks, 2011). Indeed, it may well be, as O'Connell-Davidson (forthcoming) so convincingly argues, that 'universal protection *from* the market is more pertinent to the degree of freedom enjoyed by workers than the valorization of their labour as a commodity in the mainstream labour market'. A radical politics of sex work, which can incorporate all of these factors, must not only be a critique of sex work, or of the vastly unequal positions in which people enter the labour market, but of the mandatory nature of waged work. Such a politics must not only ally with and be led by sex workers to transform their bodily encounters in the workplace, by struggling for decriminalization and organizing with sex workers vis-à-vis clients and employers or managers, but also to ground these in multiple struggles against exploitation and structural inequalities. Namely, if the commodification of sex and sexual labour is to be challenged, this must be a struggle 'against the commodification of everything', including labour (Gilbert, 2008). Such a politics would mean engaging in the production of a world in which sex workers can transform their workplaces and conditions of work, and to live in conditions in which it is possible to refuse sex work, but also to refuse work itself.

REFERENCES

Adkins, L. (1995). *Gendered Work: Sexuality, Family and the Labour Market*. Buckingham: Open University Press.

Agamben, G. (1998). *Homo Sacer: Sovereign Power and Bare Life*, trans. D. Heller-Roazen. Stanford: Stanford University Press.

Agustin, L. (2012). Sex and Work and Sex Work. *The Commoner* Winter 2012, No. 15. Available at http://www.commoner.org.uk/.

Anderson, B. and O'Connell Davidson, J. (2002). Is Trafficking in Human Beings Demand Driven?: A Multi-Country Study. IOM Migration Research Series, No. 15. Geneva: International Migration Organisation.

Barry, K. (1995). *The Prostitution of Sexuality*. New York and London: New York University Press.

Chapkis, W. (1997). *Live Sex Acts: Women Performing Erotic Labour*. London and New York: Routledge.

Chugh, S. and Hancock, P. (2009). Networks of Aestheticization: The Architecture, Artefacts and Embodiment of Hairdressing Salons. *Work, Employment & Society* 23(3): 460–76.

Cox, K. (2002). 'Globalization,' the 'Regulation Approach,' and the Politics of Scale. *In* A. Herod and M. Wright (Eds) *Geographies of Power: Placing Scale*. Oxford and Malden: Blackwell. Pp. 85–114.

Crossley, N. (1994). *The Politics of Subjectivity: Between Foucault and Merleau-Ponty*. Aldershot: Avebury.

—— (1995). Body Techniques, Agency and Intercorporeality: On Goffman's *Relations in Public*. *Sociology* 29(1): 133–49.

Cruz, K. (forthcoming). *(Sex) Work and the Limits of Law: Rights, Labour and the Spectre of the Nation-State*. Unpublished PhD thesis, University of Nottingham.

Frank, K. (2002). *G-strings and Sympathy: Strip Club Regulars and Male Desire*. Durham: Duke University Press.

Frase, P. (2012). The Problem with (Sex) Work. Jacobin Magazine. Available at http://jacobinmag.com/blog/2012/03/the-problem-with-sex-work/.

▶

Fraser, N. (1995). From Redistribution to Recognition? Dilemmas of Justice in a 'Postsocialist' Age. *New Left Review* 212: 68–93.

Gibson-Graham, J.K. (1996). *The End of Capitalism (As We Knew It): A Feminist Critique of Political Economy*. Minneapolis: University of Minnesota Press.

Gilbert, J. (2008). Against the Commodification of Everything: Anti-Consumerist Studies in the Age of Ecological Crisis. *Cultural Studies* 22(5): 551–66.

Hardy, K. (2010). *Proletaria de la vida: Sex Worker Organising in Argentina*. PhD thesis, Queen Mary, University of London.

IUSW (2012). International Union of Sex Workers. Available at www.iusw.org.

Jeffreys, S. (1997). *The Idea of Prostitution*. London: Spiniflex.

—— (2009). *The Industrial Vagina: The Political Economy of the Global Sex Trade*. London and New York: Routledge.

Jenness, V. (1998). *Making It Work: The Prostitutes' Rights Movement in Perspective*. New York: Aldine de Gruyter.

Kotiswaran, P. (2011). *Dangerous Sex, Invisible Labor: Sex Work and the Law in India*. Princeton and Oxford: Princeton University Press.

Leidner, R. (1991). Serving Hamburgers and Selling Insurance: Gender, Work, and Identity in Interactive Service Jobs. *Gender and Society* 5(2): 154–77.

McDowell, L. (2009). *Working Bodies: Interactive Service Employment and Workplace Identities*. Oxford: Wiley-Blackwell.

McNeal, M. (2012). Quoted in KayleeB. Available at http://kayleemb.tumblr.com/post/23663444013/the-claim-that-sex-workers-sell-our-bodies-is.

Mill, J.S. (1859). *On Liberty*. Mobilereference.

O'Connell Davidson, J. (1998). *Prostitution, Power and Freedom*. Cambridge: Polity.

—— (forthcoming). Liberal Fictions of Disembodiment: Prostitution, Slavery and Wage Labour.

Oerton, S. and Phoenix, J. (2001). Sex/Body Work: Discourses and Practices. *Sexualities: Studies in Culture and Society* 4(4): 387–412.

Pateman, C. (1988). *The Sexual Contract*. Cambridge: Polity.

Rivers-Moore, M. (2011). Imagining Others: Sex, Race and Power in Transnational Sex Tourism. *ACME International Journal for Critical Geographies*, Special Issue on 'Gender, Power and Transcultural Relations', 10(3): 392–411.

Sanchez-Taylor, J. (2000). Tourism and Embodied Commodities: Sex Tourism in the Caribbean. *In* S. Clift and S. Carter (Eds) *Tourism and Sex: Culture, Commerce and Coercion*. London: Pinter.

Sanders, T.L.M. (2005). *Sex Work: A Risky Business*. Cullompton: Willan.

—— (2008). Selling Sex in the Shadow Economy. *International Journal of Social Economics* 35(10): 704–28.

Sanders, T. and Hardy, K. (2012). Devalued, Deskilled and Diversified: Explaining the Proliferation of Lap Dancing in the UK. *British Journal of Sociology* 63(3): 513–32.

Schultz, V. (2006). Sex and Work. *Yale Journal of Law and Feminism* 18(1): 223–34.

Truong, T.D. (1990). *Sex, Money and Morality: Prostitution and Tourism in South East Asia*. London: Zed.

Warhurst, C. and Nickson, D. (2009). 'Who's Got the Look?': Emotional, Aesthetic and Sexualized Labour in Interactive Services. *Gender, Work & Organization* 16(3): 385–404.

Wills, J., Datta, K., Evans, Y., Herbert, J., May, J. and McIlwaine, C. (2009). *Global Cities at Work: New Migrant Divisions of Labour*. London: Pluto.

Wolkowitz, C. (2006). *Bodies at Work*. London: Sage.

x:talk (2012). English Classes for Migrant Sex Workers. Available at http://www.xtalkproject.net/.

The Socio-Economic and Legal Context of Body/Sex Work

Legal Constructions of Body Work

4

Ann Stewart

Introduction

This chapter explores the ways in which intimate, embodied and sexualized labour is regulated within the law in the United Kingdom by considering how the relationships involved are understood within law and highlighting the limitations of the existing regulatory norms and frameworks. It takes two examples wherein the human body is used as the 'material of production'. The first example involves the commercial provision of sex, the second caring for the vulnerable, particularly the elderly, undertaken predominantly within the home. The labour processes under discussion are only marginally recognized by labour law. As a result, those involved are unable to make use of its normative frame of reference, which is in part based upon addressing the risks associated with unequal bargaining power. At present commercial sex is heavily associated with the criminalized discourse of 'prostitution' and trafficking. Domiciliary-based caring involves a range of work-related arrangements undertaken by persons defined as domestic workers, social care workers/personal assistants and, very importantly, unpaid carers. We find that the legal construction of unpaid carers is located primarily within social welfare law whereas other domiciliary workers are addressed through the potential violation of their human rights.

This chapter considers the wider implications of these different legal locations, in particular the forms of legal protection available to those involved, and explores the ways in which concepts of risk, vulnerability and mutuality affect body work relationships as they emerge within law.

A short history of labour law: employees, workers and 'employment'

Modern labour law emerged from a range of relationships associated with work in the nineteenth century (Deakin, 2007; Deakin and Wilkinson,

2005). At its heart is the common law contract of employment. Two autonomous parties, the employer and the employee, enter into a free and voluntary agreement whereby the employer owes a duty to pay for work undertaken whereas the employee owes a duty to be ready, willing to work, and to obey the lawful orders of the employer. Although constructed as a mutual agreement, Pateman (1988: 118) argues that the contract in general is a specifically modern means of creating relationships of subordination. Clearly, the employment contract reflects inequality of bargaining power in the market place, placing the worker in a position of subordination. This contract of service involves not only elements of mutuality and dependence, but also of continuity. Nonetheless, it replaced archaic legal distinctions between blue collar and white collar workers (Deakin, 2007) and by the 1950s provided the basis for the 'standard employment relationship' involving 'an ensemble of institutions, along with the vertically integrated enterprise, the industrial union, the male-breadwinner family, and the state as employer and provider of services, which served as the basis of an historical compromise between workers, employers, and governments' (Fudge, 2007: 2).

This Fordist employment relationship has three objectives: '(1) to protect employees against economic and social risks, (2) to reduce social inequality, and (3) to increase economic efficiency'. It provided 'stable, socially protected, dependent, full time jobs' for male breadwinners (Fudge, 2007: 2). In the UK, conditions were regulated primarily through a system of 'collective laissez faire' backed by strictly limited legal interventions that extended protections for employees (Kahn-Freund, 1972).

While labour law provides the dominant frame of reference for the regulation of relationships for those involved in paid work, it is generally recognized to be struggling conceptually to cope with the changes that have occurred in the global economy since the 1970s. There are a wide range of problems. One such is territoriality. State laws based upon local traditions of industrial relations are not best placed to deal with the way in which multinational enterprises organize their relations of production on a global scale or with flows of migrant workers. Here, however, we are concerned with two other challenges. The *first* comes from feminist labour lawyers who question the way in which the boundaries between production and social reproduction are set and the consequential gendered impact on access to the labour market. Since the 1970s, they have been pointing out that this employment model largely ignores the ways in which women engage with the market and offers little protection to women who work in 'non-standard' ways. As more women joined the labour force, women's organizations in the UK campaigned for legal rights to ensure women's equality at work, resulting in the legislation which tackled access to and segregation within the labour market and equality of pay. A framework developed to cover pregnancy and maternity discrimination and benefits and prohibitions on sexual harassment. Some of these measures have had their origins within the European legal framework. There is an uneasy conceptual relationship between measures introduced to tackle discrimination and those incorporated within employment protection, leading to some highly complex legal issues relating to the precise scope of protection, which continues unabated (Freedland and Kountouris, 2012; McCrudden, 2012).

While a legal framework to provide women with substantive equality was developing in the UK, the labour market was restructuring. By the 1980s, new forms of flexibility were required to tackle decreasing productivity and to reposition the economy within the global market. Public services were privatized. Generally, employment relations were commercialized through the introduction of precarious forms of working, which attracted little or none of the protections offered to those categorized as employees under the Fordist model (Conaghan et al., 2002; Fredman, 2006). The male family wage disintegrated, requiring women to work to maintain household living standards.

The *second* problem, therefore, for labour law results from its basis within a Fordist model of commodity production in economies now organized around the provision of services (Albin, 2010). The commercialization of employment relations associated with the rise of a service economy, through self-employment, subcontracting and franchising, fit uneasily, if at all, into a conceptual framework based upon the contract of employment, a bilateral contract of service between an employer and an employee. A service economy draws together production and consumption in such ways that the processes of consumption affect those of production. It is a world of tripartite relationships between employers, workers and customers/clients organized through contracts for services.

What can seem like esoteric debates, relating to the distinctions between a contract of service and a contract for services, matter greatly to those involved. Organized labour has fought to limit the exploitation of employees, those with contracts of employment, backed by state legislative protections. Entrepreneurs, freely selling services in a market place, are located within a different understanding of power relationships and legal frameworks relating to contract, commercial and consumer law. Clear, if fine, conceptual distinctions between employees, workers and those trading services, disappear in the messy world of working relationships but still result in many workers having far fewer protections.

Women's work is concentrated in the service sector, which is associated with the sort of flexible working that is underpinned by commercialized relationships wherein services are freely traded. However, they tend not to be in the vanguard – the free floating knowledge workers, the independent risk takers who, it is argued, can subvert traditional relations of power through the skilful deployment of their human capital (Albin, 2010). Instead, the majority work in traditional service sectors – still closely associated with socially reproductive activities which can at the extremes hark back to pre-modern forms of relationships and where work is low skilled, commands poor wages, is provided informally and is associated with very different relations of power and risk allocation.

Since the 1980s, there have been attempts to recapture territory for labour law. In the 1990s, the Labour government utilized the language adopted within European law to provide employment-related protections based upon the concept of a worker rather than an employee (Ashiagbor, 2006). This category extended the scope of measures such as the minimum wage and working time limits to those who did not qualify as employees because they were not operating under a contract of employment or because they lacked the continuity necessary to qualify for protective measures. The European framework more generally has had significant effects through the extension of its reach in relation to anti-discrimination measures.

Additionally, the discourse of human rights with its origins in international and regional rights frameworks such as the European Convention on Human Rights has become more significant. Labour law norms as previously discussed recognize inequalities in power and the need to protect workers from economic and social risks. The normative base for anti-discrimination and human rights roots inequality within status categories (sex and disability, for example). While human rights discourse increasingly informs labour law there is an uneasy relationship.

There is a widely held view among labour lawyers that there is a need for the construction of a new employment normative base, which does more than resolve the complexities that have developed around definitions of employees, workers and the somewhat different employment definition used in relation to some anti- discrimination measures (Albin, 2010; Davis, 2007; Freedland, 2006; Fudge, 2006). The aim would be to breathe new life into its distinctive contribution, 'which is to strengthen the bonds of social solidarity against the fragmentation of the market' (Fudge, 2007: 18) and to reassert the progressive norms associated with this form of regulation (Freedland, 2003, 2006).

Body work in a service world: commercial sex services, exploitative relationships and dangerous consumers

The weakening of the ideological assumption that sexual relationships are more appropriately undertaken outside the market place in a consumer-based society has led to the 'normalization' of market satisfaction of sexual desire and the proliferation of services (Hardy et al., 2010). Market provision is however normatively contested, and this is reflected in the legal construction of prostitution and trafficking (O'Connell Davidson and Anderson, 2006). The focus here is on the provision of intimate sexual services, whether on or off street, fully recognizing that there can be a range of contexts in which these services take place reflecting different power relationships.

We can frame this labour process within labour law terms of reference. If the woman works for an employer for wages in an establishment, we would look for a contract of employment upon which to base employment protection rights. She may pay a fee, or other form of consideration, to use premises; she may provide her services via an agency and use her own premises. We would need to know how she works, part-time for how many hours, on a casual basis and so on to assess her employment status and the extent to which she is entitled to employment rights or discrimination protection. Is she working under a contract of service or a contract for services? Is she employed or self-employed?

She is providing an intimate service in which the customer plays a key role. The customer may share employing functions, but more generally it is clear that customers affect her employment conditions and her position at work. The demands of customers are likely to influence both 'hiring and firing'. Meeting the demands and expectations of the 'fantasizing consumer' for particular body images and identities is paramount in this consumer-based industry. Customers need to be 'enchanted' rather than concern themselves with the 'toiling worker' (McDowell et al., 2007).

Therefore, within this discourse we could illustrate the challenges presented by this service work and reflect on similarities to the way in which customers influence labour relations within the wider hospitality industry. Are tips to be seen as contributing towards the minimum wage? To what extent must employers take responsibility for sexual or other forms of harassment by 'third parties' (customers)? Can employers impose dress (broadly defined) codes? We would also need to consider the impact of personal relationships within consumer service provision. Many such services are provided through informal, personal relationships wherein it is difficult to establish a legal basis for worker protection. Working in informal settings, close to employers in a domestic or small establishment, may raise particular issues such as 'on call' time. This issue arises often when a presence is needed at night, for instance in a hospital, or for residential or domiciliary-based care. Is the worker entitled to be paid for such time? Realizing any protection is also very difficult. Workers tend to 'exit' rather than use 'voice' processes (Albin, 2010). Such settings are not conducive to unionization, which makes challenging decisions in appropriate fora even more unlikely.

These issues can be used to support the need to reconfigure labour law to ensure that it functions appropriately in a service-based consumer economy, not only to support economic objectives but also to recognize power relationships and to offer protections to workers.

This, of course, is not the way in which commercial sex services are discussed. Instead, they are placed beyond the margins of labour law. We see the aims of protecting employees and ensuring economic efficiency transposed into the criminal law and to a lesser extent, human rights discourse. These discourses construct the relationships in terms of dominance. The economic objective is to suppress, not facilitate the market while customers are recognized as contributing substantially to power relationships. In the trafficked body, we see recognition of the way in which particular bodies are constructed within law through their work.

Although 'prostitution' in practice can involve a contract for services, it is not legally recognized for reasons of public policy. No employment relationship is recognized in the criminal provisions which regulates relationships[1]. The employer is recast as someone causing or inciting for gain or controlling activities for gain. Providing a place of work is criminalized as the provision of a brothel. The person seeking to sell her services is impeded by crimes against soliciting and advertising. The international aspects of trading are tackled through anti-trafficking measures that criminalize the processes involved.

The normative justification for this criminalization has shifted over time, from protecting against immorality, then prohibiting public nuisance, to, in recent times, an explicit attempt to disrupt and suppress the market because of the unacceptable levels of exploitation involved, which in the case of trafficking are seen as clear violations of fundamental human rights to liberty. There has been a policy shift from constructing the service provider as a dangerous woman to seeing her as vulnerable, as a victim of exploitation who needs protection of her right not be bodily violated and exploited. We have transposed the danger on to the customer, along with those who are cast in the 'employer' role such as traffickers.

The key provision which illustrates many of these issues is Section 53A of Sexual Offences Act 2003.

Paying for sexual services of a prostitute subjected to force etc

(1) A person (A) commits an offence if
  (a) A makes or promises payment for the sexual services of a prostitute (B),
  (b) a third person (C) has engaged in exploitative conduct of a kind likely to induce or encourage B to provide the sexual services for which A has made or promised payment, and

  (c) C engaged in that conduct for or in the expectation of gain for C or another person (apart from A or B).

(2) The following are irrelevant
  (a) ....
  (b) whether A is, or ought to be, aware that C has engaged in exploitative conduct.

(3) C engages in exploitative conduct if
  (a) C uses force, threats (whether or not relating to violence) or any other form of coercion, or
  (b) C practices any form of deception.

We see here that tripartite relationships are recognized. The consumer and his power is placed centre stage. In an attempt to suppress demand, to reassert not just recognition of the toiling worker but the exploited victim, the fantasizing consumer is denied the legitimacy of agency. His desires are recast as an obligation to recognize the particular identity of the service provider – not stunning Albanian beauty, but raped and abused victim, made vulnerable by her economic location within the global economy. The potential abuse of the worker by the client and the assumed abuse by the 'employer' figure are emphasized. The interdependence of the parties is clearly recognized but wholly outside labour law.

Body work in a service world: caring

The exclusion from labour or commercial contract law in the previous example results from an explicit policy decision not to recognize the relationships. The present one concerns difficulties with fitting 'legitimate' relationships within the framework. Forms of 'care', particularly when provided in informal, domestic, personalized contexts within a network of relationships, struggle to be recognized as a work relationship or worthy of protection. Much paid care work, particularly for the elderly, is associated with irregular hours, multiple job holding, agency provision and bogus self-employment – factors which mitigate against protection within labour law. Unpaid caring by 'carers' is beyond such protection.

    Labour law is not the only legal domain which organizes the relationships involved and addresses issues of risk, vulnerability and exploitation. The work relationship involving family members is constituted within social welfare law. It grants the status of 'carer' and some rights, derived through this work relationship, although these do not provide labour law forms of protection. Some paid relationships, marginalized by labour law, are now being recognized in terms of rights. The power relationship can also attract a dominance discourse within criminal law similar to that of trafficking.

Exploitative relationships and dangerous employers

For the discourse of labour law, the margin is constituted through debates over domestic workers, which in this context include those providing paid care within informal familial settings. Feminist labour lawyers, joined now by human rights activists, have highlighted the position of such workers, who occupy a no woman's land between legal regimes organized around concepts of production and those organized in relation to social reproductive activities. Domestic work is hard to regulate but 'prone to precariousness for social (gender, race, migration and social class), psychological (intimacy and stigma) and also economic reasons' (Albin and Mantouvalu, 2012: 69).

They point to the current UK position whereby domestic workers are often excluded from the protections provided to 'workers' such as over regulation of working time, health and safety legislation, partially (if provided with accommodation) or wholly (if treated as family members domestic workers) from minimum wage requirements. Such workers cannot access anti-discrimination and equality provisions (Albin and Mantouvalu, 2012: 70–71).

Legal migrant domestic workers are even less likely be included in any protective labour law measures. Illegal status denies all employment protections. The plight of migrant domestic workers has surfaced within international labour and human discourse in recent times because of the sheer size of this group worldwide (Stewart, 2011). A discourse based upon violations of human rights, similar to that of women trafficked for the purposes of sexual exploitation, has emerged within various settings. One of which has made use of an underused article, Article 4, of the European Convention on Human Rights that prohibits slavery, servitude, forced and compulsory labour. It was invoked to expose the inadequacies within the French criminal legislation to deal with the 'servitude, forced and compulsory labour' experienced by the applicant. This ruling against the French state recognized 'modern slavery' and prompted the UK to adopt new legislation (section 71 of the Coroners and Justice Act 2009; Mantouvalou, 2006, 2010).

Slavery, servitude and forced or compulsory labour

(1) A person (D) commits an offence if
   (a) D holds another person in slavery or servitude and the circumstances are such that D knows or ought to know that the person is so held, or
   (b) D requires another person to perform forced or compulsory labour and the circumstances are such that D knows or ought to know that the person is being required to perform such labour

The position of domestic workers has also been recognized by the International Labour Organisation. The Convention on the Rights of Domestic Workers 2011 is seen as a 'landmark moment for the international labour law regime' because it addresses a specific sector of activity now clearly identified as work and incorporates a human rights approach into international labour law discourse (Albin and Mantouvalou, 2012: 67). Its provisions cover both 'civil rights, like access to justice and privacy, and social and labour rights, like working time and minimum wage' (Albin and Mantouvalou, 2012: 73). The UK government abstained in the voting on its adoption. Albin and Mantouvalou (2012: 77) quote the views of the UK representative: 'we do not consider it appropriate, or practical, to extend criminal health and safety legislation, including inspections, to cover private households employing domestic workers. It would be difficult, for instance, to hold elderly individuals, who employ carers, to the same standards as large companies'.

This quotation is illuminating: first because employed 'carers' are identified as falling within this category of worker and second because elderly clients are, by implication, seen to be particular types of employer. The suggestion here would seem to be that such a caring relationship involves competing vulnerabilities and uncertain distributions of power between the employer/client and the worker.

To understand more, we need to consider the nature of caring relationships within this 'non-standard' or marginal work context and the way in which the discourse from another area of law, associated with the fixing of social responsibility for care, constructs such relationships and addresses the associated risks.

Exploitative relationships and 'empowered' clients/consumers

Social welfare law delineates the responsibilities of the state for the welfare of vulnerable adults. The focus of legal attention here is the person in need of care who is situated within a network of relationships (Ungerson, 2000). This individual is being repositioned within a social market as *an independent consumer of care services*, as someone who chooses what they want rather than being the recipient of state-defined provision. As a consumer/client, they gain power, in theory, but given the nature of state responsibility for such care only the most intensely vulnerable are presently eligible for publicly funded services. In relation to whom does such a vulnerable consumer gain power? Their unpaid relatives, who within social welfare law are defined as 'carers'? The paid workers from whom they purchase services directly or indirectly?

Evolution of social/community care law and policy

Social responsibility for the care of the vulnerable, including the elderly, involves a range of actors, the state, market, voluntary sector and families, the relationship between which has changed substantially since its origins in the Poor Law 1834 (Lyon and Glucksmann, 2008: 111). The post-war welfare state excluded the provision of social care, viewed as residual, from the National Health Service. Local authorities were sanctioned under the National Assistance Act of 1948 to provide and to charge for specific services to those with identified forms of need. Such public assistance as was available to the elderly in general was institutionalized through provision of 'old people's homes', although those identified as having a particular need could be provided with a 'home help' who was directly employed by the local authority.

The restructuring of economic relations, which took place in the 1980s, resulted in a changed relationship between the state and the market. This involved the creation of a mixed market in welfare through splitting purchase and provision functions through compulsory competitive tendering for services. The result was privatization of services. By the end of the decade, social services departments had been recast as commissioners of state-financed, privately delivered services. Private residential homes developed rapidly, many of which were small, often family run businesses, dependent on publicly funded residents (Brown, 2010; Means et al., 2008).

More generally, there was a move in a service-based economy towards greater client choice through 'personalization' of services. Residential provision became not only prohibitively expensive for the state, but also seen as inappropriate. An increasingly effective disability rights movement lobbied for replacement of the dependency model to one based upon user empowerment and rights. Local authorities began to commission community care, particularly domiciliary-based services, which stimulated a market in agencies to provide these. This mixed market is now constituted by a large number of small businesses and voluntary organizations providing care homes, domiciliary services, and a small number of large providers. The sector remains under-capitalized, with small profit margins and high risk, deeply dependent on public funds (Stewart, 2012).

Employment relations within the social service provision have been reconfigured. State employed social workers operate as care brokers, buying packages of care (Ungerson, 2000). Social care workers (including personal assistants) undertaking body work are now located primarily within the private sector (70 per cent). This workforce is low skilled, low paid, predominately female (90 per cent), two-thirds of whom provide care for the elderly (Lyon and Glucksmann, 2008: 112). The commercialization of relations has resulted in the predominance of 'non-standard' and precarious work arrangements. As we have seen, such workers attract few employment protection rights, enabling the economic risks associated with restructuring to be passed on to them.

There is another group of workers, invisible to labour law, who undertake 'social' care. Family law in the UK places no legal responsibility on adult children to support parents or other relatives. Nonetheless, the 1948 welfare system was predicated upon the assumption that such informal care would be provided within the dominant societal model of the male breadwinner/female homemaker model. Although this model has been superseded, the assumptions relating to the provision of informal care have not. Approximately six million people, now termed 'carers', undertake such work in the UK. It is estimated that if valued their yearly cost would be roughly equivalent to that of the NHS; without it the public systems would collapse (Buckner and Yeandle, 2007). The manifest tensions between paid work and care responsibilities coupled with the financial and social consequences of demographic changes, which see a significant rise in the proportion of very elderly people in the next decades, has spawned anxious debates over a crisis in care (Stewart, 2012).

The present legal and financial systems are generally recognized by policy makers as wholly unfit for purpose (Stewart, 2012). The Law Commission in 2011 made recommendations for a comprehensive new legal framework that forms the basis for forthcoming legislation. It places the individual client at the normative core of its proposals. While local authorities retain the responsibility for assessing individual needs within a framework which sets the eligibility criteria for the provision of services, the overall objective is to enable clients (or advocates on their behalf) to choose the services they want to ensure their well-being. There will be further development of the direct payments/individual budgets framework that enables the individual client to use public funds to buy services, leading to further commercialization in service provision. The Dilnot Commission, which also reported in 2011, tackled the highly contentious area of how to fund social care. Responsibility for funding a significant, but defined proportion of life-time caring costs is placed firmly on the individual.

Social welfare law also recognizes that there is a relationship between this newly constituted client/customer and unpaid familial carers. We have seen the emergence of a new legal identity, the carer who is defined in legislation through this relationship. However, they are now attracting separated rights that recognize that this form of work affects them as quasi workers. Carers are entitled to be assessed for services based upon their separate needs such as for time off (to purchase respite care) and as individuals experiencing exclusion from full citizenship primarily derived through their inability to undertake paid work or to participate in social life. Many carers, both working age and older, are impoverished because they cannot undertake any or enough paid work and/or because they are reliant on inadequate state welfare payments which are primarily derived through their relationship with the care recipient (Yeadle et al., 2007a, b, and c).

Because of their socially reproductive location, carers lack the indices for legal recognition of their body work as employment for the reasons discussed earlier. If a carer has a separate paid occupation that constitutes them as an employee they will attract similar rights to those offered to parents to 'balance' work and family (Employment Relations Act 1996). As workers who also care, they may also be able to rely on the anti-discrimination measures contained within the Equality Act 2010, which recognizes discrimination by association with someone with a protected characteristic (in this case disability; Stewart, Hoskins, and Nicolai, 2011).

Recognizing power relationships in body work

The elderly care recipient as customer/client in an era of consumerism is being provided with services through a range of legally constructed relationships. They may be provided with state funds to purchase (in theory) the care services they would like. The care recipient may employ a social carer or domestic worker. If supplied through an agency, there will be a contract for services with the agency but no direct employment relationship with the worker. If employed directly, there may be a contract of employment or the worker may be self-employed. A care recipient cannot use state-provided funds (direct payments) to pay relatives who live with them. They may be able to employ other family members in which case these family members may become their employees. Unpaid carers although attracting some citizen-based rights are not protected through an employment relationship despite often being the linchpin to the web of relationships necessary to meet the customer/client needs.

Who needs protection here and from what? The empowered client may be very frail and vulnerable, wholly dependent on the abilities of an agency to deliver agreed, but often meagre, services and the worker/employee to provide appropriate care. An agency worker is often under immense pressure to carry out the agreed service. They may work in difficult physical and social environments that require them to meet consumer desired, but agency prescribed, demands. They may face 'third party' harassment. Those working within bilateral arrangements, including migrant domestic workers, face similar consumer expectations without the protections potentially offered through their relationship with an agency. Determining and limiting working hours can be difficult.

Family carers are under no formal obligation to provide care, but in practice they can work very long hours, sometimes with continuous 'on call' time. More than 21 per cent of carers provide over fifty hours or more care per week (Lyon and Glucksmann, 2008: 111). They can experience harassment. At the same time, there is a rising expectation of what is involved in decent care, encouraging carers as well as care workers to acquire care skills (Dodds, 2007).

There is also growing anxiety over abuse of the elderly and vulnerable. The legal language used to address this issue varies but it is increasingly framed as a violation of human rights. As such, it places responsibilities upon the state to ensure that such abuses do not take place. It is however seen as perpetrated by both care workers and carers. Those within the sphere of labour law and, therefore, within the public realm are affected by the framework for the public regulation of care standards. Care workers are constructed as potentially dangerous workers requiring screening to alert employers/clients to this danger. Dangerous (private) carers are viewed differently (Galpin, 2010; Herring, 2009). Their abuse is absorbed into two possible policy frameworks, one analogous to child abuse, involving the language of safeguarding, the other seeing elder abuse as a continuation of domestic violence.

Conclusion

These two examples consider body work on the margins of recognition within labour law. In both instances the consumer/client is increasingly incorporated into the work–like relationships. In both cases, we see the exploitation and abuse which result from inequalities of power in working relationships being tackled through 'non-traditional' legal frameworks.

Both examples in different ways engage other areas of law to tackle issues of vulnerability, exploitation and abuse using different languages. The first locates the activity outside the realms of labour law, thereby denying its protection to those involved as workers. However, the form of regulation used, a combination of criminal and human rights discourses involving two different forms of state power, recognizes the impact of a global consumer/service economy on power relations associated with work. The law is being used not to facilitate economic relations while protecting workers against market risk, but rather it is being used to disrupt the market by criminalizing the client. The vulnerability of the worker constituted as a prostitute/trafficked person is protected through client-based interventions.

The caring example involves relationships on the margins of labour law. Many categories of workers in the informal context of home find themselves outside the protection of labour law. Those who employ 'modern slaves' attract criminal penalties. At the same time, the international labour discourse is seeking to provide domestic workers with human and labour rights. Social welfare law is providing unpaid carers, who are wholly outside the discourse of labour law, with some form of rights that nevertheless recognize the impact of their work on their lives, including the risks to their health and well-being. These rights do not offer labour law type protections. Yet developments within the social market in care are reconstituting caring through love (and obligation). The reconstruction of the care recipient as a consumer/client who assembles care services limits recognition of the complex power relationships involved in these intense body work contexts, which characterize their relations with both unpaid carers and paid workers.

Labour law as presently constituted cannot tackle relationships constituted on the borders of production and social reproduction, and also struggles to recognize the influence of consumer/clients on work relationships. Resort to criminal sanctions and to the individualistic language of human rights to protect vulnerability in working relationships is not necessarily a positive development. The first creates a particular form of worker vulnerability while invoking direct state power, whereas the second denies the relational nature of power relationships within work contexts and reconstructs these as conflicting rights. The solidarity that underlies labour law protections is lost. We need to find a way of reconstructing labour law in a way which retains its understanding of work based *relationships* and its recognition of power differentials. It will need to encompass the range of relationships that now constitute work in a consumer society and recognize the role and influence of consumers (Albin, 2010). It is clear from the two examples discussed here that body work offers particular challenges to such a reconstruction.

Note

1 See Crown Prosecution Service guidance for more details: http://www.cps.gov.uk/legal/p_to_r/prostitution_and_exploitation_of_prostitution/#a14.

REFERENCES

Albin, E. (2010). Labour Law in a Service World. *Modern Law Review* 73(6): 959–84.
Albin, E. and Mantouvalu, V. (2012). The ILO Convention on Domestic Workers: From the Shadows to the Light. *Industrial Law Journal* 41(1): 67–78.

▶

▶

Ashiagbor, D. (2006). Promoting Precariousness? The Response of EU Employment Policies to Precarious Work. *In* J. Fudge and R. Owen (Eds) *Precarious Work, Women and the New Economy: The Challenge to Legal Norms.* Oxford: Hart. Pp. 77–97.

Brown, K. (2010). The Older Person's Social Care and the Enabling Service. *In* K. Brown (Ed.) *Vulnerable Adults and Community Care,* 2nd ed. Exeter: Learning Matters.

Buckner, L. and Yeandle, S. (2007). *Valuing Carers: Calculating the Value of Unpaid Care.* London: Carers UK.

Conaghan, J., Fischl, R.M. and Klare, K. (Eds) (2002). *Labour Law in an Era of Globalisation: Transformative Practices and Possibilities.* Oxford: Oxford University Press.

Davis, A.C.L. (2007). The Contract for Intermittent Employment. *Industrial Law Journal* 36(1): 102–18.

Deakin, S. (2007). Does the 'Personal Employment Contract' Provide a Basis for the Reunification of Employment Law? *Industrial Law Journal* 36(1): 68–83.

Deakin, S. and Wilkinson, F. (2005). *The Law of the Labour Market.* Oxford: Oxford University Press.

Dilnot, A. (2011). *Fairer Caring Funding.* The Report of the Commission on Funding of Care and Support (Dilnot Enquiry). Available at http://www.dilnotcommission.dh.gov.uk/our-report/.

Dodds, S. (2007). Depending on Care: Recognition of Vulnerability and the Social Contribution of Care Provisions. *Bioethics* 21(9): 500–10.

Fredman, S. (2006). Precarious Norms for Precarious Workers. *In* J. Fudge and R. Owen (Eds) *Precarious Work, Women and the New Economy: The Challenge to Legal Norms.* Oxford: Hart. Pp. 177–200.

Freedland, M.R. (2003). *The Personal Employment Contract.* Oxford: Oxford University Press.

——— (2006). From the Contract of Employment to the Personal Work Nexus. *Industrial Law Journal* 35(1): 1–26

Freedland, M. and Kountouris, N. (2012). Employment Equality and Personal Work Relations – A Critique of Jivraj v Hashwani. *Industrial Law Journal* 41(1): 56–66.

Fudge, J. (2006). Self-Employment, Women, and Precarious Work: The Scope of Labour Protection. *In* J. Fudge and R. Owen (Eds) *Precarious Work, Women and the New Economy: The Challenge to Legal Norms.* Oxford: Hart.

——— (2007). The New Workplace: Surveying the Landscape. Paper prepared for and presented at the Isaac Pitblado Lectures, Winnipeg, Manitoba, 9–10 November 2007.

Galpin, D. (2010). Policy and the Protection of Older People from Abuse. *Journal of Social Welfare Law and Family Law* 32(3): 237–45.

Hardy, K., Kingston, S. and Sanders, T. (Eds) (2010). *New Sociologies of Sex Work.* Farnham: Ashgate.

Herring, J. (2009). *Older People in Law and Society.* Oxford: Oxford University Press.

▶

Kahn-Freund, O. (1972). *Labour and the Law*. London: Stevens for the Hamlyn Trust.

The Law Commission (2011). *Adult Social Care* No 326 HC 941 May. London: HMG.

Lyon, D. and Glucksmann, M. (2008). Comparative Configurations of Care Work across Europe. *Sociology* 42: 101–17.

Mantouvalou, V. (2006). Servitude and Forced Labour in the 21st Century: The Human Rights of Domestic Workers. *International Labour Journal* 35(4): 395–414.

———— (2010). Modern Slavery: The UK Response. *International Labour Journal* 39(4): 425–31.

McCrudden, C. (2012). Two Views of Subordination: The Personal Scope of Employment Discrimination Law in Jivraj v Hashwani. *Industrial Law Journal* 41(1): 30–55.

McDowell, L., Batnitzky, A. and Dyer, S. (2007). Division, Segmentation, and Interpellation: The Embodied Labors of Migrant Workers in a Greater London Hotel. *Economic Geography* 83(1): 1–25.

Means, R., Richards, S. and Smith, R. (2008). *Community Care: Policy and Practice*, 4th ed. Basingstoke: Palgrave Macmillan.

O'Connell Davidson, J. and Anderson, B. (2006). The Trouble with 'Trafficking'. *In* C.L. van den Anker and J. Doomernik (Eds) *Trafficking and Women's Rights in Europe*. London: Palgrave Macmillan. Pp. 11–26.

Pateman, C. (1988). *Sexual Contract*. Cambridge: Polity.

Stewart, A. (2011). *Gender, Law and Justice in a Global Market*. Cambridge: Cambridge University Press.

———— (2012). From Family to Personal Responsibility: The Challenges for Care of the Elderly in England. *Journal of Social Welfare and Family Law*. Available at http://www.tandfonline.com/doi/abs/10.1080/09649069.2012.718534.

Stewart, A., Niccolai, S. and Hoskyns, C. (2011). Disability Discrimination by Association: A Case of the Double Yes? *Social and Legal Studies* 20(2): 173–90.

Ungerson, C. (2000). Thinking about the Production and Consumption of Long-Term Care in Britain: Does Gender Still Matter? *Journal of Social Policy* 29(4): 623–43.

Yeandle, S., Bennett, C., Buckner, L., Fry, G. and Price, C. (2007a). *Diversity in Caring: Towards Equality for Carers*. Employment and Service Report Series, No. 3, University of Leeds. Available at http://www.sociology.leeds.ac.uk/circle/publications/ces-reports.php.

———— (2007b). *Managing Caring and Employment*. Employment and Service Report Series, No. 2, University of Leeds. Available at http://www.sociology.leeds.ac.uk/circle/publications/ces-reports.php.

———— (2007c). *Stages and Transitions in the Experience of Caring*. Employment and Service Report Series, No. 1, University of Leeds. Available at http://www.sociology.leeds.ac.uk/circle/publications/ces-reports.php.

Gender, Emotional Labour and Interactive Body Work: Negotiating Flesh and Fantasy in Sex Workers' Labour Practices

5

Barbara G. Brents and Crystal A. Jackson

It is a truism in some circles to say that prostitutes 'sell their bodies'. For some, the prostitute has become iconic in representing the female body's subordinated status in patriarchal sexuality (Barry, 1995; Jeffreys, 1997). Yet, in rejecting that view, one sex worker told us, 'I don't know where they got "selling your body" because wouldn't that be uncomfortable if somebody walked off with your vagina?'

As the social sciences begin to bring the body back into our understandings of social life, the gendered body's relationship to the labour process continues to be the subject of much debate. Understanding the dilemmas of body work in sex work becomes increasingly important as more work in late capitalist service economies involves the sale of bodily labour. From the commodification of appearance to intimate labour on another's body, more workers must labour on their own bodies to look 'right' in entertainment, tourism, hospitality, retail sales and even corporate management (Entwistle and Wissinger, 2006; Warhurst and Nickson, 2007; Warhurst et al., 2000; Witz, Warhurst, and Nickson, 2003). Beauticians, fitness instructors, maids, tattoo artists and piercers, undertakers, childcare workers, and a host of medical workers labour on others' bodies, touching them, manipulating them, enhancing them and healing them (McDowell, 2009; Twigg et al., 2011a; Wolkowitz, 2006).

The increasing attention to the body/work nexus provides an important frame for exploring sex work. Body work is gendered as well as material, and research exploring the negotiation of physical boundaries of the body as well as the physical senses is important (Vannini, Waskul, and Gottschalk,

2012; Wolkowitz, 2006). By using the frame of body work, we can add a more refined understanding of how the gendering process is implicated in the construction and surveillance of the body in sex work. Likewise, examining sex work can teach us much about the relation between body, emotion and labour in a variety of jobs.

In this chapter, we use Nevada's legal brothels as a case study to examine how sex workers talk about their bodies and their labour. This research comes from a larger project on Nevada's legal brothels (Brents, Jackson, and Hausbeck, 2010). We focus specifically on what prostitutes say about themselves, their bodies and their work. What does the body mean to sex workers themselves? How do they position themselves in relation to their bodies and to the bodies of their customers? We specifically look at the way sex workers talk and don't talk about bodies, how they describe the interactions and how they give meaning and value to the interactions.

What we find is that there are multiple dimensions of body work, and these dimensions can be configured into different strategies or practices by different workers. In other words, the body/work nexus must be understood as a body/emotion/work nexus involving a variety of dimensions assembled in different ways, even within similar jobs. Among these dimensions, we conceptualize interactive labour, which includes labour where clients engage the worker's body. Sex workers' thinking about their body is itself socially and culturally constructed, and how they put together strategies rests on gendered assumptions about a mind/body dualism and the stigma of dirty work. In their different constructions, workers both reproduce and resist dominant gendered constructions of the body and the devaluation of body labour. This multidimensional way of conceptualizing body work helps us understand commonalities and differences in different kinds of work.

The body and emotional labour

Beginning with Arlie Hochschild's groundbreaking study of the labour of airline stewardesses, emotional labour has become the dominant frame for understanding the labour process of the service industry. Emotional labour focuses on how service and care workers, largely women, deploy emotions as commodities and how that affects their sense of self (Hochschild, 1983). While the early literature focused on the alienating aspects of shaping one's emotions to the demands of employers, more recent research suggests that there is variety in how workers employ emotional management strategies to manage self-identity (Bolton, 2005a; Grandey, 2000). In addition, the structure, context and conditions of the job, autonomy, working conditions, length of interactions, and repetition of interactions all affect their ability to negotiate and cope with the labour (Abiala, 1999; Brotheridge and Grandey, 2002; Bulan, Erickson, and Wharton, 1997; Sanders, 2005a; Wharton, 1993, 2009; Zapf and Holz, 2006).

Body work involves direct, hands-on activities, handling, assessing, and manipulating bodies in paid labour (Twigg et al., 2011b; Wolkowitz, 2002). Empirical research on body work has focused on the field of health, medicine and care work (Diamond, 1992; Foner, 2004; Stacey, 1988; Twigg, 2000, 2004; Twigg et al., 2011a). In many of these studies, it is both the labour process as well as the cultural constraints of gender, sexuality and race that shape the experiences, value and performance of the work.

Carol Wolkowitz (2006) points out that much of the analysis of the prostitute's body itself has been largely theoretical, either essentializing the body or viewing the body as text or metaphor, without looking at the material relations that both construct mindfulness of the body and organize the work. Empirical research on sex work has drawn on concepts from the emotional labour literature (Chapkis, 1997; Vanwesenbeeck, 2005), focusing on the ways women negotiate separating 'self' from their labour through creating physical or emotional boundaries between self and work (Abel, 2011; Brewis and Linstead, 2000; Browne and Minichiello, 1995; Sanders, 2002, 2005a, 2005b). Yet this work has not necessarily focused on the body. What is clear from this research, though, is that the interaction between emotional and bodily labour is important to understand.

Research on body work also suggests that contemporary Western culture's mind/body dualism affects how service work is allocated and valued, and this further implicates emotional labour in how we view body work, especially for sex workers. In the health professions, for example, it is male doctors who do the intellectual labour whereas women do both the emotional and 'dirty' body work (Anderson, 2000; Emerson and Pollner, 1975). Certainly gender as well as race and class are also involved in allocating this 'dirty' work (Diamond, 1992). Gender also matters as female body workers stress affective components and 'caring' in their work. These workers also struggle to establish power, authority or expertise as they work against the devaluing of bodily labour. A study of gynecological nurses finds that they ascribe a gendered specialness to their 'dirty' work (Bolton, 2005b). Although devalued, emotional labour can add value to (non-sexual) service industry exchanges (Adkins, 1995, 2001, 2002; Adkins and Merchant, 1996; Hochschild, 1983, 2003; Toerien and Kitzinger, 2007). For sex workers, emotional labour can often enhance the value of their services. These findings suggest that workers struggle against the negative connotations of bodily labour (Bolton, 2005b).

Further, whereas studies of work frequently focus on employer control of gendered bodies, in today's economy independent, flexible and contingent work is increasingly the norm. Jobs from models to masseuses to care workers are independently contracted. Workers must answer to both customers and contractors in regulating their bodies and emotions to successfully earn a living, and research finds that the service triangle means that workers engage in self-surveillance. Indeed a study comparing emotional management strategies found that self-employed workers were more likely to use deep acting whereas hourly paid hair stylists used surface acting (Cohen, 2010). This makes it increasingly important to examine workers' mindfulness about their own bodies in the course of doing their labour.

The research methods

Nevada's brothels are important sites for examining the labour of prostitution in a number of ways. Sexual services in Nevada's brothels are legal. Workers are independent contractors and do not have to deal with the same stressors, dangers or risk of arrest as illegal workers. As independent contractors, brothel workers are relatively free in how they choose to perform their labour; management does not provide a script or staging instructions. There is a range of services from 30-minute sessions to multi-hourly 'dates' outside of the brothels, depending on the location. Workers negotiate contracts with brothel managers to include either shift work or one to three-week stays in-house at the brothel. The amount of control over work conditions varies somewhat among brothels. All women told us they had the power to turn down customers, although there is an economic incentive not to do so.

Nevada's brothels are also a particularly rich place for studying the diversity of sex work. Small rural brothels market primarily to working class mobile labourers, such as truckers, migrant farm workers, and miners. Suburban brothels outside of Las Vegas and Reno see these same clients, in addition to a large number of tourists and affluent clients from the nearby urban areas (Brents and Hausbeck, 2007).

The legal setting means a wide variety of workers come to one location. While workers were predominantly white, women had wide ranging occupational, educational and social class backgrounds (Brents, Jackson, and Hausbeck, 2010). Workers usually came from out of town or surrounding states.

This chapter uses the Nevada brothel industry as a case study for understanding the intersections of body, work, and emotion in a specifically gendered, sexualized workplace. We undertook a ten-year multi-method study of sexual labour in Nevada brothels, including ethnographic visits to the brothels and interviews with thirty-eight women working at brothels across the state (Brents, Jackson, and Hausbeck, 2010). The interviews were conducted in the brothels, lasting from a half hour to two hours. To understand how the women[1] defined their work, we analysed interviews for information on how workers described their labour process, their bodies, and their customers' bodies.

Multiple dimensions of body work

So what kind of labour is sex work? We found that women drew upon a range of dimensions or elements in their work that they combined into different overall strategies. Drawing on previous research on body work, we found it best to consider several dimensions, components or elements of body work to help us understand how sex workers talked about their labour.

1. Physical labour: Labour performed by the worker's body where the body is the tool.
2. Aesthetic labour: Labour performed on one's own body to produce a particular image or style that is part of the job.
3. Bodily labour: Labour managing the customer's body as the object/point of service provision.
4. Interactive bodily labour: Where the customer touches back, or the customer is allowed or encouraged to engage the worker's body, the labour involves managing the customer's manipulation of the worker's body.
5. Emotional labour on three levels:
   a. Attending to the physical sensations of customers.
   b. Attending to the emotional needs of customers, producing an emotional result in the customer.
   c. Managing and modifying one's own emotions on the job and as a result of the work.

All of these factors are apparent in several kinds of service work, including the sale of sex.

Physical labour

Brothels price services based on timed physical acts, like a thirty minute 'half and half' (begin with oral sex, then move to penetrative sex), often relying loosely on menus of physical services. It makes sense, then, that women would talk about their labour in terms of the physical acts they must perform using their own bodies. Many talked about learning the job as learning physical techniques, such as how to do the best blow jobs or hand jobs. Many also talked about the physicality of the work of being a sensing body. Emili talked about how 'the smell of a man, the way that their facial hair is kind of rough. And their bodies are hairy' defined her preference for working with men. Celeste, age 45, then at the Green Lantern in rural Nevada, but who had worked in the industry for 13 years, talked a great deal about the skills in using her body to set the pace of the encounter: 'You can set exactly, almost like a micrometer exactly, how deep they're going to go. I mean, just the benefit of one knee, yea, one knee down, it's only going that far.'

Bodily labour

Celeste also articulated much of what the women were telling us about body labour, or work managing other's bodies, in the way one had to physically feel and read another's body in order to manage the outcome.

> It's almost like choreographing a dance in bed...you have to pay attention. When you feel their buttocks tighten, or you feel a twitch here or a twitch there, what does that mean? Is that a good twitch or a bad twitch?...You've got to take stage directions well.

These stage directions, reading twitches, eye contact, hand gestures, helped women manage men's bodies to time their parties, making sure they orgasm at the right moment within the allotted time.

Aesthetic labour

Aesthetic labour undertaken on their own bodies to compete for clients is a significant part of their work. Workers either approach customers at the bar, or are chosen by customers out of a line-up, where they are required to stand, smile, and say their names with little other interaction. As such, aesthetic narratives mostly revolved around living up to clients (and other women's) standards of beauty. Women talked about using exercise facilities at the brothel, or buying clothing from the many travelling retail businesses; costume changes, exercise, hair and make-up occupied large portions of the day. Surgeries such as breast implants or 'tummy tucks' were almost standard in the larger suburban brothels.

Aesthetic labour also included self-branding, working with and marketing their bodies to fit into a niche. This was particularly important for older or larger women, and they worked at self-presentation in contrast to hegemonically beautiful bodies. For example, Angela, 27, at the rural Green Lantern said, 'They just want a woman who has meat. And I have meat.'

Emotional labour

As Twigg et al. (2011) point out, boundaries around body work are fluid and body work never involves just the body. Emotional labour was an important and complicated component of the job. There were two components to this, how women talked about evoking an emotion in the customer and how women talked about managing their own emotions.

For example, Celeste's attention to tightening of the buttocks or other physical cues ultimately required an assessment of the client's emotions as to whether this was a positive or negative experience. Zoie, in her thirties and working at the suburban Moonlight Bunny Ranch, talked about the work of eliciting an emotional response of happiness which is mixed with physical relief.

> With every man there's a plan in your head because your goal is to make them really happy. To 'get them off and get them out,' right? So as soon as you start touching them, or he's voiced to you what he likes, everything you do from that moment on is a calculated move to reach that goal.

The physical labour happens when 'you start touching them' and in the focus on managing their bodies in the 'calculated moves to reach that goal' of orgasm. But the calculation itself, the emotion work to 'plan in your head' with a goal of evoking emotion, to 'make them really happy', involves a combination of physical, bodily and emotional labour. As discussed later in this chapter, we find, as do others, that it is not just the physical release, but managing a client's emotional response that is important in sex work (Sanders, 2008).

Evoking an emotional response in the customer is often discussed as a kind of manipulation of self, involving managing one's own emotions. Ricki, 35, at suburban Miss Kitty's, talked about having to have a dual persona in enticing a customer to your room. 'You've got to be someone's fantasy. You basically have to manipulate and be someone that you're not to entice them to go to your room.' 'It's [the job is] complete acting, that's how I look at it', said Alicia. But for Alicia, the acting was less about fulfilling a sexual fantasy and more about being a counselor. 'When I act with a customer, I like to act like I'm their advisor, you know I like to listen to people, listen to their problems or their dreams or their goals.' Many studies have found that women talk about acting as a critical part of their labour (Abel, 2011; Brewis and Linstead, 2000; Sanders, 2005a).

Hiding or modifying one's own emotions is a necessary part of this. Bretney, 31, at the Moonlight Bunny Ranch talked about being homesick at the brothel, but as she said, 'Nobody wants to be with somebody that's this close to tears all the time. You know, homesick. Yeah, so you're happy, all happy.' Hochschild sees this acting as a kind of betrayal of one's inner emotions in order to match the demands and feeling rules of the job.

Another element of modifying one's own emotions on the job was the act of selling. Bev, 21, an adult film star now working at Miss Kitty's, says, 'There are a lot of us who are very quiet – and to be in this industry you have to be talking and communicate and sell yourself and your party. Sell your party more than yourself.'

For Emili, new to the industry, the upfront selling caused her the most agony: 'You think it's not a lot, it's a lot. Because you're learning how to sell yourself, you're learning how to present yourself in a way that you're valuable, your time is valuable.' Alice at the Moonlight Bunny said, 'You know if you say I want $10,000 for an hour and you don't believe you'll get it, then you won't get it. You have to believe that you'll get that money.'

For Emili, the work was intellectually difficult in a way that surprised her:

Trying to remember in what order to ask them ... You start with a Jacuzzi suite information, you let them know that it books for $500, I mean that's the booking fee for anything [activities are added on]. And that can generate whether they're willing to spend that much or not willing to spend that much just by their expression. Ya know. Then you know up or down, as far as price. Little keys, little factors, which you have to be a good listener and you have to be good at presenting.

Many also talked about those first moments when the customers had to be sold and led on what they wanted. Joyce told of the work that went into sensing the needs of a 'real shy' customer in order to evoke emotions from him:

He was very nervous and when I came back in I said, you know just let me give you a hug. And I held him and he held on to me. And I could just sense that he hadn't had the human touch. It had been a long time. Ya know?

Interactive body work

What is perhaps the most distinct element of sex work, compared to other jobs, is the interactive body work. In few other jobs does the customer touch back, or engage the worker's body as extensively as for sex workers.[2] That a client can so actively touch back is perhaps behind much of the concern about the level of control the worker can have over this intimacy. Many studies of sex workers talk about the boundary work that is necessary because of the intimate level of the exchange (Brewis and Linstead,

2000; McKeganey and Barnard, 1996; Sanders, 2002; Vanwesenbeeck, 2005).

Workers approached this in a variety of ways. Some begrudgingly acquiesced to letting the customer have the illusion of control. Jackie, in her early thirties, working at the rural Calico Club, articulated what many women told us,

> If a guy takes a long time, long time, you're like, God, you know, least amount of work for the most amount of money. That's the way I was taught, you know. And to me, it's a lot easier just to lay there, you know. It's easier than it is to give a blow job.

In other words, the work was in reducing effort.

At the same time, the sex worker must at least act like what the customer is doing is also enjoyable to them. Many workers joked 'What woman doesn't fake an orgasm?!' Jackie talked about clients being fascinated with her breasts.

> The first thing they do, bury their heads in them. And I'm wondering why this is such a fascination? You know. I just don't get it. Because it doesn't turn me on when they're doing that. You know? I have to remember to make noises. I make them up, because it doesn't turn me on.

Misty and Celeste were talking about the challenges in figuring out what customers wanted to do to you and how to respond. Misty said, 'They want to stare at you, but they don't want you to look at them.' Celeste then said, 'That's when you know right away to close your eyes and just do that "oh moans of ecstasy" thing.' Likewise, she said 'Some guys want you to touch yourself, others find that to be a total turnoff, so you have to know the cues.'

Many, however, saw clients' engagement as endearing, as a positive part of the job. For Dizyer, a long time worker in her forties, now at Angel's Ladies, clients could be 'very compassionate and very mannerly. I mean just subservient down to "Can I move my arm? Can, can I tilt this way?" And they'll have a good party.' It is interesting that she put subservient in the same category as compassionate and mannerly. Angela said, 'Sometimes when they [clients] go to a room they just want to lie down and give the girl a back massage or just get a back massage themselves.'

Other workers were likely to clearly enjoy the physicality of the sex. Even Jackie said, 'I've had guys that you'd never think they'd be that good, but were really good. You look at them like going…like, "Oh damn".'

Resistance and reproduction of gendered narratives

Although there were multiple dimensions of body work, women also had different ways of combining and arranging these dimensions into strategies or practices. In our research, we found that there were three types of general strategies into which workers combined these dimensions: body practices, caring practices and holistic practices (Brents, Jackson, and Hausbeck, 2010). These differed in how workers conceptualized their bodies, how they conceptualized what they were selling, and strategies they employed to do their jobs. Even though there was overlap, workers frequently differentiated themselves from others based on these strategies. What interests us here is how reactions to and ordering of body work as 'dirty work' differed in these practices. These strategies also reinforced or resisted traditional gendered sexualities in different ways.

Body practices were narratives of the work emphasizing physical performances of their bodies and the physical nature of the product they were selling. The women who relied on this narrative separated the physical labour from the emotional labour, emphasizing bodily skills, or the aesthetic assets of their bodies. Caring practices were narratives that emphasized the caring, affective and emotional labour they provide as distinguished from the physical sex. These emphasized the emotional labour necessary for the job, and their mental work was often contrasted with the physicality of sex. Holistic practices were narratives of practices that combined physical sex and emotional connection to provide a sensual experience that engaged body and mind, for both worker and client (Brents, Jackson, and Hausbeck, 2010).

Caring practices

Those who emphasized caring practices consistently contrasted emotional from physical labour and talked about how the job was not about 'sex', but predominantly about caring and emotion. Worker after worker talked about how they had customers who just wanted to watch TV with them, talk, or give or get a massage. One worker estimated that 30 per cent of her clients don't want sex. Ricki, from Miss Kitty's explained:

> Everybody is under the conception that it is just all about spreading your legs. Wrong, wrong…It's almost like being a psychologist, you know you're listening to people's problems, you're making them feel okay about them.

The unspoken narrative was that providing raw sexual gratification is 'dirty work'. 'It's not just sex. It's, you know, a lot more than that', said Angela. Emphasizing counselling or emotional support elevated their work defining themselves against the stigma and devaluing of body work.

At the same time, these narratives reproduced fairly traditional gender roles. Again, Ricki from Miss Kitty's explains:

> I think me being emotional and me being probably overly compassionate, and sometimes a doormat, but at the same time it benefits me in my job, because I truly care.... I think I'm a better listener because I am not there to advise, I'm there to just make you feel better.

The qualities that mattered to Ricki were highly gendered and heteronormative, reproducing the concept of women as natural caretakers of men even at the expense of being 'a doormat'. As Joyce at Angels Ladies, said, 'We just snuggled up, I just held him, ya know? And I enjoyed that, because I enjoy being that person for people.'

Another worker articulated how she sees her job as a counter to the instrumental, alienating nature of many relationships today: 'There's so much bullshit, games and stuff, ya know?' Likewise, Alicia at the Green Lantern compared the work of the sex worker against the emotional failures of women in some marriages. 'People might be in a marriage, but they are on both ends of the bed and there's no touching, there's no feeling, there's no emotion.' Her job is to truly care, give that emotion.

> But one guy the other Monday night, he paid a good amount of money too, and the time he had was an hour and a half, the sex itself probably lasted 15 minutes, but he gave me a massage, and then we ended up talking for the last half hour. We just talked, we talked about kids, we talked about wives, husbands, we talked about life. And he was just like the sweetest guy.

Several workers also said that the caring actually increased the monetary value of the interaction. In one discussion between workers, Sadie reiterated the line that the job is not about sex: 'Believe it or not, there have been customers that will come in here and don't want sex at all. They just need to lie in your company.' Joyce, however, quickly added, 'And those ones, you get paid the most, too.' The added value of caring may be because of the way it reproduced traditional heteronormative, non-commodified relationships. Several studies have shown that a kind of 'girlfriend experience' is a highly valued commodity for high end sex workers and their customers (Bernstein, 2007; Sanders, 2008). The girlfriend idea fits better with traditional gendered roles.

Body practices

Those who adopted body practices resisted the stigma and devaluing of body work in a different way. Like Bolton's gynecological nurses, they emphasized the skill of their work. As Celeste said, 'Flying by the seat of your pants in this business doesn't work, ya know. Anyone can fuck and suck.' Older women emphasized their physical skill. Zoie, in her late thirties, has been working on and off in prostitution for 16 years in various settings. 'I know what I'm doing. I've been doing it a long time. I'm pretty good at my job, even now with girls that are ten years younger than me.'

Holistic practices

Perhaps the most radical challenge to the traditional feminine narrative came from holistic workers. They rejected the mind/body dualism itself, reclaiming dirty work. They emphasized their skill, but unlike Bolton's gynecology nurses, they integrated body and mind. Holistic workers distinguish themselves from other workers, not by ignoring body work or interpreting care labour as separate from sex, but by correlating sexual pleasure with bodily and mental engagement, a skill they saw as more specialized than those of other workers who seek to 'get em in, off and out'. Holistic practices combine physical labour, bodily labour, emotional labour, and, uniquely, explicitly discuss the reciprocity of bodily exchange with the client. They were less likely to discuss controlling or manipulating the exchange and more likely to discuss building body work *with* their clients.

Magdalene Meretrix has worked in a range of venues including Nevada's suburban brothels. She describes her work as an 'exchange of sexual energy...I have been a healing force in their life. I've given them healing, unconditional love.' Bretney also talked about how she awakens in her clients 'the wonderful, fairy joy feeling that people don't always want to give themselves the permission to experience'. With holistic practices, the value of sex at work is not conceptualized as purely emotional or purely physical. Physical and emotional connections are wound together in a way that is articulated as mutually reinforcing.

In engaging body and mind for both herself and the client, holistic workers were more likely to talk about the sensual pleasure they gained from the work, resisting a narrative of self-denial. These narratives resisted the traditional gendered narrative: not only did these women enjoy sex, they enjoyed using their skill to guide a mutually enjoyable sexual encounter. Says Bretney, 31, who had been contracting off and on with the Moonlite Bunny Ranch for three years, 'I love to fuck. So it is fun for me and very athletic.' In calling the work athletic, she invokes a narrative of athleticism, self-monitoring and achievement, not just skill for the benefit of the customer. She goes on to talk about the work: 'I have my tantric customers that I like to party with because they like to use more yoga positions.' In invoking yoga, she invokes a practice that seeks to dissolve a mind/body dualism.

Finally, importantly, women with the most resources were more likely to practice holistically. Plus, the longer, more engaged interactions bring in the most money. Ruby, Bretney, Dusty and Magdalene are high earners in the suburban brothels outside of Reno and Las Vegas. They will spend a day or more with a client, particularly with repeat customers. Ruby said she once was paid over $8,000 for two days with a regular client. This practice combines bodily exchange labour, bodily labour and physical labour with all three aspects of emotional labour as women attend to the physical sensations and emotional needs of customers, as well as their own emotional needs and physical feelings.

Conclusion

Sex work is an important site to interrogate body work in the twenty-first century. To say simply that sex workers 'sell their bodies' misses the multiple dimensions and variety of strategies that these workers, and indeed all body workers, use in doing their labour. We find three important points. First, the lines between body work and emotional labour are often blurry. Second, there are multiple dimensions of body work; here we identify five dimensions: physical, aesthetic, emotional, bodily, and bodily interaction. Third, workers configure these different dimensions of body work into a variety of different strategies. Consistent with research that finds many ways to negotiate emotional labour, sex workers employ a variety of strategies to negotiate body work.

One of the important organizing elements in understanding any configuration of body work is the attention to a mind/body dualism and the stigma of body work as dirty work. The attention to this dualism is also related to gender. In caring practices, workers value affective and caring over physical or body labour. True to a traditionally feminine role, caring itself is the intrinsic reward. Women relying on body practices rejected the stigma of 'dirty work' by emphasizing bodily skill and expertise. Holistic workers provided the most radical resistance to traditional gendered ideologies by defying the mind/body dualism, and rather emphasized a mutual and fully pleasurable experience for customer and worker via spiritual and bodily connections.

It also appears that workplace organization, setting and the class and resources of workers and clients matter. We argue that the legal, semi-autonomous context allows more diversity in these sex workers' approaches to labour. Resources give workers more tools to use in negotiating the body/ mind/work nexus.

We urge much more research on diversity and variety in post-industrial embodied labour. Sex work, like sexual surrogates, pregnancy surrogates and practice models for medical students (to practice pelvic exams, for example), are unique forms of body work in that the client touches the worker. Such labour is often written off as caring, or medicalized and sterilized, or, as is often the case of sex workers, type-casted as deviant, coerced or unhealthy.

Women's labour strategies reflect how women actively define gender and sexuality, both resisting and accepting cultural constraints. These conceptions affect how they experience sexuality, pleasure, self and service work. The demands of a growing sex industry may be reshaping our understanding of heterosexuality as successful high-end workers provide holistic labour that pushes beyond dualities of mind and body.

Notes

1 We recognize that men and transgender people also engage in commercial sex, but up until 2010, only women could sell sex in the legal brothels because of a law requiring all brothel sex workers to submit to a cervical exam. In late 2009, this was overturned with the assistance of the local ACLU. Less than a handful of men have been hired since the change.
2 We thank Rachel Cohen for pointing out this fairly obvious component of sex work that we had not thought of before.

REFERENCES

Abel, G.M. (2011). Different Stage, Different Performance: The Protective Strategy of Role Play on Emotional Health in Sex Work. *Social Science and Medicine* 72: 1177–84.
Abiala, K. (1999). Customer Orientation and Sales Situations: Variations in Interactive Service Work. *Acta Sociologica* 42: 207–22.
Adkins, L. (1995). *Gendered Work: Sexuality, Family and the Labour Market.* Philadelphia: Open University Press.
——— (2001). Cultural Feminization: 'Money, Sex and Power' for Women. *Signs* 26: 669–95.
——— (2002). *Revisions: Gender and Sexuality in Late Modernity.* Philadelphia: Open University Press.
Adkins, L. and Merchant, V. (1996). *Sexualizing the Social: Power and the Organization of Sexuality.* New York: St. Martin's Press.
Anderson, B. (2000). *Doing the Dirty Work?: The Global Politics of Domestic Labour.* New York: Palgrave Macmillan. ▶

▶

Bernstein, E. (2007). *Temporarily Yours: Intimacy, Authenticity and the Commerce of Sex.* Chicago: University of Chicago Press.

Bolton, S.C. (2005a). *Emotion Management in the Workplace.* New York: Palgrave Macmillan.

——— (2005b). Women's Work, Dirty Work: The Gynaecology Nurse as 'Other'. *Gender, Work & Organization* 12: 169–86.

Brents, B.G. and Hausbeck, K. (2007). Marketing Sex: U.S. Legal Brothels and Late Capitalist Consumption. *Sexualities* 10: 425–39.

Brents, B.G., Jackson, C. and Hausbeck, K. (2010). *The State of Sex: Tourism, Sex and Sin in the New American Heartland.* New York: Routledge.

Brewis, J. and Linstead, S. (2000). 'The Worst Thing Is the Screwing' (1): Consumption and the Management of Identity in Sex Work. *Gender, Work & Organization* 7: 84–97.

Brotheridge, C.M. and Grandey, A.A. (2002). Emotional Labor and Burnout: Comparing Two Perspectives of 'People Work'. *Journal of Vocational Behavior* 60: 17–39.

Browne, J. and Minichiello, V. (1995). The Social Meanings behind Male Sex Work: Implications for Sexual Interactions. *British Journal of Sociology* 46: 598–622.

Bulan, H.F., Erickson, R.J. and Wharton, A.S. (1997). Doing for Others on the Job: The Affective Requirements of Service Work, Gender, and Emotional Well-Being. *Social Problems* 44: 235–56.

Chapkis, W. (1997). *Live Sex Acts: Women Performing Erotic Labor.* New York: Routledge.

Cohen, R.L. (2010). When It Pays to Be Friendly: Employment Relationships and Emotional Labour in Hairstyling. *The Sociological Review* 58: 197–218.

Diamond, T. (1992). *Making Gray Gold: Narratives of Nursing Home Care.* Chicago: University of Chicago Press.

Emerson, R.M. and Pollner, M. (1975). Dirty Work Designations: Their Features and Consequences in a Psychiatric Setting. *Social Problems* 23: 243.

Entwistle, J. and Wissinger, E. (2006). Keeping Up Appearances: Aesthetic Labour in the Fashion Modelling Industries of London and New York. *Sociological Review* 54: 774–94.

Foner, N. (2004). *The Caregiving Dilemma: Work in an American Nursing Home.* Berkeley: University of California Press.

Grandey, A.A. (2000). Emotion Regulation in the Workplace: A New Way to Conceptualize Emotional Labor. *Journal of Occupational Health Psychology* 5: 95–110.

Hochschild, A.R. (1983). *The Managed Heart: Commercialization of Human Feeling.* Berkeley: University of California Press.

——— (2003). *The Commercialization of Intimate Life: Notes from Home and Work.* Berkeley: University of California Press.

McDowell, L. (2009). *Working Bodies: Interactive Service Employment and Workplace Identities.* Boston: Blackwell.

McKeganey, N.P. and Barnard, M. (1996). *Sex Work on the Streets: Prostitutes and Their Clients.* Buckingham and Philadelphia: Open University Press.

▶

Meretrix, M. (2001). *Turning Pro: A Guide to Sex Work for the Ambitious and the Intrigued.* Emeryville: Greenery.

Sanders, T. (2002). The Condom as Psychological Barrier: Female Sex Workers and Emotional Management. *Feminism and Psychology* 12: 561–66.

——— (2005a). 'It's Just Acting': Sex Workers' Strategies for Capitalizing on Sexuality. *Gender, Work & Organization* 12: 319–42.

——— (2005b). *Sex Work: A Risky Business.* Cullompton: Willan.

——— (2008). Male Sexual Scripts: Intimacy, Sexuality and Pleasure in Commercial Sex. *Sociology* 42: 400–17.

Stacey, M. (1988). *The Sociology of Health and Healing: A Textbook.* New York: Routledge.

Toerien, M. and Kitzinger, C. (2007). Emotional Labour in Action: Navigating Multiple Involvements in the Beauty Salon. *Sociology* 41: 645.

Twigg, J. (2000). *Bathing – The Body and Community Care.* New York: Routledge.

——— (2004). The Body, Gender, and Age: Feminist Insights in Social Gerontology. *Journal of Aging Studies* 18: 59–73.

Twigg, J., Wolkowitz, C., Cohen, R.L. and Nettleton, S. (2011a). *Body Work in Health and Social Care: Critical Themes, New Agendas.* Malden: Wiley-Blackwell.

——— (2011b). Conceptualizing Body Work in Health and Social Care. In J. Twigg, C. Wolkowitz, R.L. Cohen, and S. Nettleton (Eds) *Body Work in Health and Social Care: Critical Themes, New Agendas.* Malden: Wiley-Blackwell.

Vannini, P., Waskul, D.D. and Gotschalk, S. (2012). *The Senses in Self, Society, and Culture: A Sociology of the Senses.* New York: Routledge.

Vanwesenbeeck, I. (2005). Burnout among Female Indoor Sex Workers. *Archives of Sexual Behavior* 34: 627–39.

Warhurst, C. and Nickson, D. (2007). Employee Experience of Aesthetic Labour in Retail and Hospitality. *Work, Employment & Society* 21: 103–20.

Warhurst, C., Nickson, D., Witz, A. and Cullen, A.-M. (2000). Aesthetic Labour in Interactive Service Work: Some Case Study Evidence from the 'New' Glasgow. *The Service Industries Journal* 20: 1–18.

Wharton, A.S. (1993). The Affective Consequences of Service Work: Managing Emotions on the Job. *Work and Occupations* 20: 205–32.

——— (2009). The Sociology of Emotional Labor. *Annual Review of Sociology* 35: 147–65.

Witz, A., Warhurst, C. and Nickson, D. (2003). The Labour of Aesthetics and the Aesthetics of Organization. *Organization* 10: 33–54.

Wolkowitz, C. (2002). The Social Relations of Body Work. *Work, Employment & Society* 16: 497–510.

——— (2006). *Bodies at Work.* Thousand Oaks: Sage.

Zapf, D. and Holz, M. (2006). On the Positive and Negative Effects of Emotion Work in Organizations. *European Journal of Work and Organizational Psychology* 15: 1–28.

The Frontline Costs of the Southern Cross Decline

6

Joe Greener

In 2011, Southern Cross, the largest provider of elderly residential care services in the United Kingdom (UK), announced that it was ceasing operations. Southern Cross' decline and eventual termination is reasonably well documented by journalists, although these reporters usually cite the fall of share prices and the involvement of Blackstone, the private equity fund, as critical to the company's failure (BBC, 2011b; Peston, 2011). However, while in 2008 a number of papers reported on the drastic increase in deaths in Southern Cross homes (*Financial Times*, 2011a), since then little reporting has focused on degrading service standards in the company. Indeed, there has been little discussion at all of the frontline effects of the financial failure of Southern Cross. In part, this chapter explores some of the frontline effects of Southern Cross' struggling profit margins for workers and residents.

However, looking across the mass media more generally, cases of abuse and neglect in care homes for the elderly consistently grab headlines. A recent example was the secretly filmed *Panorama* investigation, which showed four carers engaging in forms of mild negligence, with another seen perpetrating more serious, deliberate abuse (*BBC*, 2012). All staff involved were dismissed but Forest Healthcare, the company which owned and operated the facility, were not subject to any form of rebuke. Accounts of ill-treatment usually emphasize the individual responsibility of frontline workers for providing quality care and resisting abuse. Similar constructions of negligence in care work are also observable in much of the official policy produced on care standards. In the recent draft of *Delivering Dignity*, a preliminary report on the NHS Confederation investigation into how to improve care in hospitals and care homes, the first of ten key recommendations states that 'staff must take personal responsibility for putting the person receiving care first' (Commission on Dignity in Care for Older People, 2012: 5).

These policy and media discourses individualize blame and fail to recognize that the characteristics of care relationships emerge from the economic and social conditions which surround the giving and receiving of care (Greener, 2012; Tronto, 1993). As such, in contrast to these typical media and policy accounts of care, and drawing on ethnographic research conducted during 2009, I argue that far from being the fault of frontline workers, it is the structural circumstances within which caring occurs that pushes workers into harmful or undignified practices. In this investigation of one Southern Cross care home, I suggest that it was the drive for profit that produced such inadequacies in care. The discussions that follow have relevance beyond this one empirical example and may be more generally telling of commercialized care services.

Privatization and care

In recent years, there has been a growing scholarly interest in the concept of care (England, 2010; Mitchell et al., 2003; Phillips, 2007). Much of this literature emphasizes the importance of 'care' as a key human relationship (Bubeck, 2002; Kittay, 1999). A number of writers focus on the supposed incompatibility of 'commodification' and 'care', especially the in/compatibility between the values and principles thought to define high-quality affective relationships and those which guide profit maximization. It is argued that commercial objectives that give primacy to increasing margins undermine the values of care (Nelson and England, 2002). For instance, factors that are critical in delivering a quality service, such as staffing levels, are seen as simply production costs and become targets for cost cutting (Folbre, 2006). While some analysts, such as Zelizer (2005) or Held (2002), are more concerned with the relation between 'love' and 'money' on a conceptual level, a growing body of literature examines the relationship between care and profit in formal care situations through an organizational or labour process lens. These studies deal with the complex juncture between routines, practices, organizational motives and relations of employment, including the relations between the cared for and the carer (Diamond, 1992; Lee-Treweek, 1994, 1996, 1997; Lopez, 2006, 2007).

For example, in a detailed study of the routines of institutional care, Timothy Diamond (1992) argues that the increasing standardization and rationalization of caring is inevitable when profit motives take primacy over care. 'Patients are produced', Diamond states, and the job of caring is 'organizationally produced as menial and mechanical, industrially streamlined to complement the making of patients' (1992: 166). Diamond's analysis of privatized care emphasizes the quantification, systematization and regimentation of the work. His ethnographic account uncovers the role of commercial aims in creating particular ways of living for the residents, namely restrictive, undignified lifestyles lacking in personal freedom and even access to basic needs. Another example traces aspects of the relation between workers and care recipients to the pressures facing care assistants, whose dirty, difficult and low-paid working conditions engender a form of resistance to care work (Lee-Treweek, 1997). This resistance takes shape as a callous disposition leading them to engage in insensitive and even punitive acts towards the receivers of their care.

A number of authors have highlighted the inherent distinctiveness of care work, suggesting that cost cutting in this sector is likely to lead to severe service degradation. Folbre (2006: 351) argues that although economists assume that, as elsewhere, competition leads to improvements in efficiency and output, in the care sector what she calls 'over-commodification' frequently undermines rather than improves care service standards. For example, Lopez (1998) compared three Pennsylvania nursing homes subject to varying threats of privatization across a range of variables relating to care quality, and found deterioration in staff-to-resident ratios, access to medical supplies, worker turnover rates and wages in all three homes, including the home that remained publicly owned and managed. However, the worst deterioration in capacity to meet residents' needs was found in the home that, while it remained in county ownership, was managed by a private company, and the home sold outright to a private company suffered the greatest deterioration in service quality. Another example is McGregor et al. (2005), whose comparative study of staffing levels in nursing homes across the United States shows that private sector homes had the lowest staff to service user ratios.

These findings are mirrored in the UK context, where working conditions in terms of pay and turnover rates have been found to be worse in private sector elderly care homes than in non-profit or public sector facilities (Skills for Care, 2010). Migrant workers, with less purchase on the labour market than UK-born workers, are also overrepresented in the UK's for-profit sector, another indicator of poor conditions and rewards in this sector (Cangiano et al., 2009; UNISON, 2009).

It can be suggested that the downgrading of both employment rights and care conditions that often transpires in the wake of the formation of business agendas in care homes is an articulation of inherent tendencies in labour processes driven by capital accumulation. Labour process analysts suggest that two major strategies exist to improve capital's profitability (Jaros, 2010; Thompson, 1989), either increasing productivity or decreasing the costs of the labour process (Thompson, 1989: 42). Yet unlike more traditional industrial activities, those that focus on bodies, or 'body work' industries (Twigg, 2000; Wolkowitz, 2006), are limited in how they can reorganize production in line with increasing efficiency. Body work demands the co-presence of a worker and recipient for activities to take place and body work labour processes are inflexible in their requirement for real, lived human labour; workers who perform body work cannot easily be replaced with machinery (Cohen, 2011; Twigg et al., 2011). Bodies are also 'complex, unitary and responsive' (Cohen, 2011: 21), meaning that as a material in a production process they pose certain problems. For instance, they cannot be separated into different parts worked on in disparate locations. Cohen argues that there is a 'naiveté' about current cost-cutting agendas in health and social care facilities because they fail to recognize just how inflexible the use of embodied and present labour is in these occupations (Cohen, 2011: 19).

This sociological literature previously outlined reveals some of the innate problems in commodifying caring relations. Employing a range of different arguments, these and other authors suggest that market and profit values are at odds with the principles of care, nurturance and intimacy (Held, 2002; Nelson and England, 2002). This chapter focuses on one elderly residential care home in the UK. It shows how, in this case, the structural pressures to increase profit in a large care-providing company produced grave consequences for frontline staff and the care they were able to offer. The following section gives an overview of the Southern Cross' recent history, which contextualizes my later discussion.

Southern Cross

Prior to formally announcing its break-up, on the 11th of July 2011, Southern Cross Healthcare Group (Southern Cross from herein) owned in the region of 800 residential care homes, employed more than 40,000 workers and had the potential to provide care to over 37,000 vulnerable adults (Southern Cross, 2009: 10). In the previous ten to fifteen years, Southern Cross had undergone rapid growth, emerging as the largest supplier of elderly residential care in the UK (Scourfield, 2007). The business was founded in 1996 and by the early 2000s owned 140 care homes. After 2002, the organization's capacity grew substantially in a short period. Southern Cross obtained backing from a New York-based private equity firm, Blackstone Group, in 2002 and bought out a number of large care home property owners and operators (Scourfield, 2007). To illustrate, the company acquired 39 homes in April 2001, 26 homes in February 2002 and 193 homes in November 2005 (Scourfield, 2007). This expansion continued throughout the decade prior to its collapse. Even as late 2007/2008, Southern Cross reported that they had increased the number of beds they offered by 3,121 through the attainment of another 62 homes (Southern Cross, 2008: 7). In that year alone, this represents a growth of 9.1 per cent in beds offered. By the end of financial year 2009, Southern Cross was the leading provider of elderly residential care in the UK with over 740 care homes and 37,000 beds nationwide.

While the expansion of Southern Cross continued right up to the announcement of their closure, the reasons behind their unwavering commitment to this strategy are rather obscure. Southern Cross Group was a public limited company (PLC), meaning they sell shares of their business to any willing buyer. Southern Cross Annual Report and Accounts (2008) gives an overview of company performance for the period beginning September 2007 and ending September 2008. The chairman's statement from 2008 indicates the company's crisis:

> This has been a very difficult year for Southern Cross after a promising debut in 2006 as a listed company. Our share price has fallen from an average of 564p in the first quarter to an average of 119p in the last quarter. (Southern Cross, 2008: 4)

The chairman goes on to outline the proposed strategy aimed at improving long-term business success. He formalizes out the company's plans for 'improving quality of service', 'lowering costs' and 'maximizing cash flow' (Southern Cross, 2008: 4). He also highlights his desire to continue growing the firm by leasing homes directly from landlords and developers.

Later on in the 2007/2008 Annual Review, the costs of Southern Cross operations are expanded on in greater depth. The major difficulties are identified as fee rates, staff costs, occupancy difficulties and rent (Southern Cross, 2008: 10). The total revenue for the company in 2007 to 2008 rose £157.5 million from the year before due to the expansion in the number of homes (Southern Cross, 2008: 11), but payroll costs also rose 4.4 per cent on the previous year (Southern Cross, 2008: 11). Southern Cross argued that they faced pressure from both the national minimum wage and the working time directive. Although occupancy rates (number of beds filled) were 0.6 per cent lower than the previous year, fee rates increased to £522 in 2008 (Southern Cross, 2008: 11). Despite the unstable outlook and struggling share price, however, the 11 board of directors at Southern Cross cleared just under £2.1 million in benefits and pay in the year 2007 to 2008 (Southern Cross, 2008: 40), and just over £2 million in 2008 to 2009 (Southern Cross, 2009: 46). In total, £16.5 million was paid out in share dividends[1] in 2007 to 2008 (Southern Cross, 2008: 62), but none were paid in 2008 to 2009.

In addition, it has recently been revealed that when Southern Cross became a public limited company in 2006, floating itself on the stock market, significant bodies of wealth were generated not only for Blackstone but also for some of the Southern Cross board members. By 2007, the equity company had made £600 million through various deals to do with Southern Cross (GMB, 2011). According to the Financial Times (2011b), four of the board directors between them had cleared in the region of £35 million through selling their shares. However, after the initial period, profits began to slow and eventually halted altogether.

The financial review for 2008 to 2009 showed some improvements in their overall operations, from a 'business' perspective, but it was still plain that the company were experiencing difficulties (Southern Cross, 2009). Occupancy rose, increasing revenue, and Southern Cross secured a 4.6 per cent increase in the rates charged (Southern Cross, 2008, 2009). Even so, it failed to halt a decreasing share price which fell by a further 11 pence. Overall, profitability also remained questionable. A pre-tax loss of £19 million was announced (Southern Cross, 2009). The company spent over £530 million on pay, over £110 million on running costs and just over £290 million on rent. However, in the year 2008 to 2009, it managed to reverse the trend of rising debt and reduce overall debt from £64 million to £33 million. The high level of labour costs – considerably more than half of total revenue – reflects the unavoidably labour intensive nature of care work (Cohen, 2011; Twigg et al., 2011).

The final dive occurred in the year 2010 to 2011. There are two theories that can be expounded in order to understand the recent history of Southern Cross. The first is that the company was attempting to achieve monopolization over the residential care market. Importantly, the fees paid for care to Southern Cross largely come from local authorities. Local authorities are keen to drive down care fees in their areas and they have considerable power in determining rates. Even for privately paying residents the rates are set, to a degree, by local authorities (Age UK, 2010). If a company such as Southern Cross can achieve a monopoly on a local market, its bargaining power is increased because local authorities may have little power to choose an alternative source for care services. Scourfield (2007) has argued that this strategy is mirrored by many of the top elderly residential care providers in what he dubs a process of 'caretelization'.

The more cynical explanation for the failure of Southern Cross would be that Blackstone Capital's mission in Southern Cross was from the outset to plunder. Blackstone and some of Southern Cross' directors have always denied this accusation, pointing out that Southern Cross was operating well when it was sold (*Financial Times*, 2011b). As stated earlier, Blackstone bought Southern Cross for £162 million in 2004, leading to a number of large acquisitions, which increased the size of the company three-fold, and then floated the company on the stock market in 2006. Yet, as Mundy and

O'Connor report (*Financial Times*, 2011b), in 2007 four of the top management at Southern Cross sold their shares, netting roughly £35 million between them. It would seem possible to suggest that those at the top of Southern Cross were aware that the company might not be as profitable in the long run as the share price at that time indicated.

'Meadowvale Care Home'

The research on which this chapter is based took place between 2008 and 2009 for the author's PhD. The study was an 8-month covert ethnography during which I worked in the home for between 24 and 36 hours a week. Prior to accessing the home covertly, many private sector care homes in the area where the research took place were asked if they would take part in research – all rejected. Covert methods were chosen because it was impossible to access a home of this sort for this type research overtly. The home, which for the purposes of anonymity is given the pseudonym 'Meadowvale', was owned by Southern Cross. The needs of the residents were wide-ranging. Residents suffered from numerous mental, cognitive and physical impairments. However, the most common health or social care issue faced by the residents was dementia of various types.

The running of a care home demands a considerable variety of different employees, including management, administrative, maintenance, food preparation and cleaning staff. However, the backbone of the staff was the registered nurses and numerous care workers. The care workers were divided between care assistants and senior care assistants, although there was little difference between what was expected of these two roles.

My official title was 'care assistant' and my primary responsibility can be summarized as performing personal care. The work itself was, as in many social care facilities, highly structured around certain time periods (Goffman, 1961). Duties and sets of duties were incorporated into a generalized routine and performed at certain times of the day. The care assistant's work was easily defined as body work in that it mostly consisted of attending to the basic bodily needs of residents, including physically moving and handling residents' bodies, or cleaning their bodies and the spaces around them (Twigg, 2000; Wolkowitz, 2006). Furthermore, cleaning work involved the handling of substances which originate from bodies, another defining feature of care work which is often noted in the literature (James, 1992; Stacey, 2005).

Before moving on, it is right to identify a certain weakness with the subsequent discussion about Meadowvale care home and the implications of this for more generally analysing Southern Cross. The following data explored are based on a relatively short period of working in the care home and is essentially one case study. The benefit of this is that it provides a rich and in-depth representation of living and working within the walls of a Southern Cross establishment. On the down side, the generalizability of the argument may be questionable because it is still only one home and it is possible, if unlikely, that the observations presented were only true for this one home. The author hopes that through the analysis of Southern Cross' accounts given near the start and by reference to other studies this difficulty is overcome, at least to a degree.

Declining standards at Meadowvale

While I was employed by Meadowvale, there were between 25 and 35 residents. The management staffed the home at a ratio of 1 worker to 5 residents (which at the time was the minimum imposed by the local authority). This ratio fell considerably short of the labour required to complete the tasks, which were set out by management. In addition, when workers called in sick or were expected to leave the home to assist a resident to the hospital, they were not replaced by agency staff. On one particular occasion, three workers were absent because of illness, resulting in myself and one other care worker being the only staff on shift within the entire home. My colleague and I had attempted to attend to the needs of more than 25 residents.

The work set out for the care assistants was unfeasible, even at the imposed one-to-five ratio. Davies (1994) also suggests that conflicts between time and processes are common in care work and are exacerbated when organizations are attempting to make cuts. Yet it was not only staffing which presented an opportunity for savings. Meadowvale's management engaged in other cost-cutting strategies and all aspects of the service were at risk of having expenditure removed or reduced. For example, budgets for activities, events and staff meals were halted and the funds for food for residents were reduced significantly. Charges were introduced for new staff, including for uniforms and charges for criminal record checks.

These attempts to reduce costs at Meadowvale reflected a broader companywide strategy. In one of the company's annual reports the chairman, Ray Miles, states that cost pressures currently stem from three main sources: 'legislation, regulation and the minimum wage' (Southern Cross, 2008: 6). Ray Miles also states that reducing production costs is a key strategy for the company the coming months and years (2008: 7).

Cost rationalization, abuse, mistreatment and neglect

The initial discussion highlighted the struggling profitability of Southern Cross in the years leading up to my participant observation of practices in the care home, while the previous section suggested that the company were engaged in strategies to reduce operating outlay both in Meadowvale and across the larger operation. This section focuses on how care was organized at Meadowvale, highlighting the failure of the labour process to successfully meet the needs of the elderly service users.

While completing the workload was largely impossible, the majority of care workers did retain a sense of duty (this commitment to caring ethics amongst even the lowest paid workers has been highlighted in a range studies; see for example Dodson and Zincavage [2007]). Most of the workers attempted to complete the workload, although many tasks were left outstanding at the end of each day. Throughout shifts workers were consistently negotiating which tasks to complete and which tasks to leave undone within the limited time they had. The pressure to complete the work was consistently felt by the care assistants, even if the workload was never achieved and workers were forced to prioritize which residents most required which type of assistance. Three residents in every shift were supposed to be given baths, for instance, but often not a single bath was given. Instead, workers gave bed baths in the morning, which were much quicker to administer. Usually residents did not receive a proper wash for days.

The work was controlled by a system of record keeping. During shifts workers were required to keep records on each individual resident. This included making a note of what each resident ate and drank, when they had used the toilet and what caring tasks had been completed on them (such as bed baths). Managers used these records as evidence that the work had been undertaken. The implications of this were that management's control over tasks ordinarily operated through bureaucracy rather than direct supervision – workers were chastized when they failed to fill in the appropriate forms rather than when tasks had not been finished. This system of control over the work sat uncomfortably between Friedman's (1977) concept of 'responsible autonomy' and its alternative, 'direct control'. Thus, while workers were responsible for keeping records up to date, they simultaneously had no control to shape caring routines, as each single job was set out for them in detail. Taken in combination, the method of bureaucratic control and the deficient staffing levels meant that falsification of the records was pervasive. In order to protect their jobs, care workers felt that they had no choice but to record that a level of care had been given even though, in reality, it had not.

The true extent of this neglect at Meadowvale was, therefore, formally unknown. In essence, workers often had little idea about whether certain duties were completed or not. Often, all care charts were completed towards the end of the shift when many of the residents had gone to bed. One particular problem was in noting the amount of fluids that each resident had consumed, because all staff would be serving drinks throughout the day. Himmelstein et al. (1983) argue that dehydration is a key predictor of poor care. At Meadowvale, training courses encouraged staff to assist residents in drinking a minimum of 1500 millilitres of fluids a day. This was rarely achieved for many of the residents, but in the forms it was simply noted that residents had imbibed the appropriate 1500 millilitres. A truthful account would have recognized that the care assistants often had no idea how much fluid residents were drinking daily and that in many cases the amount was inadequate. The workers on the whole recognized the importance of promoting high levels of fluid intake in the home and attempts were made to give out as much fluids as possible, even if the practices fell considerably short of an acceptable level of care.

Care practices surrounding nutrition suffered similar difficulties. Some of the residents who needed feeding and took a particularly long time to finish eating did not always receive enough food. Residents with problems swallowing could take as long as an hour or an hour and a half to finish a meal and required one-on-one assistance from a worker for this whole period. The pressure to move on to the next task or set of tasks meant workers often discontinued feeding residents before their meal was finished.

Other forms of time-saving methods, which were potentially dangerous, revolved around the use of machinery. Most of the apparatus utilized in care work is aimed at securing the safety of residents and workers during moving and handling rather than at increasing efficiency. Hoists, slings, stand-aids and moving straps were the commonest types of equipment used (and misused) at Meadowvale. A hoist is a crane-like piece of equipment used in tandem with the slings. The slings are fitted underneath a resident and then the edges are attached to the hoist. The arm of the hoist then raises the resident up off where they are sitting or lying, moves the resident over a chair, wheelchair, bed or toilet and lowers them onto it. Hoisting is a reasonably dangerous procedure because for a short period the resident is in mid-air supported only by the sling. Safe use of this machinery depends on two staff members working in cooperation – one operates the hoist while another steadies the resident in the sling. Without two workers there is a danger that the recipient could start to rock, potentially leading to injuries from collisions with nearby furniture or with the machine itself. Furthermore, it is crucially important that the correct size of sling is used. If a sling is too large or too small for the person being hoisted, there is a danger that they could slip out of the hoist. Incorrect usage of hoists in health and social care facilities has led to injury and even death in the past (BBC, 2011a; Health and Safety Executive, 2011).

During my time at Meadowvale, incorrect use of hoists occurred frequently. During shifts which were particularly arduous, either because of a shortage of staff, or simply because the routine had been displaced for some other reason, staff would use hoists without the assistance of a colleague. In addition to this, certain equipment was also in short supply. There were only a small number of slings available and in order to save time searching for a suitably sized sling, staff resorted to choosing the one closest to hand.

Another piece of equipment, known as the 'the strap', was the simplest of the moving and handling devices, but was perhaps even more hazardous. According to the training given in the home, the strap was never supposed to be used. A moving strap is a canvas belt which fits around the upper torso of the person being moved. It fastens behind their back and is easily adjustable to different sizes. On either side of the strap there are handles so that those providing assistance can help lift the care recipient. During a moving and handling training course delivered by a manager from the regional headquarters, we were instructed that the strap should never be used. However, the strap, although requiring two care assistants, was much quicker to use than either the hoist or the stand-aid. For this reason, the strap was frequently used on residents who either had some strength in their legs or were easily lifted. The strap is the lifting technique which is most vulnerable to human error and poses a severe risk of falling for the care recipients (see also Lopez, 2007: 234). Managers, it seemed, realized the time-saving nature of the strap and, therefore, allowed its usage to continue yet resisted openly encouraging its use.

Importantly, when discussing the misuse of machinery it is crucial to highlight that many of these practices not only endangered the residents, but also the staff. Using the strap or using the hoist without assistance increased the risk of back injuries for employees. The workers accepted that many of these practices were potentially harmful, but engaged in them in order to increase the amount of care that residents received. They were not acts of pointless disregard or deliberate maltreatment, they were labour-saving strategies which allowed workers to attend to the care needs of as many residents as possible within given time periods. This sheds some doubt over Lee-Treweek's (1994, 1997) analysis of care workers engaging in misconduct as a form of resistance to the graft and grime of care work. Workers, it can be suggested, are unlikely to engage in behaviour that puts themselves at risk as well as others. Rather than being a form of abuse or neglect, often workers partook in unsafe practices in order to get around to as many patients as possible and to deliver all of the care required.

Incontinence care in the home can also be seen as stopping seriously short of quality provision. Incontinence pads were used as a labour-saving device, rather than as a last resort for managing residents' toileting habits. Medical literature around incontinence care shows that if care recipients are regularly assisted to the toilet at predictable intervals (a practice often named 'voiding') the frequency of incontinence can be significantly reduced or even eliminated (Ouslander and Schnelle, 1995). However, effective voiding requires recurrent and temporally predictable management of toileting habits, essentially increasing the labour time required. Workers at Meadowvale received regular training on delivering better incontinence care from the regional continence nurse, but the practice of voiding was never instituted into the routines at the home during any periods of observation.

At Meadowvale, pads were fitted to many residents as a matter of course and no attempt to prevent instances of incontinence was made during any shifts that I worked. Certain individuals with better communication skills were able to demand assistance to the toilet but for most it was simply expected that they go to the toilet in their incontinence pads. As Diamond explains, fitting a particular resident 'into a diaper' can be more 'labour saving, cost effective, time-and-motion efficient, profit accountable and documentable' (1992: 180). The residents with the greatest physical immobility and limited cognitive awareness were subject to the most neglectful of practices around their incontinence. They were simply left in incontinence pads, often for four hours at a time, and if staffing levels were low, for even longer. Some of these residents may have soiled their incontinence pad ten or fifteen minutes after it had been fitted.

Care staff simply did not have access to adequate resources to deliver better standards of care. The routines and care practices often put workers and residents at risk and confined residents to a life of indignity. However, Meadowvale's employees and managers did not resist these practices, they engaged in them 'haphazardly but systematically', to use Lopez's (2007: 234) vocabulary. During the time that this participant observation took place Southern Cross was in a period of severe financial difficulty. It seems that while many of these neglectful practices at Meadowvale were not especially new, there was certainly little scope for improvement in the standards of care within the desire for the company to accumulate more profit.

Conclusion

The previous discussion regarding practices in the home points towards a particular type of labour process in which frugality and intensification reigned supreme. It was also obvious that further cuts were being made, such as the residents' food budget, various entitlements for the staff and entertainment funds amongst others, and there was certainly no scope for improving the service. A few members of the care team had worked in the home prior to its purchase by Southern Cross and they described waning standards of service provision since then. They said that, previously, qualified nursing staff had been heavily involved in delivering day-to-day care such as feeding and washing. Moreover, according to them, eight care assistants and two nurses per shift had been normal under the old owners, compared to only one nurse and five care assistants during the period of my fieldwork. This experience replicates findings found in many other studies which suggest that the quality of care in private sector care homes is defined by lower staffing levels, lack of funding and generally worse quality care than in non-profit (Lopez, 1998; McGregor et al., 2005).

As the very beginning of this chapter discussed, populist media accounts of care often focus at the point of care delivery, blaming the people who carry out the work. These accounts are individualistic and centre on the incompetence, heartlessness or even wickedness of particular care workers. Contrary to this type of vision, care work, like all forms of work, is both performed and received within a particular political and economic landscape. The routines, practices and tasks expected from the workers and consequently the relations between these workers and the residents are inseparable from the structural conditions which set the context within which the production of care services can occur. As Lopez shows in his study, the 'routine rule violations' (Lopez, 2007: 231) that workers engaged in were a result of both official and unofficial routines. Managers were often aware that workers were failing to follow the correct, safe procedures but turned a blind eye in order to allow workers to complete more of the workload. Both Lopez's and my findings bring into question Lee-Treweek's (1994, 1996, 1997) notion that callous practices engaged in by workers are a form of resistance. While the notion of resistance cannot be discounted in its entirety, overemphasizing the concept fails to recognize the significance of informal pressures that force workers to engage in neglectful malpractice which in fact is tolerated by management.

Southern Cross offers an excellent example of the broader challenges that face private sector care providers. Southern Cross' predicament is a reflection of many of the intrinsic difficulties in profit-driven care and the current political context in which care takes place. The current market conditions of the elderly care sector are particularly tough, reflected in the fact that double the number of care homes went into administration in 2011 than the previous years (*Guardian*, 2011). As was set out near the beginning of this chapter, Southern Cross itself recognized that insufficient funding was a major constraint on generating better profits (Southern Cross,

2008: 7). Even so, whereas it is obvious that Southern Cross has faced difficulty in balancing the books in recent years, over the past ten years generous amounts of wealth have been accrued by certain individuals. Even in the years leading up to the company's final failure, the 11 members of the board of directors cleared £2.2 million in benefits and pay in the year 2007 to 2008 (Southern Cross, 2008), and then just over £2 million in 2008/9 (Southern Cross, 2009).

The practices and routines followed in the home have a direct link with the wider financial decline of Southern Cross, adding weight to the argument that the marketization of care leads to standards that spiral downwards. According to the neoliberal logic, free and unfettered competition in the market weeds out weaker competitors and therefore leads to efficiency savings across the system. Yet this ignores two important points. First, in remaining competitive, achieving savings can become crucial to commercial success in terms of capital gains, but it can also impact the frontline of service delivery. In attempting to remain competitive managers at Meadowvale, at least during the period of research, maintained minimal staffing levels that in turn had serious implications for how work was arranged. Second, competition between providers means that each may seek to lower the costs of delivery, leaving some struggling and forced to engage in the most extreme forms of labour process reorganization.

Care itself is problematic to reorganize through the use of machinery or novel management strategies without leading to decaying standards (Cohen, 2011; Folbre, 2006; Himmelweit, 2005). The success of care services largely depends on staffing ratios and sufficient time to deliver care. When private companies such as Southern Cross are faced with the need to improve profitability, they are faced with fewer options than the managers in many other sectors. With fewer possible opportunities to increase profitability, the providers are more likely to look for savings through reducing costs, especially the major cost of care which is labour.

Proponents of care marketization argue that competition operates as a force for good (Megginson and Netter, 2001; Savas, 1987; Sheshinski and López-Calva, 1998). In reality, when enterprises are in periods of crisis, rationalizing costs has detrimental effects for workers and service users. Inevitably, the continuation of a UK social care system based on competitive markets means other large providers will fail. The findings show that these wider competitive forces create a tendency for providers to restructure, reorganize and rearrange care services in such a way that the ultimate effect is increasing neglect, mistreatment and general failures in the standard of care. This study suggests that it is ultimately those receiving these services, in this case frail elderly people, as well as the low-paid workers who deliver frontline care, who pay the gravest costs of this market failure.

Note

1 Understanding Southern Cross' accounts is difficult. They published their review of accounts from September to September rather than for the tax year (April to April). This leads to what appears to be some inconsistencies or discrepancies. For instance, the company reported losses, not profits, in both the reviews of accounts 2008 and 2009 but also reported paying out dividends in 2008.

REFERENCES

Age UK (2010). Care Homes: Finding the Right Care Home. London: Age UK.
Baines, D. (2005). Pro-Market, Non-Market: The Dual Nature of Organizational Change in Social Services Delivery. *Critical Social Policy* 24(1): 5–29.
BBC (2011a). Newport Council Fined over Michael Powell's Hoist Death. Accessed 21 February 2012 at http://www.bbc.co.uk/news/uk-wales-south-east-wales-14907525.
———— (2011b). The Financial Lessons of Southern Cross. Accessed 21 February 2012 at http://www.bbc.co.uk/news/business-13630394.
———— (2012). Regulator Criticised After Woman Assaulted in Care Home. Accessed on 9 May 2012 at http://www.bbc.co.uk/news/health-17777113.
Bubeck, D.G. (2002). Justice and the Labor of Care. In E.F. Kittay and E.K. Feder (Eds) *The Subject of Care: Feminist Perspectives on Dependency.* Oxford: Rowman & Littlefield.
Cangiano, A., Shutes, I., Spencer, S. and Leeson, G. (2009). *Migrant Care Workers in Ageing Societies: Research Findings in the United Kingdom.* Oxford: COMPAS.
Cohen, R.L. (2011). Time, Space and Touch at Work: Body Work and Labour Process (Re)organisation. *Sociology of Health & Illness* 33(2): 189–205.
Commission on Dignity in Care for Older People (2012). Delivering Dignity: Securing Dignity in Care for Older People in Hospitals and Care Homes. A Report for Consultation.
Davies, K. (1994). The Tensions between Process Time and Clock Time in Care-Work: The Example of Day Nurseries. *Time & Society* 3(3): 277–303.
Diamond, T. (1992). *Making Grey Gold: Narratives of Nursing Home Care.* London: University of Chicago Press.
Dodson, L. and Zincavage, R.M. (2007). 'It's Like a Family': Caring Labor, Exploitation, and Race in Nursing Homes. *Gender & Society* 21(6): 905–28.
England, K. (2010). Home, Work and the Shifting Geographies of Care. *Ethics, Place and Environment* 13(2): 131–50.
Financial Times (2011a). Southern Cross Run on Failed Business Model. Accessed 21 February 2012 at http://www.ft.com/cms/s/0/102a1a4a-8-ae5–11e0-b2f1–00144feab49a.html#axzz1vmwpdi00.

▶

Financial Times (2011b). Southern Cross Chiefs Netted £35m. Accessed 21 February 2012 at http://www.ft.com/cms/s/0/21084f7e-8e2a-11e0-bee5-00144feab49a.html#axzz1odPRO8Q2.

Folbre, N. (2006). Nursebots to the Rescue? Immigration, Automation, and Care. *Globalizations* 3(3): 349–60.

Friedman, A. (1977). Responsible Autonomy versus Direct Control. *Capital and Class* 1(1): 43–57.

GMB (2011). Southern Cross: The Cross We Have to Bear, the Greedy and the Gullible. London: GMB. Accessed 8 June 2012 at http://www.gmb.org.uk/pdf/SX%20Gullible%20and%20Guilty%20v7b.pdf.

Goffman, E. (1961). *Asylums: Essays on the Social Situation of Mental Patients and Other Inmates*. London: Penguin.

Greener, J. (2012). Response to Delivering Dignity in Our Hospitals and Care Homes. Accessed 9 May 2012 at http://www.hope.ac.uk/news/newsitems/name,2275,en.html.

Guardian (2011). Doubling in Number of Care Home Firms Collapsing into Administration. Accessed 10 May 2012 at http://www.guardian.co.uk/business/2011/nov/14/care-home-administrations-double.

Health and Safety Executive (2011). Bupa Care Home Company Fined After Resident Death. Accessed 21 February 2012 at http://www.hse.gov.uk/press/2011/coi-wm-45611.htm.

Held, V. (2002). Care and the Extension of Markets. *Hypatia* 17(2): 19–33.

Himmelstein, D.U., Jones, A.A. and Woolhandler, S. (1983). Hypernatremic Dehydration in Nursing Home Patients: An Indicator of Neglect. *Journal of American Geriatrics Society* 31(8): 466–71.

Himmelweit, S. (2005). Can We Afford (Not) to Care: Prospects and Policy. GeNet Working Paper, No. 11. Accessed on 8 June 2012 at http://www.genet.ac.uk/workpapers/GeNet2005p11.pdf.

James, N. (1992). Care = Organisation + Physical Labour + Emotional Labour. *Sociology of Health & Illness* 14(4): 488–509.

Jaros, S. (2010). Core Theory: Critiques, Defences and Advances. In P. Thompson and C. Smith (Eds) *Working Life: Renewing Labour Process Analysis*. Basingstoke: Palgrave Macmillan.

Lee-Treweek, G. (1994). Bedroom Abuse: The Hidden Work in a Nursing Home. *Generations Review* 4(1): 2–4.

——— (1996). Emotion Work in Care Assistant Work. In V. James and J. Gabe (Eds) *Health and the Sociology of Emotions*. Oxford: Blackwell.

——— (1997). Women, Resistance and Care: An Ethnographic Study of Nursing Auxiliary Work. *Work, Employment & Society* 11(1): 47–63.

Lopez, S.H. (1998). *Nursing Home Privatization: What Is the Human Cost?* Harrisburg: Keystone Research Centre. Accessed 21 February 2012 at http://keystoneresearch.org/sites/default/files/krc_nursing_home_priv.pdf.

——— (2006). Emotional Labor and Organized Emotional Care: Conceptualizing Nursing Home Care Work. *Work and Occupations* 33(2): 133–60.

▶

————(2007). Efficiency and Fix Revisited: Informal Relations and Mock Routinization in a Non-profit Nursing Home. *Qualitative Sociology* 30(3): 225–47.

McGregor, M.J., Cohen, M., McGrail, K., Broemeling, A.M., Adler, R.N., Sculzer, M. et al. (2005). Staffing Levels in Not-For-Profit and For-Profit Long-Term Care Facilities: Does Type of Ownership Matter? *CMAJ* 172(5): 645–49.

Megginson, M.L. and Netter, J.M. (2001). From State to Market: A Survey of Empirical Studies on Privatization. *Journal of Economic Literature* 39(2): 321–89.

Mitchell, M., Marston, S. and Katz, C. (2003). Life's Work: An Introduction, Review and Critique. *Antipode* 35(3): 1–26.

Nelson, J.A and England, P. (2002). Feminist Philosophies of Love and Work. *Hypatia* 17(2): 1–18.

Ouslander, J.G. and Schnelle, J.F. (1995). Incontinence in the Nursing Home: Diagnosis and Treatment. *Diagnosis and Treatment* 122(6): 448–49.

Pollock, A. (2004). *NHS PLC: The Privatisation of Our Health Care*. London: Verso.

Savas, E.S. (1987). *Privatization: The Key to Better Government*. New Jersey: Chatham House.

Scourfield, P. (2007). Are There Reasons to Be Worried about the 'Cartelization' of Residential Care? *Critical Social Policy* 27(2): 155–80.

Sheshinski, E. and López-Calva, L.F. (2003). Privatization and Its Benefits: Theory and Evidence. *CESifo Economic Studies* 49(3): 429–59.

Southern Cross Healthcare (2008). *Southern Cross Healthcare Annual Report and Accounts*. Darlington: Southern Cross Healthcare.

————(2009). *Southern Cross Healthcare Annual Report and Accounts*. Darlington: Southern Cross Healthcare.

Stacey, C.L. (2005). Finding Dignity in Dirty Work: The Constraints and Rewards of Low-Wage Home Care Labour. *Sociology of Health & Illness* 27(6): 831–53.

Thompson, P. (1989). *The Nature of Work: An Introduction to Debates on the Labour Process*, 2nd ed. Basingstoke: Macmillan.

Tronto, J. (1993). *Moral Boundaries: A Political Argument for an Ethic of Care*. New York: Routledge.

Twigg, J. (2000). Care Work as a Form of Bodywork. *Ageing and Society* 20(4): 389–411.

————(2006). *The Body in Health and Social Care*. London: Palgrave.

Twigg, J., Wolkowitz, C., Cohen, R. and Nettleton, S. (2011) Conceptualising Body Work in Health and Social Care. *In* J. Twigg, C. Wolkowitz, R. Cohen and S. Nettleton (Eds) *Body Work in Health and Social Care: Critical Themes and New Agendas*. Malden: Wiley-Blackwell.

UNISON. (2009). *UNISON Migrant Workers Participation Project: Evaluation Report*. London: UNISON.

Wolkowitz, C. (2006). *Bodies at Work*. London: Sage.

Zelizer, V.A. (2005). *The Purchase of Intimacy*. Oxford: Princeton University Press.

Hairdressing/Undressing: Comparing Labour Relations in Self-Employed Body Work

Teela Sanders, Rachel Lara Cohen and Kate Hardy

Introduction

Since 'body work'/'body labour' has been conceived as a specific form of labour (Gimlin, 2002; Wolkowitz, 2006), studies across various forms of labour have begun to utilize the concept to discuss existing and emerging forms of work that have the body at their centre. Typically, these have focused on a single empirical location, a specific occupation or labour process. To date, less work has employed a comparative framework, comparing and contrasting differing forms of body work/labour. In this chapter we compare two forms of body work/labour. We use the term 'body labour' because we are discussing forms of paid activity that focus on the body in the waged labour market (see also Kang, this volume).

Body labour is a key component in expanding markets in service work and personal services (Cohen, 2011; McDowell, 2009). In such services, the intimate physical proximity of worker and worked-upon exacerbates the possibility that workplace interactions may be sexualized. In many forms of work, employers explicitly or implicitly condone such sexualization (Warhurst and Nickson, 2009) and workers may exert considerable effort in desexualizing, or resisting the sexualization of their labour (Kang, Chapter 10; Oerton, 2004). Meanwhile sex work, in its multiple forms, has been argued to be fundamentally different from other kinds of work (O'Connell Davidson, 1998), yet this argument has not been based on direct comparison between sex work and other types of human service work. This is notable, because even a brief comparison suggests a number of similarities, including, but not limited to, the issue of sexualization. Within the leisure industry many occupations require sexualized, semi-dressed bodies (usually, but not always, female), which are expected to be complemented by flirting, teasing, sexualized banter and humour (Adkins, 1995; Tyler and Abbott, 1998). Comparisons have, however, tended to focus primarily on the sexualization of 'legitimate' occupations, rather than more specifically on similarities in the structures, organization and dynamics of labour process mechanisms between work in the sex industry and elsewhere that are central to the analysis here.

This chapter draws on two sets of empirical data to examine the convergences and divergences between labour in two types of body work: stripping and hairdressing. We do this in order to begin to develop a tentative framework for comparative research on body work. The first study is of hairstylists and barbers in a city in the North of England, which involved semi-structured interviews with over 70 stylists and a self-completion survey of stylists in 131 salons or barbershops (Cohen, 2010b). The second is a study of strippers from a large scale mixed methods project that included a survey of 197 dancers and 70 interviews with dancers, other workers and managers across the UK's strip clubs and pubs (Sanders and Hardy, 2012). These two studies have key similarities, both in terms of methods and research focus: specifically, both studies concerned female dominated occupations in which self-employment status is ubiquitous.

Sex work, including stripping, is argued to involve the body in ways that distinguish it from other forms of work (as discussed by Fazzino and Selmi in Chapters 8 and 9). Yet comparing stripping with another form of work enables us to highlight that which makes it similar to, as well as different from, other service work. Examining two occupations in which a significant proportion of workers are independently contracted, or have wages based on commission, also allows us to examine the implications of these structures of employment across two very different settings. Of course, in one the core labour process involves dressing the body of another, whereas the other is characterized by the undressing of one's own body. Yet in both, customers are recipients of the worker's embodied performance. In the following we analyse the ways in which workers perform different types of interactive service labour (aesthetic, emotional and body labour), exploring the distinct labour processes of the two occupations, before concluding with a consideration of the labour relations under which both sets of workers work.

The labour of hairdressing and stripping

At first sight, the types of labour involved in both hairdressing and stripping are self-evident. Whereas hairdressing requires the manual labour of cutting, shaping, washing and dying the hair of another person, stripping requires workers to dance, take their clothes off and present their naked body to customers (Colosi, 2010; Egan, 2005). In the former, the primary site of labour is constituted by the body of another. As such, it more closely resembles 'body work' than stripping, in which the primary site is the worker's own body. Such simplistic representations, however, disguise the multiple and converging forms of labour that (mostly) women in both industries are required to provide in order to perform their jobs. This includes aspects of *aesthetic labour* and *emotional labour*, as well as the multiple forms of *body work/labour* or *corporeal labour* that we discuss in this chapter.

Aesthetic labour

Although 'body work/labour' has tended to refer to the manipulation of the bodies of others, there has been increasing acknowledgement of the necessity for workers to work on their own bodies as a precondition for working on the bodies of others (Chugh and Hancock, 2009; Wainwright et al., 2011). Thus, aesthetic labour, which is common in other service areas (Warhurst and Nickson, 2007), can be seen across sites of body work, for example the masculinized physical bulking up of bouncers referred to by Korczynski in Chapter 2 of this collection (and in Hobbs et al., 2002), or, in feminized occupations, the desexualization of therapeutic masseurs (Oerton, 2004). In line with this, and in order to perform their jobs, both hairdressers and strippers were required to perform aesthetic labour, managing the presentation of their own bodies in order to court and maintain custom.

Dancers carried out a high level of corporeal self-maintenance through applying fake tan, bronzing powder, heavy cosmetics, perfume and costumes (Barton, 2006; Colosi, 2010; Price, 2000). Similar to Fazzino's description in Chapter 8 of the temporary bodily alterations professional porn actors make on themselves, the participant observation study by Frank (2002: 172) describes the self-grooming necessary to 'costume' her naked body: accurate trimming of pubic hair, shaving, covering up bruises and scars, taking care not to smudge, polishing nails, filling in facial lines, and removing grey hairs were everyday routines. Such detailed attention to the display of the naked body can be understood as a process of self-presentation: 'these strippers show us that the body is 'selved' or re-selved through the labour of self-presentation' (Wolkowitz, 2006: 139).

Such labour may be understood as self-evident in erotic dance performance as, after all, the gaze of the customer focuses on the commodified image of the dancers' bodies; their aesthetic labour is commodified like that of a model or promotional worker, albeit with a more sexualized emphasis. Hairdressers did not have to produce their own naked bodies, but were, especially at the start of their career, often required to remake themselves. Tony, salon manager in a large franchised chain, describes this:

> We've just taken on these eight [trainees] and it's, not bizarre, but it's really interesting, to see what changes they've gone through from being little sixteen year old, don't let any of them hear this, but dweebs, to nice little trendy little young men and women now.... we've got this girl, who looked like she was on the school playground, you know what I mean, she'd got no personal skills, and just being there three four months she's changed, and that's nice to see. I'm not saying you have to be that overly highly different and fashionable but just that little bit more pride in your appearance. I don't like to see loads of gold or anything like that. One of the girls, when she started she must have had about 25 gold chains on, and a ring on every finger. That's all gone. I think that looks cheap as hell.... And she's getting a bit more style to her. It's nice to see them coming through.

Saliently, Tony later acknowledges that, notwithstanding a standardized aesthetic and fashion criteria for hiring promoted by his corporate head office, he cannot afford to select stylists on the basis of aesthetics because 'if we did that every single time we'd never end up with any staff, because half of them haven't got a clue'. In light of this 'cluelessness', Tony takes an active role, supporting his trainees as they navigate the tricky boundary between 'sixteen year old dweebs', 'cheap' and 'fashionable' to develop an appropriately individual aesthetic that is nonetheless bounded by conformity to the company style.

Notably this 'style' discourse hides an important underlying issue: that young working class workers are being aesthetically re-made to fit a middle class aesthetic, which for instance excludes excessive gold jewellery. The production of an appropriately classed body was also evident in some other strip clubs, where managers would talk with distaste about dancers with piercings and tattoos, with some venues operating zero tolerance on body art, preferring temporary and traditional elements of feminization and sexualization such as cosmetics and tanning.

One difference between stripping and hairstyling was that while demand for aesthetic labour was relatively consistent across strip clubs, salons varied greatly in this regard. Tony's salon, in common with those included in other research on the aesthetics of the salon (Chugh and Hancock, 2009; Lee et al., 2007), was typical only of a sub-set of high-priced establishments. Elsewhere aesthetic requirements were much weaker. For example, in 'shampoo-and-set' establishments ageing bodies were more common amongst both clients and workers, while salons located within working class residential estates less consciously orchestrated bodily aesthetics, relying on uniforms if anything (a temporary aesthetic modification used in 42 per cent of salons surveyed) to convey appropriate professionalism. Thus, hairstylists' aesthetic labour varied with the social identities of those on whom they performed body work and the spatialities in which they did so.

In contrast, dancers were not only required to achieve a particular *degree* of bodily presentation, but to conform to a fairly specific aesthetic ideal. Such an ideal included large breasts, tanned skin, lithe, firm bodies, long hair and heavy make-up:

> I don't like the way I look sometimes but I know it earns me money, I don't like being covered in fake tan all the time which is weird and patchy and comes off all the time. I'm not a high maintenance person, but I have to do it. I know a girl who's got her eyebrows tattooed on, her lips tattooed on, botox, three boob jobs, this that and the other. It's all because of work and she's not happy. She's not done it to make herself feel happy or because that's the body image she wants. (Xana)

Some dancers' bodies were therefore transformed not only within, but also outside workspaces, in some cases with long-term or irreversible effects. As Xana suggests, the construction of the working body/dancing 'self' was often problematic, contradicting workers' desired extra-work self-presentation. Other dancers concurred:

> To be honest, I'm quite a scrubber outside work. I've got false hair because I tried to make myself look Barbie bimbo like the rest of them. Boob jobs you can claim back on expenses, because they never would have considered them before. I'm even considering getting one and I don't even agree with boob jobs. I'd say 60% of the girls at least have them; you do have to conform to earn the money. (Danielle)

Much like the trainee stylist with too many gold chains, dancers are, therefore, forced to remake themselves – albeit to gendered, rather than classed conformity – creating alternative embodied identities for the workplace that do not always correspond to their private selves.

Despite pressure to achieve bodily aesthetics, some dancers noted client preferences for 'natural' looking women or stated that women with various body types successfully secured clients and money:

> All guys really want to see is a girl who's confident and can use their body in a seductive way.... I think all guys have their own taste anyway.

I've asked a guy for a dance before and he's said 'oh no, your bum's not big enough' or 'your boobs are too big, I prefer smaller boobs'. (Jodie)

Requirements for embodied representation had material impacts on dancers' bodies. For example, the ways dancers were encouraged to dress, combined with standing around for long periods of time waiting for customers, had detrimental effects on their health. As Nancy described,

I've got a varicose vein. . . . They think it's from standing up all the time. Standing up, five nights a week, maybe six nights a week, so I would say that from doing that I've actually caused damage to myself and your knees, your knees go too. Sometimes someone probably could get some compensation.

The industry fashion preference for extremely high-heeled Perspex shoes exacerbated women's physical issues, such as back problems. Lack of facilities to make hot food, cold temperatures within the clubs and slippery floors or poles also presented health and safety risks, threatening women's bodily well-being. Indicating the lower requirements for feminized aesthetics in hairstyling, stylists wear more comfortable footwear, but nonetheless similarly suffered back problems. In their case, this was related to the physical conditions required for body work on a seated client: the need to stand for long hours and, especially, to manipulate heavy blow dryers.

Hustling/emotional labour

Real differences in dancers' earning potential arose not only from conformity to the 'stripper aesthetic', but also from variable skills in performing emotional labour and 'hustling' for customers, that is, persuading or subtly coercing customers into purchasing their time/labour. Colosi (2010: 103) argues that 'hustling skills' consist of four types: the ego boost, bimbo act, empty promise and the pity plea. In each case, performances are designed to convince customers to pay for a private dance, preferably several, and possibly time in the VIP suite, where the most money can be made (approximately £250 per hour).

The importance of hustling is borne out by several respondents who had just started dancing but had not, and did not intend to, go on a pole. They believed that they could earn enough by hustling, flirting, doing 'sex talk' and enticing men with private dances:

I'd say it's 50% looks and the rest is what you can say and how you can say it. Because basically you are conning people. Of course they're getting something for their money, basically it's like being an Avon lady, innit?

You've got to be like 'here's the product I'm selling you and it's really good. It's better than all the rest.' (Yasmin)

In this brutally honest account of 'conning' men to spend money, Yasmin relates stripping to more generic sales persona, albeit a highly personalized form of selling, one that relies on the merging of public and private relations (Biggart, 1990). Yasmin's account, however, provides an unambiguous example of Goffman's (1959) 'cynical performance'.

Rhiannon, a dancer who had previously worked in hairdressing, identified a relationship between emotional labour skills in the two sectors:

Being confident and having good conversation skills, and being nice, even if you are not, you have to come across as quite complimentary.... I don't think I could have done it without the hairdressing really as you need to hold a conversation.... Before I was hairdressing, I was pretty under-confident and I had quite bad anxiety and couldn't really speak to many people.

Like dancers, hairstylists' performance is highly dependent on their ability to perform emotional labour (Cohen, 2010b). This is partly because the ability to 'do being friends' underpins stylists' ability to develop regular clienteles, or 'followings'. As followings are constructed, and stylists' work becomes increasingly oriented around repeat, rather than novel, relationships with clients, so their need to perform aesthetic labour or signify their trendiness also decreases considerably. Thus, it is not simply that senior stylists come to 'naturally' embody aesthetics that trainees consciously acquire, but also that these aesthetic qualities are of diminished importance as they establish themselves. In this process, emotional labour is critical, but also, as Natalie suggests, becomes easier as 'you get to know people and you can have good old chats with them'. The ways stylists perform the emotional labour required to construct a following nonetheless varied significantly with labour relationships; for example, where stylists were employees and less immediately dependent on clients for their income, their emotional labour was far more bounded than where their income, like dancers', depended directly on individual clients (Cohen, 2011).

The 'cynical performance' seen in dancing is also found in hairstyling. Here it tends to be oriented around two, not always corresponding aims. Like dancers, stylists' short-term aim is to get clients to spend more, whereas the long-term aim is the establishment of a following, as described previously. The extent to which different workers operate within one or other of these is often reliant on their employment relationship. Where workers are either self-employed or paid on commission (only accruing on 'repeat' clients, requesting the stylist by name), one way of achieving both aims is to 'hustle' colours (hair dye). This increases the price and, equally importantly, the need to return to the salon for a touch-up:

> Colours are…because that's where the money is really. It's not really a matter of persuading [clients]. It's just you recommend the colour to people anyway, because a lot of colours…it works both ways – it will complement the haircut so, it's better for the client to have a colour. It is more beneficial for us but it's beneficial for the client as well. (Josh)

Of course, stylists' ability to retain clients is not only dependent on such cynical performance but also, as previously discussed, the importance of 'friendliness' for developing client-followings was nearly universally acknowledged.

For many dancers simply making the 'conversation' required to hustle was the most difficult form of labour:

> The getting naked bit is easily the – the most straight forward, easy bit of the job. The hardest part of the job is talking to people and trying to find something that – that is interesting to talk to them like, 'cos some of them can be just boring. (Janna)

Similarly, stylists' need to 'learn' conversational skills was frequently offered as a rationale for relatively long apprenticeships (two to three years) and for the superiority of salon-based, over college-based, training.

In light of the often huge social distance between strippers and their clients, as well as between hairstylists and their clients, it is hardly surprising that the requirement to carry on extended conversations is often onerous. In this context, the reliance on stock topics and phrases or teasing and flirtation may be a way of containing and coping with clients whose habitus is unfamiliar:

> If it's an old lady, you don't like go 'alright love' [adopts a 'street' accent] and all this lot do you! Some people, like this regular lady who comes in, she's like that [adopts a 'posh' accent]. So you, you've got to change your way….They're not going to come back if you're boring are they? (Tina)

Whereas Tina suggests that she merely 'changes her ways', distinctly classed and generational 'ways', by adopting more polite language, the 'manufactured identities' (Sanders, 2005) dancers create can be much more developed. Employing a combination of aesthetic and emotional work on themselves, some dancers adopt the strategy of the 'girlfriend experience' by pretending to desire customers and even promising or inferring a relationship beyond the club: a performance which is becoming an increasingly core component of the sex industry (Bernstein, 2001).

Body work/corporeal labour

The ways in which touch between worker and client is managed and organized is a key point of difference between hairdressing and stripping. Hairdressers' core labour involves the manipulation of the body (hair) of clients, necessitating almost constant contact between hairdresser and client. In contrast, regulations governing dancers' labour prohibit contact, or allow only mediated contact. In both instances, however, the customer adopts a relatively passive, seated position, thus allowing (female) workers a (limited) degree of control over another's body.

Although the hairdressing client experiences almost constant physical contact during a salon visit, this contact need not involve the same hairstylist over the whole period. Critical in this context is the 'trainee', paid at a rate well below the minimum wage (at the time of this research in 2002/3 £50 to £60 per week). Large salons are organized on the basis of high trainee churn. Thus, Tony's salon takes on eight new trainees per year, retaining fewer than half that number the second year and employing only a select few stylists on completion of training. Trainees do miscellaneous work around the salon, including a lot of sweeping and tidying up, but they also learn how to work on hair and (as seen previously) develop the requisite aesthetic and emotional labour. Having developed the skills to work with clients, trainees facilitate a styling division of labour, performing relatively low-skill body work (such as drying or washing hair) and enabling higher earning qualified stylists to concentrate on more skilled body work. To make this system fully effective, trainees must, however, learn to manipulate the pace of body work, passing clients on to skilled stylists only when they are ready to see them. Typically, for example, an 'Indian Head Massage' is added to the hair-washing process to delay it, yet because the client experiences constant work on her head (the appropriate body part), she does not recognize this as a delay. That salons increasingly offer some form of head 'massage' with a wash is thus partially related to attempts to upscale (and increase the price of) services, but part of the attraction of this 'treatment' is also that it allows workers some temporal control over otherwise temporally intractable processes (Cohen, 2011).

Notably, much body work performed by trainees occurs at points in the labour process when verbal interaction is difficult, for example because of the water stream necessary for washing hair or the noise created by blow dryers. As such, there is an analogy with the hierarchy of body labour found in other occupations (such as medicine). In both instances, those at the bottom of the occupational hierarchy concentrate on body work, while those with higher occupational status may have more limited interactions with the body or their interaction is limited to specific parts or processes, but importantly are simultaneously required to exercise verbal and emotional communication (Twigg, 2000).

Unlike the constant touch required of hairstyling, in the UK strip industry, most clubs operate a 'no-touching' rule, colloquially 'the three foot ban'. This is either written into the club rules of engagement for dancers or constitutes a key licensing condition under which the clubs and, therefore, the dancers operate. Usually, the only time when dancers and clients may legitimately come into contact is when the customer is led to the private space for dancing or to exchange money. In some London boroughs, customers are required to sit on their hands or place a cushion on their lap while the dance takes place, putting an object in the way in order to ensure no touching takes place.

Although these rules were industry-wide, dancers emphasized the importance of some physical contact with customers and their everyday practices, usually tacitly agreed amongst dancers and managers, involved specific forms of physical contact. These ranged from sitting very close and brushing customers' shoulders, tactile playful interactions or more intimacy such as holding or stroking customers' hands while they talked. This was primarily a component of dancers' attempts to hustle.

Some dancers criticized the no-touching rule, claiming that it interrupted the flow of providing a private intimate dance, instead constructing the dance as an artificial interaction, something which challenged the authenticity of their performance and put men off paying for further dancers/ time. Although a less obvious issue in hairstyling, questions about authentic touch also emerged at times, most often during discussions of health problems, especially dermatological issues such as psoriasis. Skin disease is a relatively common occupational hazard for stylists who handle chemicals (in dyes, perming agents, etc). Latex gloves provide a barrier, but produce a synthetic feeling (and symbolically alienating) touch. To avoid this, stylists tended either to tolerate ongoing skin problems or change their job role. For example, one stylist switched from women's hairstyling to barbering (requiring less frequent handling of chemicals).

Touch in hairstyling is one-way (worker to client). Amongst dancers, it was also seen as more acceptable for dancers to touch clients than vice versa, as body work focused on the body of the client is less aligned with prostitution where, somewhat uniquely, the customer is allowed and expected to initiate touch (as Brents and Jackson discuss in Chapter 5 and Hardy details in Chapter 3).

Overstepping boundaries relating to touch could lead to dancers' breaking the unofficial 'tacit rules' put in place by other dancers (Colosi, 2010). Allowing customers to touch their bodies, or other excessive touching (for example, masturbation) was constituted as offering 'dirty dancing' and frowned upon by dancers who felt that it degraded stripping/dancing. It also meant that dancers unwilling to engage in such practices would be put out of competition or pressurized by customers expecting all dancers to offer more than striptease, leading to a race to the bottom (Sanders and Hardy, 2012) and reflecting tensions described in studies of other sites of sex work in which touch is formally prohibited but informally condoned (Parreñas, 2010).

Labour relations in hairdressing and stripping

Strippers and many stylists operate as self-employed 'independent contractors', despite most working in a single workplace. Moreover, unlike many independent contractors (although similar to taxi drivers and a few others) independently contracted dancers and hairstylists are required to pay the club or salon owner to work on their premises.

Employing workers as 'independent contractors' shifts the risk over securing income sufficient to pay wages from owners to workers and means owners can abrogate responsibility for workers' health. This is especially advantageous where custom varies so that it is difficult to calculate the right ratio of worker-bodies to customer-bodies and fixed-hours employment contracts become costly (Cohen, 2011), while potential health (and harassment) issues are a disincentive for owners to engage with formal health and safety requirements, which they would have to if the establishment employed over five staff.

In general, dancers paid between £20 and £80 in order to work a shift and recruit customers within the clubs. Dancers are often also required to pay clubs commission on private dances (30 per cent). In addition, many clubs operated fining systems whereby dancers were charged up to £100 for breaching 'house rules' set by the club, such as chewing gum, having a mobile phone on the floor, turning up late or missing a shift or wearing the wrong item of clothing.

Much like dancers who 'rent' floor-space in a club, many hairstylists 'rent chairs'. They are engaged in various contractual arrangements. Some simply pay a proportion of all their takings to the salon as 'rent' (sometimes, but not always, with a capped minimum payment). In these cases, chair-renting was very much like commission-based work (another employment relationship common in hair salons). Other chair-renting stylists pay a fixed 'rental' per day, with an agreement on how many days holiday, when the fee was not due, were permitted. For dancers, mechanisms for taking time off varied; whereas some clubs enabled them to be entirely flexible, others demanded a retainer fee if dancers wished to have time off yet remain on the rota.

Independent contracting has often been associated with 'flexibility', although not always in workers' interest (Kalleberg, 2003). Flexibility was, however, a core reason offered by women for working in stripping. The job enabled women to select shifts to suit them and to fit in around other life engagements including educational courses and other work (Hardy and Sanders, forthcoming). Hairstyling, especially mobile hair styling (Cohen, 2010a), was similarly seen as providing a degree of flexibility. In hairstyling, flexibility largely involved female stylists moving to part-time work (very common in the industry) or to mobile work after having children (Cohen, 2010a). In practice, however, styling was not very flexible. For example, salons required most stylists to work late shifts on Friday evenings as well as working Saturdays. Indeed a surprising number of stylists took time out from hairstyling (a relatively skilled occupation) to work in unskilled retail jobs, for example as a supermarket cashier, because this allowed them to fit shifts around childcare. Temporarily withdrawing from styling limited stylists' maintenance of a following and often had the consequence of limiting their opportunities if and when they chose to return to salon-based work. Therefore older stylists, where they had not become owners of their own salons, tended to be based in suburban, and less expensive, salons. (This, of course, was also related to ageist aesthetics as previously discussed.) As such, the myth of flexibility was evident in both occupations, although not always the reality.

Despite dancers' apparently independent status, they experienced differing levels of autonomy. Some clubs strictly dictated the costumes and clothing worn by dancers, whereas others allowed dancers more freedom to select outfits. For instance, some clubs determined and checked the length of dress (which changed after midnight), along with the style (for example, sequins or frills), garters and the colour of underwear. Chair-renting hairstylists' autonomy also varied greatly, including their ability to determine their own schedule (starting/ending times/days off); the rates they charged customers; and the styling products they used. Whether other rules were imposed also varied, for instance relating to clothing, structure of the client-interaction or length of appointment. As such, where stylists were, like dancers, independent contractors, their body labour was both controlled by salon owners but also impacted by the pressures of self-employment.

The pressure of stylists' job and client demands, refracted through particular employment relations, sometimes prevented them from having sufficient breaks. For instance, Paul, a self-employed stylist who often worked alone as sole owner-operator, highlighted this:

> [The] worst thing is when you don't have time to eat and time to go to the toilet. Yeah, can be difficult. If you go past when you should go to the loo, but you don't get off to the loo when you should, which isn't a good thing....Well you've got to go when you've got to go, but I mean, you tend to hold yourself, which is stupid, can't be any good really. It can be very stressful. If you're behind and someone comes late and things don't go quite right. It can be very stressful.

Here the immediate pressure of clients, especially the unpredictability of clients' temporality, exacerbates the difficulties of being a solo worker. Later in the interview, Paul highlighted the difficulty of taking sick leave as a self-employed worker, describing working through a bout of kidney infection and diarrhoea because 'You have to come in. Don't have a choice. You work whatever state you're in. You're self-employed.'

Conclusion

Both hairdressing and dancing involved multiple forms of intersecting labour – aesthetic, emotional and body. Notably these forms of work were required both to sell the product and make money, as well as to establish the boundaries and relationships with customers necessary to ensure repeat and/or prolonged commercial interactions. Although these techniques have been a common thread within commentary on stripping (Boles and Garbin, 1974; Deshotels and Forsyth, 2005), understanding these strategies as an intertwined combination of aesthetic, body and emotional labour demonstrates the complexities of labour undertaken by women in the strip industry, and aligns this work with other forms of work in which the body of both worker and customer is centre stage.

The labour process of both occupations had similar health and corporeal impacts, specifically on workers' backs and feet from standing up. It is perhaps worth highlighting that the physical positions in which body work and sex work can be performed are limited, albeit in different ways. Although the body is central to each labour process, strippers, unlike hairstylists, are not supposed to be in physical contact with customers. On the other hand, workers in both industries had their own bodies shaped into acceptable classed and gendered bodies. Some workers heavily resisted the encroachments of these changes in their non-work lives and identities, whereas others accepted their respective work identities and bodily alterations as an integral part of who they were.

As independent contractors, both strippers and hairdressers were reliant on self-generated income on a daily basis. Both industries have variable (and somewhat unpredictable) custom on any day, meaning that both stylists and dancers face problems taking sufficient breaks while at work, taking holidays or planning financially. Stripping was, however, significantly more insecure than hairdressing, in which the construction of a 'following' provided a form of security. Strip club regulars tended not to last for such a long duration. Familiarity also eases a central tension in all body work – how to produce trust in an intimate embodied interaction (Eayrs, 1993). To a limited extent, a similar evolution in trust occurs in the longer term commercial relationships that strippers sometimes forge with 'regulars' (Egan, 2003). Yet strippers' usual commercial interactions are one-offs, given that visiting strip clubs is largely considered a luxury or one-off entertainment (for stag parties, birthdays, etc).

Hairstyling also encompasses more variety in employment relations than dancing. This may simply be the product of an earlier wave of regulatory attention to 'disguised wage workers' in the sector (Druker et al., 2005). In comparison to dancing, it is also a sector in which most 'owners' are simultaneously workers (and also largely female). Thus, the social relations between owners and workers in the sector is less clearly defined than it is in dancing, which usually has a clear demarcation between the self-contracted dancers (often transient workers with minimal allegiance to the club) and more permanent management and salaried staff.

This comparative analysis highlights both similarities and differences in the body, aesthetic and emotional labour performed by a group of service workers (hairdressers) and sex workers (strippers). Although hairdressing is a more stable, secure and less stigmatized form of work, both occupations have high rates of self-employment, instabilities in remuneration and demands for particular intersecting forms of aesthetic, emotional and body labour. Not insignificantly, the disadvantages and negativities associated with providing aesthetic, emotional and body labour in such insecure contexts are largely shouldered by women, and increasingly younger working class women, alienated from other sections of the labour market.

REFERENCES

Barton, B. (2006). *Stripped: Inside the Lives of Exotic Dancers*. London: New York University Press.

Bernstein, B. (2001). The Meaning of the Purchase: Desire, Demand and the Commerce of Sex. *Ethnography* 2(3): 389–420.

Biggart, N.W. (1990). *Charismatic Capitalism: Direct Selling Organizations in America*. Chicago: University of Chicago Press. ▶

Boles, J. and Garbin, A. (1974). The Choice of Stripping for a Living: An Empirical and Theoretical Explanation. *Sociology of Work and Occupations* 1(1): 110–23.

Chugh, S. and Hancock, P. (2009). Networks of Aestheticization: The Architecture, Artefacts and Embodiment of Hairdressing Salons. *Work, Employment & Society* 23: 460–76.

Cohen, R.L. (2010a). Rethinking 'Mobile Work': Boundaries of Space, Time and Social Relation in the Working Lives of Mobile Hairstylists. *Work, Employment & Society* 24: 65–84.

——— (2010b). When It Pays to Be Friendly: Employment Relationships and Emotional Labour in Hairstyling. *Sociological Review* 58: 197–218.

——— (2011). Time, Space and Touch at Work: Body Work and Labour Process (Re)organisation. *Sociology of Health & Illness* 33: 189–205.

Colosi, R. (2010). *Dirty Dancing. An Ethnography of Lap-Dancing*. Cullompton: Willan.

Deshotels, T. and Forsythe, C. (2005). Strategic Flirting and the Emotional Tab of Exotic Dancing. *Deviant Behavior* 27: 223–41.

Druker, J., White, G. and Stanworth, C. (2005). Coping with Wage Regulation: Implementing the National Minimum Wage in Hairdressing Businesses. *International Small Business Journal* 23: 5–25.

Eayrs, M.A. (1993). Time, Trust and Hazard: Hairdressers' Symbolic Roles. *Symbolic Interaction* 16: 19–37.

Egan, D. (2003). 'I'll Be Your Fantasy Girl, If You'll Be My Money Man': Mapping Desire, Fantasy and Power in Two Exotic Dance Clubs. *Journal of Psychoanalysis, Culture and Society* 8(1): 109–20.

Frank, K. (2002). *G-strings and Sympathy: Strip Club Regulars and Male Desire*. London: Duke University Press.

Hardy, K. and Sanders, T. (forthcoming). The Political Economy of 'Lap Dancing': Flexibility, Precarity and Women's Work in the Stripping Industry. *Work, Employment & Society*.

Hobbs, D., Hadfield, P., Lister, S. and Winlow, S. (2002). 'Door Lore': The Art and Economics of Intimidation. *British Journal of Criminology* 42(2): 352–70.

Isaksen, L.A. (2002). Masculine Dignity and the Dirty Body. *NORA – Nordic Journal of Feminist and Gender Research* 10: 137–46.

Kalleberg, A.L. (2003). Flexible Firms and Labor Market Segmentation: Effects of Workplace Restructuring on Jobs and Workers. *Work and Occupations* 30: 154–73.

McDowell, L. (2009). *Working Bodies: Interactive Service Employment and Workplace Identities*. Chichester: Wiley-Blackwell.

O'Connell Davidson, J. (1998). *Prostitution, Power and Freedom*. London: Polity.

Oerton, S. (2004). Bodywork Boundaries: Power, Politics and Professionalism in Therapeutic Massage. *Gender, Work & Organization* 11: 544–65.

Parreñas, R.S. (2010). Cultures of Flirtation: Sex and the Moral Boundaries of Filipina Migrant Hostesses in Tokyo. In E. Boris and R.S. Parreñas (Eds) *Intimate Labors*. Stanford: Stanford Social Sciences. Pp. 132–47.

Price, K. (2000). Stripping Women: Workers' Control in Strip Clubs. *Current Research on Occupation and Research* 11(1): 3–33.

Sanders, T. (2005). 'It's Just Acting': Sex Workers' Strategies for Capitalising on Sexuality. *Gender, Work & Organization* 12(4): 319–42.

Sanders, T. and Hardy, K. (2012). Devalued, Deskilled, and Diversified: Explaining the Proliferation of Striptease in the UK. *British Journal of Sociology* 63(3): 513–32.

Twigg, J. (2000). Carework as a Form of Bodywork. *Ageing and Society* 20: 389–411.

Wainwright, E., Marandet, E. and Sadaf, R. (2011). The Means of Correct Training: Embodied Regulation in Training for Body Work among Mothers. *Sociology of Health & Illness* 33: 220–36.

Warhurst, C. and Nickson, D. (2007). Employee Experience of Aesthetic Labour in Retail and Hospitality. *Work, Employment & Society* 21: 103–20.

———— (2009). 'Who's Got the Look?': Emotional, Aesthetic and Sexualized Labour in Interactive Services. *Gender, Work & Organization* 16: 385–404.

Wolkowitz, C. (2006). *Bodies at Work*. London: Sage.

Sexualizing and Desexualizing Bodies in the Labour Process

Altered Bodies, Engineered Careers: A Comparison of Body Technologies in Corporate and Do-It-Yourself Pornographic Productions

8

Lori L. Fazzino

Introduction

Pornography is an understudied occupation regarding body work and sexual labour. The dominant understanding of body work is work that an individual does on his/her own body in order to achieve certain occupational expectations (Shilling, 1993). Working on one's corporal self requires a method for doing so. Wesley (2003a: 644) conceptualizes body technologies as 'the techniques we engage to change or alter our physical appearance... [A]lthough body technologies are artificial, the technologized body passes as natural when it conforms to dominant social expectations of gendered bodies.' Body technologies contribute to the construction of the female body as a Western representation of sexualized hegemonic beauty and femininity. Further, the perpetuation of hegemonic ideals by the media normalizes the use of body technologies and contributes to the fetishization of mainstream beauty (Gimlin, 2000). This is evident in the ways advertisers and sexualizing media promote the commodification of beauty through marketplace consumption (Reichert, 2003), with the number of cosmetic surgery procedures increasing annually (Gimlin, 2002). In particular, the exploitation of adolescent girls through premature sexualization produces damaging effects on their physical and psychological developmental processes (Durham, 2008; Egan and Hawkes, 2008a; Grabe and Hyde, 2009).

My discussion of pornography is based largely on the juxtaposition of the cultural and critical feminism perspectives (Dines et al., 1998). In a wide cultural sense, pornography is understood to be sexual materials produced and sold, primary to male consumers, with the purpose of stimulating sexual arousal. The critical feminist perspective situates the cultural understanding of pornography in a web of gender inequality and power relations, asserting that pornography is *specific* sexual material that facilitates and perpetuates the sexual subordination of women. Despite all moral, religious, political, and intellectual opposition, pornography has undergone vast structural changes, increasingly being regarded as a mainstream corporate business generating annual profits reported at $10 to $14 billion dollars (Comella, 2010). It has been subject to rigorous standardization from the US federal government and medical community regarding industry labour regulations and mandated sexually transmitted infections testing. It has attempted to legitimate its business practices by rebranding itself as the adult video industry, hosting conventions where fans can interact with performers, and by broadening its presence via media technologies in a global market.

Structural changes have generated economic and cultural changes which have contributed to the fragmentation of porn culture. Movements such as *altporn* and the emergence of amateur and do-it-yourself (DIY) websites economically cater to a new generation of participant pornographers and produce what Attwood (2007: 441) calls new sex 'taste cultures' comprised of producers and consumers who challenge heteronormativity and hegemonic standards of beauty. However, little is known about the performance of sexual labour in these new subgenres. In this chapter, I explore the aesthetic labour processes of professional and amateur porn performers and the relationship between using body technologies and commodification. First, I ask how is sex embodied through work? Second, how are bodies commodified across different pornographic production structures? Third, how does the utilization of body technologies change across different commodification levels of commercial porn and DIY porn? By understanding the aesthetic labour processes of pornographic performers, scholars may be able to better address the larger issues of sexual commodification and gender exploitation.

Body technologies and the occupational performance of sex workers

The concept of 'body technologies' has been contextualized as a way to explore their role in reinforcing and challenging the relation between gender and power (Wesley, 2003a), as a technique to avoid stigmatization (Gimlin, 2002), and as an aspect of the relationship between technologies and femininity (Cole, 1993). Most of the sociological literature that addresses body technologies and erotic labour centres on escorts and exotic dancers (Barton, 2006; Egan, 2003; Ronai and Ellis, 1989; Wesley, 2003a, 2003b). The common theme among these studies is the necessary employment of body technologies for fantasy creation. In order for dancers to successfully perform erotic labour, their bodies must become desired objects necessary for the production of fantasy. Wesley (2003a: 649) identifies the relationship between erotic labour and body technologies for the exotic dancer, finding that 'To achieve the successful performance of this body, the stripper's outward appearance is thus carefully and often painfully (re)constructed via body technologies.'

Body technologies, as discussed in the literature, are classified into two categories: temporary/noninvasive or semi to permanent/dangerous (Balsamo, 1996; Wesley, 2003a, 2003b; Wolf, 2002). Temporary technologies include clothing, make-up, hair style, and hair removal, whereas technologies of invasiveness can also include unhealthy eating and binging, extreme body building and/or drug abuse. Table 8.1 presents a list of commonly used technologies.

Temporary technologies are relatively easy to access, in terms of both availability and affordability, and can have substantial impact on sexual performance. Fantasy costumes (e.g., nurse's uniform, schoolgirl, garters and stockings) are a popular technology among sex workers, enhancing one's presentation of self and redefining attractiveness (Barton, 2006). They provide erotic enhancement to sexual performances by exaggerating sexual stereotypes necessary for fantasy creation (Ronai and Ellis, 1989; Schweitzer, 2004), contribute to the creation of manufactured identities (Sanders, 2005) and are symbolic in sexual performance: the everyday act of wearing heels instantly sexualizes the body.

On the flip side, what Wolf (2002: 448) describes as 'new technologies of invasiveness' are typically more permanent and potentially deadly. In the United States, cosmetic surgery is one of the most widely used body technologies and arguably one of the riskiest (Gimlin, 2002). In 2008, Board-certified plastic surgeons performed over 10 million cosmetic and

Table 8.1   Commonly used body technologies

Temporal/Non-Invasive Technologies	Potentially Permanent/Dangerous
Clothing	Cosmetic Surgery
Make-up	Extreme Fitness
Hairstyling	Eating Disorders
Hair Removal	Substance Use
Tanning	Tattooing
Teeth Whitening	Piercing
Manicure/Pedicure/Nail Extensions	

reconstructive procedures, a 162 percent increase since 1997. Of those procedures, 9.3 million were performed on women. The most common procedure was breast augmentation, and the total amount Americans spent on cosmetic procedures in 2008 was 11.8 billion dollars. Barton's (2006) study of exotic dancers found that between 30 and 50 percent of the dancers she interviewed altered their appearance with breast implants, believing that breast size is correlated with earning capacity. Abbott (2010: 50) supports Barton's findings in her discussion of aesthetic norms of professionally pornography stating, 'Cosmetic surgeries, such as liposuction and breast augmentation, are the norm in the business...'. Norm or not, Wesley (2003b: 486) argues that these aesthetic practices are problematic, claiming that body technologies are 'creating a standard that is, by nature, unattainable'. Image saturation of sexualized bodies in the media contributes to the belief that aesthetic perfection is achievable. Trying to obtain such aesthetic standards has proven to be both highly appealing for achieving status and highly lucrative for female sex workers (Wolf, 2002). Thus, when the potential rewards outweigh the necessary costs, it is clear to see why women in the porn industry would engage in aesthetic practices that contribute to the commodification of themselves (Entwistle and Wissinger, 2006).

Having an aesthetic appeal is only half of the equation. Sexual labour, comprised of aesthetic and emotional performance, is the commodified product available for consumption in the sex industry. Sexual labour, framed as occupational performance, can be operationalized within dramaturgical analysis (Goffman, 1959). Sex workers must create idealized performances – authentic and unique illusions which the audience believes and interprets as meaningful. Delivering an idealized performance is two-fold. First, performers develop an emotional connection based on 'counterfeit intimacy' with their audiences (Ronai and Ellis, 1989). According to Egan (2006: 118), for instance, 'The dancer's labor becomes fetishistically occluded and intersects with male fantasy, operating such that male regulars come to believe that the dancers really do care about and want to have a relationship with them.' Second, idealized performances require sex workers to conform and exemplify the values of the audience, such as hegemonic beauty, desire, and sexualized femininity. Egan (2006: 118) notes that the dancer's job 'involves the performance of his desire and fantasy in order to "satisfy the customer" and make money'. If sex workers challenge the fantasy or stray from their manufactured identities (Sanders, 2005), the risk of delivering a cynical performance increases and can hinder earning potential (Egan, 2006). However, male audiences are invested in their roles as sexual voyeurs who want to define the performance as successful. Men have an active role in fantasy production when they purchase necessary technologies for the performers (Wesley, 2003a). The performance is subsidized by male producers/

consumers and defined as successful through financial compensation earned by sex workers. Thus, an authentically successful performance is one that perpetuates hegemonic masculinity and men's control over women in sexual labour relations (Garlick, 2010).

DIY porn: sexual labour or sexual leisure?

Images of sexualized bodies are ubiquitous in today's global market; sex sells and is everywhere. Coopersmith (2006: 10) identifies the Internet as the driving force that restructured the production, distribution, marketing, and consumption patterns of pornography; what he refers to as the 'democratization of pornography'. The most notable change resulting from democratizing porn is the expansive growth of do-it-yourself (DIY) porn, part of the *altporn* movement where all of the lines of status demarcation have been heavily blurred, if not completely eradicated (Attwood, 2007). Unlike traditional pornography, the DIY movement is alternative, confessional and transgressive, featuring user-generated pornographic content (Van Doorn, 2010). DIY porn changed the production, distribution and compensation structures vis-à-vis traditional porn outlets, generating profits from passing 'traffic' to partner websites, selling advertisement space, and when applicable, charging monthly membership fees (Coopersmith, 2006). DIY sites are also responsible for creating a new kind of pornographer – the amateur producer-participant where the primary focus is on new meanings of self-expression.

Amateur porn is thought of as producing a more realistic, real-world picture of sex. According to Hillyer (2004: 55), we exist in a 'culture of amateurism' where it is believed that amateur pornographers derive their motivation to produce home-based porn from love and enthusiasm, not money or obligation. Intimacy becomes embodied through sexual acts which are performed for a participatory community of like-minded individuals who value authentic over staged sexual performance. Maintaining authenticity is dependent upon a few key factors, such as cinematic setting, voracious sexual performance, a voyeuristic relationship between performers and viewers and body displays that are consistent with cultural perceptions of 'normal breast size and bodies' (Hillyer, 2004: 56). The popularity of amateur porn portraying 'normal', 'ordinary' and 'authentic' female bodies raises new questions about the commodification of the different types of sexual bodies represented on DIY sites that do not adhere to hegemonic ideals, as compared to the glamorized bodies portrayed in professional porn.

I take a mixed methods approach in this study, using a quantitative content analysis of amateur videos on a highly trafficked DIY porn site along with ethnographic observations at two professional production studios, to offer a comparative analysis of body technology representations across the professional and amateur production structures. I then provide a discussion of how professional porn actresses perpetuate hegemonic beauty through aesthetic labour, how DIY performers simultaneously reinforce some hegemonic standards while challenging others, commodification in each production structure and present new questions about gender exploitation. Finally, I offer implications for the consequences of mandated aesthetics, such as the emergence of new sexualized industries, the increased sexualization of non-sex work related industries and the broader implications these consequences have on women's value in the workplace and gender inequality.

Methods

Content analysis

One website was purposively chosen for inclusion in this study because of its affiliation with a popular network of porn sites that currently ranks 36th in the United States and 57th worldwide for Internet traffic (Alexa, 2010). This site promotes itself as one of the largest DIY amateur porn sites featuring user-generated pornographic content. Additionally, the site offers two membership options – free or premium. Free membership allows users to download pornographic content organized by video length, highest rated, most viewed, date of upload, title of video or type of content (e.g., 'anal', 'co-ed'), to post comments about the content, and to upload their own content. All uploaded content is subject to the site's *Terms and Conditions*. Premium membership, in addition to the benefits of free membership, includes access to videos from over 300 production studios that sell their content to various DIY porn sites.

Sampling technique

On this particular DIY site, video clips are 'tagged' with keywords that describe their content and then organized into specific categories. There were forty categories featured on the free member portion of this website at the time of data collection that were subject to exclusion based on the following criteria: sexual orientation, sexual acts and appearance type. I excluded some because the empirical focus of this study is on heterosexual amateur videos. This is consistent with Evans et al.'s (2010) claim that heterosexuality is a sexually hegemonic idea. I also excluded categories that specifically advertised multiple partners (e.g., 'threesome', 'group', 'bukkake') and acts that did not require intercourse (e.g., 'masturbation', 'toys', 'fetish'). To ensure aesthetic variations, I also excluded race-specific (e.g., 'Asian', 'ebony', 'Latina') and specified physical categories (e.g., 'big tits', 'blonde', 'brunette'). After these exclusions, my sampling frame comprised thirteen viable categories. I conducted a simple random sample of five categories ('anal', 'cumshot', 'Point-of-View', 'pubic', and 'reality') and conducted a systematic random sample of 20 clips from each category (Taylor, 2005), 100 in all. I took screen shots of each category's web page in order to reflect the population of clips available at the time of data collection and downloaded clips from each category over a period of five days in November 2010. In the event that I randomly selected a clip that did not fit my parameters, the following clip was substituted.

Coding scheme and interrater reliability

Clips were coded for the uses of various body technologies employed by the performers. Table 8.2 presents a list of variables in the coding scheme, which was adapted and modified from Wesley's (2003a) study of body technologies among exotic dancers.

Table 8.2 Variables recorded for content analysis

Category (Anal, Cumshot, POV, Pubic, Reality)
Clip Title
Performer's Race (White, Black, Hispanic, Asian/Pacific Islander, Unable to Tell)
Body Technologies

Performer's Physical Appearance
  Body Style (Slim/Skinny, Average, Muscular, Chubby, BBW)
  Hair Length (Short, Medium, Long)
  Hair Color (Blonde, Brunette, Red, Black, Other)

Costuming
  Clothing (Erotic/Fantasy, Fetish, Everyday Wear, Nude)
  Shoes (Stiletto Heel/Platform, Everyday Heels, Tennis Shoes, Barefoot, Other)
  Make-up
  Nails

Cosmetic Surgery
  Breast Augmentation (Implants, Reduction, Natural, Unable to Tell)

Body Maintenance
  Tanning
  Pubic Hair (Natural/Unshaven, Slightly Trimmed, Most Trimmed, Bare)
  Eyebrows (Natural, Waxed/Threaded)

Ornamental Modification
  Tattoos
  Piercings

Production Type
  Amateur
  Pro-Am
  Professional

I was the principle coder in this study. I used a second coder, a female graduate student, in order to provide a reliability check as described in Neuendorf (2002). The additional coder was given four hours of training on the definitions of the various body technologies. She was shown visual examples of the content that represented each technology. Prior to analysis, she was tested through repeated practice in order to demonstrate accurate knowledge of the definitions and measure intercoder agreement. At the onset of the coding process, both coders were provided with coding sheets and category definitions. We watched the clips independently, analyzed the actresses' appearance and marked all the technologies the actresses appeared to have used. After independent coding was complete, 20 per cent of the sample size was randomly selected for reliability. Interrater reliability was assessed through the use of Cohen's kappa statistic (Neuendorf, 2002) and calculated for each dependent variable. All kappas were above .70, which indicates an acceptable level of reliability. As the principal investigator, I analyzed the remaining 80 per cent of the sample.

Ethnographic observations

I am not a stranger to the adult video industry, having had a brief stint as a columnist for an adult Internet news site. Due to my status as a former insider, I decided to conduct an ethnography using the access that very few researchers have. In February 2011, I conducted ethnographic observations on the set of five professional adult video film productions from two West coast companies over a period of three days. Professional production companies differ from pro-amateur and amateur productions in that they are regarded as being 'reputable companies with high budgets' (Abbott, 2010: 61). The first company I observed is one of the five largest production companies in the United States and has won numerous adult entertainment awards. This company employees roughly 15 to 20 contract performers at any given time. The pay scale of contracted starlets is ambiguous, although known benefits of being contracted include marketing and promotion by a well-funded company, opportunities to interact with fans through bookings to sign at sex-oriented retailers and conventions, and opportunities to supplement income by feature dancing on the strip club circuit. The second company I conducted observations at was a small, Internet-based company headed by an award-winning producer, director, photographer and actress. Although this company did not retain contract performers, it did consistently release extremely successful high-quality productions.

On the mornings of my data collection sessions, I observed the arrival of scheduled female performers and the aesthetic processes that transformed ordinary women into porn stars. While on set, I jotted observations in my research journal and typed jottings up as field notes at the end of each day. Field notes were coded according to three criteria that included: (1) the variables used in the content analysis; (2) the use of additional body technologies not previously accounted for; (3) variation among the technologies between the Internet and video performances. I had the chance to assess the physical appearance of 13 porn actresses and observe both the permanent and temporary modifications made for their occupational performances. However, because of their busy filming schedule, I was unable to engage in any dialogue with the actresses and conducted only field observations.

A limitation of only using field observations is the inability to get a complete understanding of what is happening in places other than the observed field. As I discuss in the findings section, all of the professional actresses were extremely thin. Field observations alone did not provide me with enough information to determine how the actresses engaged in body maintenance practices to manage their weight, both on and off the set (Entwistle and Wissinger, 2006). Observations only suggest that universal thinness appears to be a highly mandated aesthetic expectation of professional porn actresses. The lack of performers' accounts and my inability to address weight management technologies should be considered when interpreting these findings.

The body spectacular: aesthetic corporeality of commercial and DIY performers

When you're having sex, you're at your most vulnerable. Only a handful of women look good fucking: everyone has a little cheese here and there. Most girls have to battle eating disorders at some point from seeing themselves jiggling naked on camera so much. (Jenna Jameson, Top American Porn Star and former owner of Club Jenna [Jameson and Strauss, 2004: 329])

In professional porn productions, sexualized bodies had a uniformly hegemonic aesthetic: Caucasian, slim, blond, and implanted. Consistent with Attwood's (2007: 449) description of professional porn stars as 'spectacular but inhuman', the porn actresses I observed had bodies that were hyper-technologically modified. Although it was February on the West coast and the women walked into the studios wearing winter clothing, I immediately noticed their physical frames. These women were extremely thin and had obvious breast implants – large circular globes that were disproportionate to their bodies. All of the actresses maintained very long hair of similar length that cascaded down their backs; four brunettes, nine blonds. Each woman maintained a tan which was observable from tan lines left by their g-string panties. Only a few of the actresses had tattoos and/or piercings that were able to be removed or concealed with make-up when necessary.

Race was represented differently in each production sphere. One hundred per cent of professional porn actresses were Caucasian, whereas the DIY sample reflected some racial variation. An overwhelming percentage of the sample (73 per cent) were Caucasian, followed by Hispanic (15 per cent), Black (9 per cent), and Asian/Pacific Islander (3 per cent). Like the professional actresses, 97 per cent of the DIY sample were coded as slim. Forty-four per cent of the sample had blond hair and like their professional counterparts, most women in the DIY sample (80 per cent) maintained long hair. Unlike the professional actresses, the majority of DIY performers had natural breasts (69 per cent); only 31 per cent of the sample had breast implants. Seventy-nine per cent of the DIY performers had multiple tattoos and piercings, which they did not conceal. Consistent with previous research on sex work and body technologies, the most popular technologies on the DIY site were erotic clothing (55 per cent), manicured nails (97 per cent), groomed pubic region (90 per cent), and tattoos and/ or piercings (79 per cent). Make-up was the single most ubiquitous technology, employed by 99 per cent of the DIY sample. Figure 8.1 provides a visual illustration of the percentage of performers using body technologies represented on the DIY site.

Consistent technologies across the performance spheres were make-up, costuming, nail maintenance, and pubic region grooming; however, there was an observable difference in the quality of the technologies that were used. When the professional actresses arrived for their shoots, without professional make-up or hair styling, their sexual personas were unrecognizable, and they looked like ordinary women. Hence in order to achieve

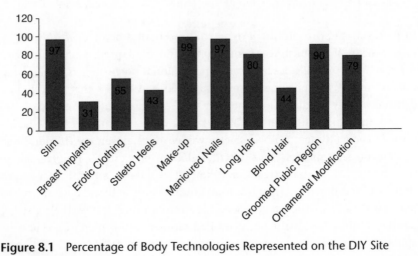

Figure 8.1 Percentage of Body Technologies Represented on the DIY Site

aesthetic standardization, professional actresses spent between two and four hours doing aesthetic labour. Hair styling, make-up, waxing, hand/foot nail maintenance, and tanning services were all done on set by professional technicians provided by the studios. Make-up application, which included the use of false eye lashes, was typically the longest part of the aesthetic process, and make-up was continually reapplied during the shoot as needed. Additionally, wardrobe stylists were employed by production studios to oversee costumes selection and fittings. Professional costuming technologies included accessories, such as stockings, garters, shoes, and jewellery, which were often adorned with markers of femininity, such as lace, bows or jewels. The use of high-quality, elaborate costumes served a dual purpose, acting as a temporary body technology that alters appearance and as a prop that contributes to the creation of an authentically fanciful story line. Although performers in the DIY sample used make-up as a technology, it was not heavily applied nor did the performers use false eye lashes as a technology. The costumes that were used by the DIY performers often consisted of bras and panties, simply lingerie or normal everyday clothing. Costumes representing a fantasy role (e.g., nurse, school girl) were much less elaborate. Accessories were not widely used on the DIY site, with the exception of jewellery such as rings and earrings.

Discussion

The Economy of Sexual Labour and Sexual Leisure

Delivering a sexual performance is the work of professional porn actresses who exist in an aesthetic industry. During my field observations, it became clear that the labour of their sexual performances is very much a labour of aesthetics resulting in the simultaneous commodification of bodies by production companies and actresses. Professional production companies with high investments in contract performers have a lot at stake. By providing technologies to their actresses, professional studios are able to mandate a specific aesthetic, the expense of which was just the cost of doing business. It has been reported that some professional adult film companies not only promote the idea of breast implants to their contract performers, but pay for them as well (Amis, 2001). Abbott's (2010) study of why women pursue a career in porn suggests that at the professional level, money and fame are primary motivations. As such, the willingness to invest a high amount of time managing their appearance was a small price actresses paid for the expected return. The fact that breast enhancements were a common technology used by all of the actresses I observed suggest that breast size and profitability were correlated by both producers and performers.

Of the 13 actresses I observed, nine did not have a contract with a specific studio. These actresses better represented the majority of performers in the porn industry who approach their jobs as sexual entrepreneurs, always trying to book the next job; they are their own bosses. Like the fashion models studied by Entwistle and Wissinger (2006: 791), these actresses are 'freelance aesthetic labourers'. The construction and commodification of their sexual performances is self-managed, requiring a deeper investment of the self. As such, aesthetic labour is more nuanced than being a corporeal embodiment of an employer's desired aesthetic, as first proposed by Witz et al. (2003). Entwistle and Wissinger (2006) conceptualize aesthetic labour as an embodied practice of combining corporeal work with emotional management. This form of labour is applicable to *all* professional porn actresses, especially those without contracts. Although not having a contract means greater occupational freedom, emotional distress can ensue from managing the pitfalls of increased occupational risks and unfavourable labour conditions. The porn industry is especially known for having a high burnout rate among new talent. Jenna Jameson, one of the most successful actresses in the industry's history, discusses the many pitfalls in the porn industry, saying that 'The biggest challenge is the psychological preparation you need before you walk in the door...never allow them [boundaries] to be crossed. If you do, it will break you down and you won't have longevity' (Jameson and Strauss, 2004: 326). Thus, the ability to embody aesthetic labour on a deeper level is critical for successful freelance performers. My former status as an industry insider contributed to my familiarization with the work of most of the actresses I observed. These performers were able to maintain their popularity and increase their staying power. Thus, a successful actress is one who has learned to become an 'emotion manager', maintaining not only her body but preserving her 'self' (Hochschild, 1983: 164).

To examine the aesthetic differences across production structures, I turn to a discussion of the motivations for participation on DIY sites and what its consumers value. Although the DIY site used in this study does not provide compensation for user-generated content, there is no shortage of amateur videos available for consumption. Consistent with Abbott (2010), money is rarely cited as a motivation for DIY participation. In a postmodern society, the relationship between new media, power and identity (re)construction provides an alternate explanation for participation. DIY sites provide a virtual space for mediated exhibitionism (Jones, 2010) where women can expose their nude bodies, devalue modesty and chastity, and redefine the gendered power relation. The 'sexual self', according to Van Doorn (2010: 426), 'is realized by making it available for continuous surveillance, in search of the visual "truth" of sexual bodies and their pleasures'. Rather than rejecting sex, embodied sexuality re-appropriates power in the hands of women by providing 'a positive economy of the body and pleasure' (Foucault, 1977: 190). Female participants see themselves through what Waskul and Radeloff (2010: 212) call the 'erotic looking glass'. The erotic looking glass process facilitates the reenchantment of sexiness of corporeal bodies that do not conform to culturally hegemonic standards by finding acceptance among an anonymous virtual audience who also reject idealized aesthetic standards (Waskul, 2002). Whereas generating profits was the impetus for professional studios to provide and actresses to use multiple types of high-quality body technologies, the relative lack of technologies among the amateur performers indicates that they did not have the same level of commitment to remaking the body. As a result, amateur performers more authentically represented embodied sexuality though their aesthetic non-conformity. Participation for pleasure rather than money raises questions about the nature of commodification on these sites.

Conclusion

Not motivated by economic gain, amateur performers engaged in few technologies and represented a more 'alternative' aesthetic, indicating that DIY sites are not labour performance spaces, but rather public spheres of personal pleasure. As such, amateur performances are better defined as sexual leisure. Although some hegemonic ideals were represented in both production spaces, others were not. Representations of slimness and hair colour/length among professional and DIY performers reflect how the social construction of beauty, femininity, and power have been reified by Western women and are continually externalized through aesthetic practices (Synott, 1987; Weitz, 2001). However, DIY porn places a great emphasis on producing aesthetically diverse content of 'normal', 'ordinary' bodies that will satisfy a wide range of sex taste cultures, presenting sexual performances done for pleasure rather than profit (Hillyer, 2004). The fact that amateur porn represents 'real' people engaged in authentically pleasurable sex acts is appealing to its voyeuristic consumers, compared to commercialized porn, which promotes a specific type of fantasy characterized by sex with an unattainable glamorized performer. As such, the use of body technologies is nuanced between performance spheres. Body work is a structural requirement in the commercialized sphere where profits are contingent upon the sexual labour of performers. Conversely, in amateur DIY spheres where pleasure and sex are embodied through performance, body technologies are minimized; body work is a matter of agency. Aesthetics are not mandated on DIY sites, because the focus is intimacy creation between sexual performers and voyeuristic consumers. Thus, intimacy and authenticity are increased in DIY genres when viewers with sexual schemas can transpose themselves into the scene and believe that they can possibly have sex with the performer *because* she is ordinary (Barcan, 2002). I argue that DIY sites specialize in commodifying intimacy and authenticity rather than sexualized hegemonic bodies, capitalising on the desire and voyeuristic nature of their viewers.

The fact remains that the majority of the porn industry's revenue comes from commercial sex. Notably, sex work is one, if not the only, occupational sector in which women earn more than men by exploiting their capacity for aesthetic labour. The professional actresses in this study strategically objectify themselves through corporeal work, using body technologies as props necessary for creating fantasies through embodied sexual performances. By choosing to engage in a high level of aesthetic labour, performers promote themselves as sexy, strong, successful women, commodifying their sexualized images *in* the male-dominated porn industry rather than *by* the male-dominated porn industry. Both producers and performers are dependent upon one another for high investment returns. This nonetheless begs a question worthy of further inquiry – to what extent is gender exploitation problematic in high commodified porn work if women agree to and benefit from exploitative occupational relationships with the employing production studios? On the surface, it may appear that sex workers are simply exercising their agency by choosing this career, but a deeper look will reveal the reification of gender inequality through structural limitations, such as occupational advancement and pay disparity, associated with non-sex work industries. Confronted by limited opportunities for *real* economic stability, as long as it is a viable option some women choose sex work.

Pornography has been studied from a variety of perspectives with an increased interest focusing on the structural consequences of pornography on mainstream labour industries. Although some women chose a career in pornography for a variety of reasons, the proliferation of pornographic imagery continues to encourage the use of body technologies, which contributes to the normalization and perpetuation of unattainable physical standards for women in all labour industries, especially service industries. Perhaps gender exploitation is not a problem for consenting women who agree to and participate in the sexualization and commodification of their bodies, however, gender exploitation and inequality are perpetuated through sexualizing women in non-sex related occupations. A growing number of employers in retail and hospitability industries are hiring female employees as 'models' in order to mandate a specific aesthetic (Farfan, n.d.). The sexualization of low-skilled occupations has severe consequences. By incorporating mandated aesthetic qualifications into hiring rubrics, the only women who have access to these jobs are those with the 'right' aesthetic qualifications, reducing the viable applicant pool and exponentially increasing the competition. Further, the emergence of new occupational titles, such as 'bikini baristas' is a relatively recent phenomena within the last decade that has created a hybrid industry based on the convergence of sexual appeal and non-sex related services (Roberts, 2011). The marginalized occupational status of women in most labour industries is further devalued when sexual aesthetic value trumps job capability. There is less emphasis on the barista's efficiency or the quality of the product, but rather how good she looks making and serving the product.

There is a clear need for more research on the aesthetic labour processes of women in all labour industries. Future research should examine the narratives of female workers in the porn industry and in traditional and emergent sexualized service industries in order to get a better understanding of the relationship between aesthetic labour, commodification, and exploitation. For all we know, females workers, like the production studios, engage in aesthetic practices because it's just the cost of doing business.

Acknowledgements

I would like to thank Barb Brents, Teela Sanders, and Rachel Cohen for proving helpful comments on previous versions of this chapter. An earlier version of this was presented at the 2011 International Labour Process Conference, Leeds, United Kingdom.

REFERENCES

Abbott, S.A. (2010). Motivations for Pursuing a Career in Pornography. In R. Weitzer (Ed.) *Sex for Sale: Prostitution, Pornography, and the Sex Industry*, 2nd ed. New York: Routledge.

Alexa Web Information (2010). Traffic, Stats, and Site Info: Pornhub.com. Accessed 3 November 2010 at http://www.alexa.com/siteinfo/pornhub.com.

Amis, M. (2001). A Rough Trade. *The Guardian*. Accessed 14 November 2011 at http://www.guardian.co.uk/books/2001/mar/17/society.martinamis1.

Attwood, F. (2007). No Money Shot? Commerce, Pornography and New Sex Taste Cultures. *Sexualities* 10: 441–57.

Balsamo, A.M. (1996). *Technologies of the Gendered Body: Reading Cyborg Women*. Durham: Duke University Press.

Barcan, R. (2002). In the Raw: 'Home-Made' Porn and Reality Genres. *Journal of Mundane Behavior* 3(1). Accessed 7 January 2012 at http://www.mundanebehavior.org/issues/v3n1/barcan.htm.

Barton, B. (2006). *Stripped: Inside the Lives of Exotic Dancers*. New York: New York University Press.

Cole, C. (1993). Resisting the Canon: Feminist Cultural Studies, Sport, and Technologies of the Body. *Sociology of Sport & Social Issues* 17: 77–97.

▶

Comella, L. (2010). Remaking the Sex Industry: The Adult Expo as a Microcosm. *In* R. Weitzer (Ed.) *Sex for Sale: Prostitution, Pornography, and the Sex Industry*, 2nd ed. New York: Routledge.

Coopersmith, J. (2006). Does Your Mother Know What You *Really* Do? The Changing Nature of Computer-Based Pornography. *History and Technology* 22(1): 1–25.

Dines, G., Jensen, R. and Russo, A. (1998). *Pornography: The Production and Consumption of Inequality*. New York: Routledge.

Durham, G.M. (2008). *The Lolita Effect: The Media Sexualization of Young Girls and What We Can Do About It*. New York: Overlook.

Egan, D.R. and Hawkes, G. (2008). Endangered Girls and Incendiary Objects: Unpacking the Discourse on Sexualization. *Sexuality & Culture* 12: 291–311.

Entwistle, J. and Wissinger, E. (2006). Keeping Up Appearances: Aesthetic Labour in the Fashion Modelling Industries of London and New York. *The Sociological Review* 54(4): 774–94.

Evans, A., Riley, S. and Shankar, A. (2010). Technologies of Sexiness: Theorizing Women's Engagement in the Sexualization of Culture. *Feminism and Psychology* 20(1): 114–31.

Farfan, B. (n.d.) Hooters, Lane Bryant, and Whole Foods Face Weight and Obesity Discrimination. Accessed 7 March 2012 at http://retailindustry.about.com/od/companynewsanalysis/a/hooters_obesity_weight_discrimnation_retail_workplace_lawsuit_hiring_employment_2.htm.

Foucault, M. (1977). *Power/Knowledge: Selected Interviews and Other Writings 1972–1977*. New York: Pantheon.

Garlick, S. (2010). Taking Control of Sex?: Hegemonic Masculinity, Technology, and Internet Pornography. *Men and Masculinities* 12(5): 597–614.

Goffman, E. (1959). *The Presentation of Self in Everyday Life*. New York: Anchor.

Grabe, S. and Hyde, J.S. (2009). Body Objectification, MTV, and Psychological Outcomes among Female Adolescents. *Journal of Applied Social Psychology* 39: 2840–58.

Hillyer, M. (2004). Sex in the Suburban: Porn, Home Movies, and the Live Action Performance of Love. *In* L. Williams (Ed.) *Pam and Tommy Lee: Hardcore and Uncensored*. Durham: Duke University Press.

Hochschild, A. (1983). *The Managed Heart*. Berkeley: University of California Press.

Jameson, J. and Strauss, N. (2004). *How to Make Love Like a Porn Star: A Cautionary Tale*. New York: Harper-Collins.

Jones, M.T. (2010). Mediated Exhibitionism: The Naked Body in Performance and Virtual Space. *Sexuality & Culture* 14: 253–69.

Neuendorf, K.A. (2002). *Content Analysis Guidebook*. Thousand Oaks: Sage.

Reichert, T. (2003). *The Erotic History of Advertising*. New York: Prometheus.

Roberts, H. (2011). Bikini Baristas Pole Dance and Flash Their Breasts for Tips at Drive Through Espresso Stand. Accessed 15 January 2011 at http://www.dailymail.co.uk/news/article-2030247/Bikini-baristas-pole-danced-flashed-breasts-tips-drive-espresso-stand.html.

Ronai, C. and Ellis, C. (1989). Turn-Ons for Money: Interactional Strategies of the Table Dancer. *Journal of Contemporary Ethnography* 18: 271–98.

Sanders, T. (2005). 'It's Just Acting': Sex Workers' Strategies for Capitalizing on Sexuality. *Gender, Work & Organization* 12: 319–42.

Schweitzer, D. (2004). Striptease: The Art of Spectacle and Transgression. *The Journal of Popular Culture* 34: 65–76.

Shilling, C. (1993). *The Body and Social Theory.* London: Sage.

Synott, A. (1987). Shame and Glory: A Sociology of Hair. *British Journal of Sociology* 38(3): 381–413.

Taylor, L.D. (2005). All for Him: Articles about Sex in American Lad Magazines. *Sex Roles* 52: 153–63.

Van Doorn, N. (2010). Keeping It Real: User-Generated Pornography, Gender Reification, and Visual Pleasure. *The International Journal of Research into New Media Technologies* 16(4): 411–30.

Waskul, D. (2002). The Naked Self: Being a Body in Televideo Cybersex. *Symbolic Interaction* 25(2): 199–227.

Waskul, D. and Radeloff, C.L. (2010). How Do I Rate?: Web Sites and Gendered Erotic Looking Glasses. *In* F. Attwood (Ed.) *Porn.com: Making Sense of Online Pornography.* New York: Peter Lang.

Weitz, R. (2001). Women and Their Hair: Seeking Power through Resistance and Accommodation. *Gender and Society* 15(5): 667–86.

Wesley, J.K. (2003). Exotic Dancing and the Negotiation of Identity: The Multiple Uses of Body Technologies. *Journal of Contemporary Ethnography* 32: 643–69.

———(2003). Where Am I Going to Stop?: Exotic Dancers, Fluid Body Boundaries, and Effects on Identity. *Deviant Behavior* 24: 483–503.

Witz, A., Warhurst, C. and Nickson, D. (2003). The Labour of Aesthetics and the Aesthetics of Organisations. *Organisation* 10(1): 33–54.

Wolf, N. (2002). *The Beauty Myth: How Images of Beauty Are Used against Women.* New York: Harper-Collins.

From Erotic Capital to Erotic Knowledge: Body, Gender and Sexuality as Symbolic Skills in Phone Sex Work

9

Giulia Selmi

Introduction

In a recent article, Catherine Hakim (2010) suggested the concept of *erotic capital* as a personal asset; an addition to the well-known economic, social and human capital that people can turn to in order to successfully manage their social interactions. In Hakim's understanding, erotic capital is a combination of aesthetic, visual, physical, social and sexual attractiveness to other members of a given society, especially to members of the opposite sex, that people can exploit (as they do other forms of capital) in order to achieve economic or social benefits. In the field of sex work, the exploitation of one's erotic capital is more evident than in other working activities because the exchange between seller and buyer depends exactly on a sexual or emotional performance. As suggested by Sanders (2005), sex workers capitalize on their sexuality as a business strategy to financially achieve the most they can from each interaction with customers.

In this chapter, I discuss the concept of erotic capital and sexual capitalizing in the case of phone sex workers selling sex to male customers, by looking to the micro-discursive practices and strategies workers use to successfully manage the call with the customers. Phone sex is a type of virtual sex work (Velena, 2003) that refers to sexually explicit or emotional conversations between two persons via telephone. Commercial phone sex services offer this sexual or emotional experience over the phone through premium-rate calls during which certain services are provided and for which prices higher than normal are charged. Unlike a normal call, part of the premium-rate call charge is paid to the service provider, thus supplying businesses with their revenue. Sex workers do not have any economic transaction with customers, but are paid by the sex phone company in proportion to the length of the call. Therefore, it occupies a 'border area' of the sex industry, so to say, where sex is sold, but through technology and voice, without any corporeal involvement with the customer. By virtue of the absence of the physical body, phone sex workers have to translate the sexual and/or emotional intercourse in a competent narrative that fits clients' needs and desires and whose success or failure (both in economic and interactional terms) depends on their professional ability to discursively mobilize suitable corporeal, sexual and gender resources and make clients feel the interaction is 'real', despite the mediation of the phone.

Are we having sex here? Sex work, language and technology

Selling sex on the phone means inscribing the sexual experience in the space made available for interaction by technology – and doing it so well that the client is willing to pay for it. The technologically mediated modality of the sexual interaction and its commercial nature raise some questions.

The first specificity of a phone sex call is that, in order for sex to be sold on the phone, the client needs to 'believe' they are having sex 'for real'. In Goffman's words (1974), if asked 'What is going on here?' the client needs to be able to answer, 'I am having sex with a woman with a determined body, determined erotic preferences, and a determined biography who is, in turn, having sex with me.' Should the client believe the woman – like the character in Robert Altman's *Short Cuts* – is wearing pajamas, cooking and feeding her kids while faking an orgasm for him, such a conversation would lose its authenticity. The first matter of interpretation in phone sex work is therefore what 'for real' is and how it makes the conversation possible. The question is: in what circumstances does someone calling a sex phone service believe the interaction to be real? A possible answer is: real is what exists as an ontologically and objectively given reality and exists outside and independently from the subject that can experience it, observe it, and measure it *per se*.

A more adequate answer can be found in those interpretations that define reality as an inter-subjective construction and discuss it in terms of a 'sense of the real' (Schutz, 1962, 1974). In this perspective, the question of reality is not advanced in frontal terms – there is an external world and a subject that knows it and verifies it on the basis of its objective qualities – but as a situated, inter-subjective product created by interaction. Therefore, what matters is what is real for the actors in a specific relationship. The consequence is that multiple realities – or sub-universes of reality (James, 1901) or finite provinces of meaning (Schutz, 1962) – can exist, and specific accents of reality are bestowed upon them by actors. Real is what we pay attention to and deem real when we do; in James' (1901: 643) words, 'Every world is real in its own way while attention is paid to it; but reality leaves when the attention does.' At the same time, though, real is what not only we, but all those we interact with, deem is real. Here, reality is the product of the actors' significant actions – a tight net of interconnected meanings resting on the contingent, negotiable agreement of the individual actors in the situation (Damari, 2008). In this perspective, what happens 'for real' during a sex phone call is what customer and operator define and negotiate as real within their conversation, at least until something catches their attention that breaks their inter-subjective agreement.

In the case of phone sex services, however, we have a commercial interaction in which customer and operator occupy different positions. The customer needs to believe the situation is real enough to pay for it, whereas the operator/worker needs to support this belief in order to make the most commission she can from each conversation. We could say that operators have the task of maintaining the client's perception of reality in the situation they have created, by preventing another reality – e.g., the one where their bodies are situated – from crashing into the space of their conversation, diverting attention and making this temporary version of the world disappear (Goodman, 1988). In any digital context, participants share a common time, but not a common space, because the space made available by technological infrastructures gathers their 'now' but not their 'here' (Backhaus, 1997). Using again Schutz's terminology, we could say that this is a world of associates – contemporaries with whom it is possible to experience a form of tele-copresence (Zhao, 2004). This is a form of electronic proximity produced by simultaneous interactions in digital spaces whereby individuals are able to operate, and, in the end, make real the situation they share, albeit contemporary to and qualitatively different from the one they are materially situated in.

If it is true that social interaction is not only a communicative interaction, in phone-mediated interactions, characterized by the absence of non-verbal elements and intentionality, interlocutors only interact through language. By talking and interpreting correctly the sense of their utterances, operator and client cooperate in the construction of the meaning of their interaction and, consequently, its success or failure. Such negotiations, as well as the very production of meaning, however, should not be interpreted in terms of 'formal correctness' of the sentences. In talking, social actors refer to and show various forms of cultural knowledge (Van Dijk, 1997) that lay the basis for a successful interaction in which the interpretation of the utterances takes into consideration the subjects' cultural positioning, and rests on a mutual cultural understanding of what is being named and how, including all its embodied feature, like the tone and inflexion of the voice. Let us think for example about the different meanings the phrase 'take your clothes off' can take on within a phone sex call and a gynaecological exam, or 'I am going to spank you' between father and child or between two people engaged in a BDSM[1] session. The meaning of these sentences emerges from the actors' shared pre-understanding of the situation and the extra-linguistic universes the single utterances refer to. In the case of phone sex calls, we have culturally and socially situated conversational interactions, the outcome of which depends on the ability of operators and clients to understand the meaning of their utterances on the basis of a shared cultural repertoire.

Within phone sex services, however, we need to add a further extra-linguistic element: money. The preservation of the reality agreement needs to comply with specific time constraints in order to be effective in work terms. Phone sex is not only a form of *cyber-sex*, but of *cyber-sex work* – if customers are looking for a satisfactory sexual or emotional experience, operators work for a financial reward. On the one hand, their earning depends on the number of minutes of conversation accumulated over a month – the more and the longer conversations they have, the more they earn. On the other hand, for legal reasons, the conversation automatically interrupts after a set number of minutes (which varies depending on the provider and technology used), and the customer needs to call back in order to continue the conversation. In a sense, therefore, if the reality agreement framing the conversations is a condition of success that is shared by non-commercial technologically mediated sexual interactions, the time-profit constraint is what qualifies phone sex as a work interaction. In the daily work routine, this means that operators need to be able to lock in their reality agreement with customers to ensure that the conversation lasts as long as possible, namely, long enough for the client to call back when the line breaks up and, ideally, for him to become a regular customer. Starting from this theoretical framework, this chapter explores the discursive micro-practices by which phone sex services operators manage this ecology of elements – the sense of reality, speech, time – in order to successfully interact with customers.

Research setting and methodology

The accounts presented in this chapter originate in fieldwork I carried out between May 2007 and September 2008 in two erotic call centres in Italy: one small and home-based and one medium-sized and office-based. These are referred to respectively as 'Kappa' and 'Lambda'. Three women aged 25 to 45 work in the centre called Kappa, from 8 am to 12 pm with three shifts of five or six hours each; while centre Lambda has 10 employees (8 women and 2 men) aged 20 to 55 working from 8 am to 12 pm on working days and 24 hours a day during the weekend. I used a case study research strategy (Eisenhardt, 1989; Stake, 1994) and qualitative data collection techniques and analysis. Data collection involved participant observation and interviews. Observation took the form of following the workers during their shifts of work, as well as spending time together outside the workplace. I audio-recorded nearly 15 hours of calls between the operators and their customers. For privacy and ethical reasons, I recorded the operators' voices only; I did not want to record clients' voices without their explicit consent and it would have been impossible to gain consent without breaking the 'reality agreement' on which phone sex work is built. Alongside the observation, I conducted repeated interviews in the field (recommended by Spradley, 1979) with all the operators working in both call centres, as well as with the two managers, achieving a total of 34 interviews. These were conducted in order to gain further information on issues that had emerged but remained implicit during the observation.

Characters in search of an author: identities, bodies and stories

The first element I wish to focus on relates to the operators' discursive construction of a corporeal identity. As it is easy to imagine, operators use pseudonyms. This happens in other lines of sex work and is a way to symbolically separate one's private self from work as well as to protect one's privacy and minimize risks (Brewis and Linstead, 2000; Oerton and Phoenix, 2001; O'Neill, 2001). Although the interaction between client and operator is always mediated by the phone, operators still perceive a high-risk level that a fake name helps control. However, my fieldwork highlighted how pseudonyms in phone sex services also serve to identify and support the different gender identities performed during conversations.

On the phone, operators cannot take for granted their self-presentation, but need to construct it discursively in each conversation. In a phone interaction, operators cannot rely on the visual resources that support face-to-face interactions in terms of setting, appearance and manner. On the one hand, the interaction cannot rely on a material setting other than the 'empty' space created by the phone. On the other hand, operators cannot rely on their 'bodily capital' nor on symbolic elements such as clothes. Thus, a pseudonym is not enough to support a role; what is needed is a narrative construction of specific corporeal identities that fit customers' expectations. As highlighted by Lisa when comparing her online role-playing experience and her work as sex phone operator:

You have to tell them who you are, you know, like every conversation starts with hi, what's your name. For example, I role-play online, right?

It's the same thing, you have to create a character in order to play with others, they don't know who you are and if I'm playing Naruto[2] I won't be a hobbit, but a ninja, because that's a ninja game. Here it's the same, this is a sex game and you have to play a real woman, not a hobbit (laughs). (Lisa, Lambda Centre)

Therefore, the first prerequisite for managing the relationship with the customer is to tell him *who you are*, because speech is the only resource available for acting in this context. What is even more important is *to play a real woman*, or to be able to construct, through narrative, a gender identity that fits the customers' expectations. If staying within Lisa's game metaphor, we can say that the 'material' for identity construction in role playing is provided by the shared story of the game, here it can be found in the symbolic universe of femininity. The second element for managing the relationship is to tell him *how you look*, which is the very first question every customer asks at the beginning of the conversation. As it has been noted in studies on online communication (Boler, 2007), the consolidated habit of asking for *asl* – age, sex, location – at the beginning of the conversation suggests that despite the material body being absent, it is still necessary to locate the other person, starting from his/her corporeal characteristics, to be able to interpret the communication and to confirm one's expectations of his/her identity. Although the material body is 'elsewhere', constant reference to it is essential for meaningful communication. The prerequisite of these conversations is that the operator is always providing a detailed description of 'how she looks' (such as the colour of her hair and eyes, how big her breasts or how long her legs) for the interaction to get started; the discursive mobilization of the body in its most material feature, in fact, is the necessary element that allows the following erotic and emotional interactions to be located in the physical place where they *should be* and without which the conversation would not be meaningful.

However, the body operators evoke is not just *a* body, but refers to the mainstream canons of femininity, as Elisa points out when answering my question on how she chooses which body to perform:

C'mon, you too know what they have in mind, right? Don't you watch TV? Take Pamela Anderson's breast, the ass of Angelina Jolie, Arcuri's legs and here is the the body you need. They look for the woman they don't have as girlfriend or wife, and we perform the woman who would like to be. Wouldn't you like to have your ass like Angelina Jolie? (Elisa, Lambda Center)

If in phone sex the material body is absent, what is present is a gendered social body. This is a body operators transform into a readable text through a set of cultural codes that determine its mode of recognition for the customer (Butler, 1993). To construct and read this text the operators not only refer to the body, but re-invoke specific gender stereotypes for the client to be able to actually *see* the interlocutor with whom he expects to talk.

To successfully manage a phone sex conversation, the next step involves the proper narrative. In order to manage the different incoming calls, operators use highly codified and repetitive conversational scripts that draw on traditional gendered symbolic universes. This means that operators need to be able to inscribe their embodied identities within precise cultural scenarios that the clients can immediately recognize. It is the extremely stereotypical nature of this performance that makes the interaction solid and intelligible, because it allows the operator to inscribe the narrative in a socially shared imagination and make the gender performance immediately readable to the client. Butler (1993: 5) argues that what bestows reality status on any gender performance is 'the ability to compel belief by creating a natural effect'. During phone sex this happens through the narrative activation of specific gender stereotypes. For instance, at a request for a young woman, operators often stage a gender performance evoking a sexually inexperienced, passive femininity, which places the client as the one who sets the rules of the game and leads the sexual interaction. The following conversation is a significant example:

> The phone rings, Lara answers by playing the switchboard lady. She puts the client on hold and tells me his name is Marco, he is 50, and is looking for a young woman. She resumes the conversation and introduces herself using a shrill, girlish voice: 'Hi honey I'm Silvia what's your name? // Marco what a nice name, where are you calling from? // Turin? What a nice city I'm from Milan// How do I look like? I'm slim and small, but I have huge tits, I'm a blonde with blue eyes. I'm wearing a little dress that would drive you crazy...and you?// Wow, you are a really handsome man. What do you do, Marco?//Oh you must be an important man then! // What do I do? I go to university sweetie, I study literature // Am I single? Of course I am sweetie, I'm too young to have a boyfriend! // You want to know if I'm naughty, honey? No I'm not, I'm a little girl, I don't know much about this stuff, you're making me blush// So you're a sex god? Oh my, honey// I learn fast though sweetie, tell me what you want me to do // Oh I'm really blushing, I have never done this // I swear honey you are the first // You have to teach me honey, because I really don't know where to start, I really needed to met someone like you to start doing naughty things.'

In this case, Lara performs a young woman who knows nothing about sex and also finds it embarrassing. She uses a shrill, girlish voice that supports her narrative and a self-presentation – beautiful, small, light hair and eyes – that consolidates the client's expectation also in aesthetic terms. In activating this performance, Lara uses the 'cultural' hints provided by the client. Her gender performance activates a repertoire of innocent femininity, ignorant of sexual desire and pleasure, that can nonetheless be led astray by the right Pygmalion. The client is then positioned as the one in charge of the relationship because, thanks to his experience, he can teach the young, naïve woman how to pleasure a man with oral sex. If the operator positions herself as the innocent virgin, the client becomes a skilled 'don Juan', able to seduce and possess her while his counterpart repeatedly confirms his virility. This very uneven symbolic positioning, emphasized by Lara all through the conversation, bestows further meaning to the sexual interaction and makes it believable to the client.

In other words, the interaction is not only supported by the description of a sexual act (in this case, oral sex), but by its being inscribed in a competent gendered narrative that allows the client to collocate the operator and himself in specific models of gender presentation and erotic desire. Lara creates a work performance that mobilizes dominant gendered symbolic universes of what belongs with masculinity and femininity (Gherardi, 1995). We could say that operators draw on what Martin (2003) defined as 'gender practices', that is, the cultural, social, discursive and bodily repertoire available to individuals for doing gender: a *set* of potential actions that individuals know are available for being acted, asserted, performed and mobilized to manage interactions. In phone sex calls, this mobilisation is exclusively discursive and can (needs to) attach itself to dominant narratives in order to ensure the cultural intelligibility of the interaction and the successful outcome of the conversation. In other terms, these (discursive) gender practices are what bring into existence, within the space of the phone call, the different women named by operators and allow clients to identify them and perceive them as 'real women'. It is by constantly citing the gender norm (Butler, 1990) that operators manage to 'play a real woman' and guarantee the performance's authenticity and cultural intelligibility.

Gender tactics, reflexivity and resistance

I have so far illustrated how in order to successfully manage interactions with the client operators need to mobilize dominant gender repertoires that fit the client's cultural expectations, and how mobilising this gender vocabulary secures the intelligibility of the conversation. Using Connell's (1987) definition, we can say operators use forms of 'emphasized femininity'. That is they use gender performances conforming to female subordination and oriented to complying with male desires. In a certain perspective, such symbolic and discursive resources used by operators can be identified as 'powerless' discourses (Lakoff, 1975), that is, narratives that position (and reproduce) female subordination to male speech and desire. However, during my fieldwork I realized how operators are able to appropriate and reflexively negotiate such repertoires to make them 'powerful' discourses (Hall, 1995) and to use them to manage conversations to their own advantage, in terms of both profit and quality of work. Echoing De Certeau's (1980) well-known distinction, we could define this process as a 'gender tactic' that opens windows for redefining meaning to the advantage of individual workers within the wider and more consolidated 'gender strategies' culturally and socially configuring the context in which operators (but not only) live and work. After the first few days of fieldwork, I pointed out to operators that the women they staged for clients were very traditional, essentially passive, and with bodies virtually non-existent in 'real' life. Sara's emblematic answer was:

> And what should I tell them, that I have hairy legs, small breasts, and want to be an astronaut? Look, it doesn't work this way, they'll hang up on you. The tits, the nurse, and the desperate housewife work, the little girl too, but that's about it. (Sara, Kappa Centre)

I felt stupid and, thinking back, I realized I had mistakenly conflated the narratives activated by operators and their personal gender positioning. In addition, I had momentarily lost sight of these conversations' professional nature – in other terms, their need to be profitable. As Sara highlights, there are performances that work and others that don't: that is, narratives that allow for a successful interaction with the customer and others that can make him hang up. Operators need to be aware of this in order to drive the conversation to their own advantage. Models of femininity that do not fit 'the norm', such as women with hairy legs, small breasts or high levels of investment in their work and career, are not attractive, and, there-fore, not functional to the operators' goals – to keep the client on the line and earn as much as possible. On the one hand, this speaks of the opera-tors' reflexive positioning and their awareness of the limits of the sym-bolic gender imaginary they can draw on for creating their narratives. On the other hand, it suggests such reflexivity is necessary in order to manage interactions with clients, because it guides the different processes on which the creation of work identities and narratives is based. Indeed, the ability to strategically use these stereotypes emerges with the very creation of the characters:

> Anyway, the best liked are Anna and Alba. Everybody wants them, can you believe? Alba is powerful, she is a dominatrix, while Anna is the

sweet one, sort of dumb too...they keep calling back, again and again, until it happens [orgasm]. Do you think anyone would call for me? I don't think so. (Lara, Kappa Centre)

Like Lara, all operators spot their best identities, that is those who best intercept the clients' expectations, thus making them call back and increase operators' earnings. By highlighting that the client would not call *for her*, Lara exposes the 'inauthenticity' of the performances mobilized for clients and, at the same time, the awareness that in this very fake authenticity of stereotypical feminine traits lies the effectiveness and functionality of the characters. If, then, technological mediation requires the discursive creation of complex work identities, because speech is the only resource available, for these words to 'sell' operators need to create 'good identities' that – like Anna and Alba – can engage clients and keep them coming back. Although they use dominant, traditional gender repertoires and place themselves in a position of subordination to male desire, operators are aware that such positioning is part of 'the rules of the game' and that by exploiting those rules they can turn the conversation to their advantage. The space of the phone call has its rules and being aware of the gender rules governing the interaction allows the operator to convince the client to call (back) and, therefore, her to earn. The mobilisation of dominant gender repertoires is thus a reflexive competence used by operators to manage and manipulate male sexuality and desire by tactically using the very gender norms that would want them subordinate.

However, if, in most cases, operators aim at keeping the client engaged as long as possible, sometimes they do receive calls they wish to interrupt. In this case, motives are not of economic character, but related to the quality of work, and the need to manage situations perceived as unpleasant. For instance, some customers are verbally aggressive or disturbing (by insulting or belittling) or, especially on weekend nights, in altered states of mind because of alcohol or drugs. Interrupting the call may seem simple at first; it would be enough to hang up as is usually done in ordinary phone interactions. However, the fieldwork revealed that this is a more complex matter in phone sex; if faced with unpleasant situations, operators try to ensure that the client is the one to hang up. This is because of an *unwritten* rule of the trade caused by pressure of the management, who do not want the operators to ever hang up the phone on a customer, even in those cases when the details makes their work difficult or unpleasant. Therefore, in order to interrupt the conversation without having problems with the management, operators need to act tactically within the reality agreement itself. If mobilising a successful narrative in terms of gender and sexual repertoire guarantees the conversation's solidity and duration, 'incorrectly' using such repertoires allows to break it without violating the reality agreement rules, as in this conversation excerpt:

> It's late at night, in the main room there are Elisa, Susanna, Silvia, and me – so far, phone have been ringing a lot. Elisa's phone rings, she goes through the switchboard routine, puts the client on hold for a few seconds, and tells me his name is Marco, he is calling from Genoa, and she thinks he is a bit out of it. Then she resumes the conversation: *'Hi honey I'm Jessica what's your name? // Marco, what a nice name! Where are you calling from sweetie?// you want to know if I'm a whore? // If I'm a whore like all the women? What did women do to you, sweetie? //* She puts him on mute and tells me and her colleagues: he says he doesn't have issues with women (laughs) sure! // *So, sweetie, what do you tell me this late at night // No, dear, a whore?* (while saying this again she gives us an annoyed look) *Who is going to pay for me anyway, honey? I'm pretty plump you know, my figure is not what it used to be // Oh no, dear, no diets, I don't think about diets, in fact I enjoy eating very much, and cooking too. I don't have much time though, what with work and the kids . . .* at this point the client hangs up and Elisa comments *here we go again, you mention kids and they beat it* raising general hilarity.

The conversation starts as usual: the operator introduces herself and asks the client for the routine information. Before it develops along the conventional lines (e.g., physical description or presentation of the character performed by Elisa), though, the customer insistently addresses the operator as 'whore'. Elisa's first reaction is to interpret such bitterness towards herself and women in general as a client's 'problem' and her first tactic is to adopt a listening attitude. Marco, however, insists on being offensive, Elisa shows discomfort, and the conversation shifts onto a different level. In order to manage the conversation and stop the client's offensive behaviour, Elisa stages a gender performance that does not fit his expectations. If, presumably, the customer called expecting to find a young, beautiful, sexually uninhibited woman completely available to his desires (and insults), the interlocutor he finds is a mature, plump woman (so much that nobody would pay for her), who appreciates food (which consolidates the description of her no longer slim body), and has a job and kids that take away time from the things she likes (which contributes to undermining the stereotypical image he had in mind). This is basically a performance that violates the cultural intelligibility of the enacting of gender, aesthetic and sexual stereotypes shaping phone sex interactions. This inadequate performance is what challenges the fragility of the interaction and breaks it 'from within', leading the client to end the conversation himself.

Therefore, operators' reflexive ability in managing interactions with clients emerges not only in the use of traditional gender repertoires, but also in their subversion – if the conversation 'works' when built on traditional gender plot, it 'fails' when this is subverted. If the operators are indeed able to do gender for clients in order to meet their expectations, they are also able to undo gender (Butler, 2004). Clearly, Elisa's gender performance is not subversive in itself; in fact, it mobilizes an extremely stereotypical gender repertoire, although different from the ones usually mobilized in phone sex. Her performance is, however, contextually subversive and it allows her to strategically resist workplace rules.

Conclusion

Using Licoppe's (2006) terminology, we can define phone sex as a conversational achievement (*accomplissement conversationnel*) enacted through technological mediation: the verbal exchange between client and operator is what creates and consolidates the work activity. Drawing on Austin (1962), we could call it a *performing narrative* that needs, on the one hand, to be bestowed illocutionary force. That is, the operator must have the ability to materialize the gender, sexual and bodily dimensions necessary for the interaction within the conversational space created by the phone. On the other hand, it needs to be bestowed perlocutionary force – to be able to produce real arousal or emotional involvement in clients.

This performing narrative draws from an ecology of knowledge that I suggest we call *erotic knowledge*. It is by competently mobilising this form of knowledge that operators are able to align sexuality, gender, corporeal features and pattern of desire in order to both provide the client with the 'fake authenticity' necessary to support the conversation and to use the time constraint to their own advantage, thus securing their gain. It is not just 'erotic capital' as defined by Hakim (2010), but expert knowledge that is developed in the specific context of interaction where it needs to be mobilized. If, on the one hand, it finds its roots in socially shared imaginaries of sexuality, gender, and the body, on the other hand it is created and consolidated on the job. It is in the daily interaction with clients and colleagues that operators learn to translate these elements into competent narratives, and to manipulate theirs and customers' emotions and sexuality. Furthermore, it is a form of reflexive knowledge that is competently activated by operators on the job, but deactivated in the private space, thus maintaining the experiential distinction between the 'strategic' performance of self aimed at preserving the reality agreement and one's positioning outside the space of the phone call.

In this sense, although narratives mobilized during the phone call position operators as sex objects to the client's desire, in order for the interaction to be perceived as authentic and last, their very ability to mobilize these specific narratives make them *sex experts,* custodians of a capital of erotic knowledge by which they can manage their work and make profit. If sex workers, then, are often regarded as subaltern or deviant subjects because of the sexual and emotional content of the work, the analysis presented in this chapter suggests that operators are able to reflexively use erotic knowledge in order to 'make profit (*capitalizing*) from sexuality'. In this sense, as suggested by Sanders (2005), sex work becomes a space where it is possible to explore the ways different, new erotic and sexual meanings are activated and performed – and can be regarded as forms of knowledge available for mobilisation in the work context. In this perspective, erotic knowledge is expert knowledge that allows operators to inscribe the complex geometries of sexuality into technology (Plummer, 2002), thus managing the clients' erotic and emotional desire to their own advantage and gain.

Notes

1 Acronym for Bondage Domination Sadism Masochism.
2 Naruto Generation is a game set in Japan in which players interpret a war between different ninja armies. For more information, see http://www.narutogeneration.altervista.org.

REFERENCES

Austin, J. (1962). *How to Do Things with Words.* Oxford: Oxford University Press.

Backhaus, G. (1997). The Phenomenology of Telephone Space. *Human Studies* 20: 203–20.

Bell, S. (1994). *Reading, Writing and Rewriting the Prostitute Body.* Bloomington: Indiana University Press.

Brewis, J. and Linstaed, S. (2000). 'The Worst Thing Is Screwing' (1): Consumption and the Management of Identity in Sex Work. *Gender, Work & Organization* 7(2): 84–97.

Butler, J. (1990). *Gender Trouble: Feminism and the Subversion of Identity.* London: Routledge.

——— (1993). *Bodies That Matter: On the Discoursive Limits of 'Sex'.* New York: Routledge.

——— (2004). *Undoing Gender.* New York: Routledge.

Cavarero A. (1995). *In Spite of Plato: A Feminist Rewriting of Ancient Philosophy.* New York: Routledge.

▶

Connell, R.W. (1987). *Gender and Power: Society: The Person and Sexual Politics.* Stanford: Stanford University Press.

Damari, C. (2008). *La percezione della realtà in Alfred Schutz ed Erving Goffman. Un problema di frames.* Pisa: Pisa University Press.

De Certeau, M. (1980). *L'invention du quotidian.* Paris: Gallimard.

Duranti, A. and Goodwin, C. (Eds) (1992). *Rethinking Context: Language as an Interactive Phenomenon.* Cambridge: Cambridge University Press.

Eisenhardt, K.M. (1989). Building Theories from Case Study Research. *Academy of Management Review* (14)4: 532–50.

Goodman, N. (1978). *Ways of World Making.* Indianapolis: Hackett.

Hakim, C. (2010). Erotic Capital. *European Sociological Review* 26(5): 499–518.

Hall, K. (1995). Lip Service on the Fantasy Line. *In* K.E. Hall and M. Bucholtz (Eds) *Gender Articulated: Language and the Socially Constructed Self.* London: Routledge. Pp. 183–216

James, W. (1901). *The Principles of Psychology.* London: Macmillian and Co.

Lakoff, R. (1975). *Language and Women's Place.* New York: Harper & Row.

Licoppe, C. (2006). La construction conversationelle de l'activité commerciale. Rebondir au telephone pour placer des services. *Reseaux* 135–36: 125–59.

Martin, P.Y. (2003). 'Said & Done' vs. 'Saying & Doing': Gendered Practices/ Practicing Gender at Work. *Gender & Society* 17: 342–66.

Oerton, S. and Phoenix, J. (2001). Sex/Bodywork: Discourses and Practices. *Sexualities* 4(4): 387–412.

O'Neill, M. (2001). *Prostitution and Feminism.* London: Polity.

Plummer, K. (2002). La sociologia della sessualità e il ritorno del corpo. *Rassegna Italiana di Sociologia* 43(3): 487–501.

Sanders, T. (2005). 'It's Just Acting': Sex Workers' Strategies for Capitalizing on Sexuality. *Gender, Work & Organization* 12(4): 319–42.

Schutz, A. (1955). Don Quijote y El Problema de la Realidad. *Anuario de Filosofia,* vol. 1.

——— (1962). *Collected Papers,* vol. 1. The Hague: Martinus Nijhoff.

Spradley, J.P. (1979). *The Ethnographic Interview.* Orlando: Harcourt Brace Jonanovich College Publishers.

Stake, R.E. (1994). Case Studies. *In* N.K. Denzin and Y.S. Lincoln (Eds) *Handbook of Qualitative Research.* London: Sage.

Velena, H. (2003). La prostituzione virtuale. In AA.VV. *Porneia. Voci e sguardi sulla prostituzione.* Padova: Il Poligrafo.

Zhao, S. (2004). Consociated Contemporaries as an Emergent Realm of the Lifeworld: Extending Schutz's Phenomenological Analysis to Cyberspace. *Human Studies* 27: 91–105.

'What Does a Manicure Have to Do With Sex?': Racialized Sexualization of Body Labour in Routine Beauty Services

10

Miliann Kang

After Minhee Cho[1] immigrated to New York City from Seoul in 2003, she immediately sought work at a nail salon. She explained, 'My hairdresser told me that I should work in a nail salon because it was a very popular and easy job for Korean women...easier than a grocery store or laundry. But my husband argued with me, saying people would think I was a low woman, even like a prostitute. I couldn't believe it and argued back, "What does a manicure have to do with sex?"' Minhee, who goes by the name Minnie at the salon, ignored her husband's protests and found a job as a nail technician. She is now a skilled manicurist and has accommodated to performing all aspects of this work, from its physical to its emotional demands: 'It's not a problem for me to have physical contact. I don't feel closer to the customer, because the customer is paying me money for a service. It's just my job – I don't put my emotions into it. I think that customers do feel closer when we give them really good and exceptional service.'

Minhee insists that a manicure has nothing to do with sex and that any positive feelings that arise in the exchange derive from exceptional service rather than sexual desire or objectification. For her, the dynamics of physical contact do not foster a sense of either emotional closeness or sexual intimacy, as she views this contact simply as a necessary part of the service that she is paid to perform. However, whereas most manicurists and customers interviewed for this study expressed similar sentiments, their constructions of the meaning of nail salon work contrast with those of certain customers, policy makers and popular representations that insist on sexualizing the manicure and the body contact that occurs in this exchange.

The impetus for this article came from a puzzling public reaction to my book, *The Managed Hand: Race, Gender and the Body in Beauty Service Work* (Kang, 2010). An ethnography of service relations in Asian-owned nail salons in New York City, the book examined these sites to explore the dynamics of what I refer to as 'body labour', the paid exchange of physically and emotionally intimate services and the increasing commercialization of body-related services. Although the book focuses on mundane beauty services, I was surprised that the first several media inquiries that I received all focused on the sexualization of this work. Although I intentionally downplayed these themes and emphasized labour rights and occupational safety and health issues such as toxic chemical exposures, low wages, lack of breaks, and the emotional and embodied challenges of performing this work, pundits seemed intent on sensationalizing issues such as whether nail salons sometimes serve as a front for sex work and trafficking.

A possible connection between 'trafficking', especially 'sex trafficking', and nail salons has been identified by several sources. The US State Department's 2010 Trafficking in Persons Report lists nail salons as one of the most high-risk sites for trafficking, asserting, 'Trafficking occurs primarily for labor and most commonly in domestic servitude, agriculture, manufacturing, janitorial services, hotel services, construction, health and elder care, hair and nail salons, and strip club dancing' (US State Department, 2010). Criminal justice authorities in various locales have determined enough cause for suspicion of trafficking in nail salons to warrant investigation (Martin, 2010). While acknowledging these concerns, I am wary of the blanket categorization and criminalization of various forms of work that span a broad spectrum of sexual commerce, illegality and exploitation. In any case, this article is not about 'trafficking', however it might be defined, and does not track or assess its actual incidence in nail salons. I have not investigated this question myself and it is very difficult to collect empirical data or to evaluate claims that nail salons are involved. My reason for mentioning it is rather to indicate the existence of an elision between nail salon workers and sex work that is emerging in the US, and which forms part of the wider context for examining the concerns raised by nail salon workers and managers.

How is it that certain types of body labour performed by certain groups of people become sexualized, whereas others do not? What are the specific characteristics of body labour, the contexts in which it is performed, the workers who perform it and the discourses of race, gender and sexuality surrounding it that lead some forms of body labour to be sexualized, and not others? How do workers, owners and customers fuel, deflect, deny and complicate the sexualization of this work? In particular, why do nail salons, which overwhelmingly perform mundane beauty services, so easily become conflated with sex work? This conflation relies upon and reproduces what I refer to as the 'racialized sexualization' of Asian women in the body service sector, and of immigrant women workers more broadly in various forms of service work. The concept of racialized sexualization delineates processes in which specific historical and situational racial constructions imbue certain kinds of services and service providers, especially those engaged in contact between bodies, with sexual meanings, whether or not the work entails commercialized sexual exchanges.

The editors' invitation to contribute to this volume serves as an opportunity for me to address this persistent sexualization of nail salon work, its context and consequences. Body labour encompasses a wide range of services, from massages, to haircuts, to cosmetic surgery to sex work. Some forms of body labour clearly involve sexual commerce, but others just as clearly do not, yet still become laden with sexual meanings. In this chapter, I discuss manicurists' attempts to de-sexualize and de-stigmatize their work by emphasizing their technical skills and emotional management of customer relations. In contrast, I discuss how a small but significant minority of both men and women customers sexualize this exchange, and how the dynamics of body labour make workers vulnerable to racialized sexualization. Finally, I discuss the significance of these findings for theoretical linkages between body studies and intersectional frameworks for studying race, gender, immigration and labour, specifically for those examining the conflation of racialized bodies with sex work, disease and other forms of social pollution.

Sexualization of body labour

What is body labour, how is it performed in specific sites, such as Asian-owned nail salons, and what dynamics shape the sexualization of this work? Elsewhere, I have developed the term 'body labour' to refer to paid work which involves direct contact with the body and attention to the physical and emotional comfort, pleasure, health and/or appearance of customers who purchase these services (Kang, 2003, 2010). Body labour entails work in which bodies are simultaneously the instruments, the sites, and the objects upon which embodied services are performed for a wage. In contrast, I use 'body work' as a generic term encompassing both paid and unpaid work *on* the body. This work focuses on maintaining, improving or enhancing the health, comfort, pleasure or appearance of the body, one's own or another's. 'Physical labour' refers to work *by* the body as the tool or vehicle of labour, whether or not it involves actual contact between bodies. Thus, the term 'body labour' focuses specifically on the exchange value of services performed both *on* the body and *by* the body for a wage or other form of compensation.

While drawing distinctions among body work, physical labour and body labour, I recognize significant overlap in these concepts. Furthermore, I acknowledge the lively debate among body scholars with regard to defining the boundaries and performance of body work, in particular, whether such work must involve actual servicing of others' bodies or whether attention to one's own body (its appearance, comportment or constitution) also qualifies as body work (McDowell, 2009; Wolkowitz, 2006). Finally, I build upon Hochschild's (1983) concept of emotional labour. The extensive management of feelings also comprises a significant dimension of body labour, as workers must negotiate their own feelings regarding the corporeality of their work while also attending to the feelings of their customers in embodied service exchanges.

This article also engages with the scholarship on sex work, which has challenged the pervasive lumping together of a range of labour practices within a single, catch-all category, arguing instead for greater precision in differentiating and documenting a continuum of sexual services whose performance and categorization is shaped by the global politics and economics of migration and security (Aradau, 2008; Bernstein, 2007; Kempadoo, 2004; Parreñas, 2011; Shah, 2011). In this chapter, I build on this discussion by developing the concept of 'racialized sexualization' to refer to work that is given racial and sexual meanings by customers, workers or public discourse, whether or not it involves direct sexual contact, stimulation or innuendo. I discuss how even routine, non-sexual body labour such as manicuring has the potential to be given sexual meanings due to its association with bodies, intimacy and pleasure, even if its actual practices do not involve direct sexual provisions. Thus, while it is not sex work, manicuring work can become sexualized in certain customer interactions and service contexts, and this process is heightened when it involves the labour of racialized migrant women. Thus, nail salon work carries the stigma of sexualized work as a result of the gendered and racialized dynamics of physical contact, emotional intimacy and sensual gratification in services performed by Asian immigrant women.

Research methods

Data collection for the study on which this chapter draws spanned over a decade, with several distinct periods of intensive fieldwork and over one hundred semi-structured interviews. The most extensive research was conducted over fourteen months from 1997 to 1998 in New York City and focused on Asian (mostly Korean) nail salon workers and owners, black and white customers and community leaders, and industry representatives and workers of other ethnicities (Vietnamese, Latina and Eastern European). With the help of research assistants, I then conducted both new and follow-up interviews and participant observation intermittently from 2003 to 2010, concentrating in these later interviews on talking with members of labour rights, public health and community organizations regarding organizing and regulatory efforts to upgrade work in the nail industry. In addition, I conducted dozens of informal interviews with owners, workers, and customers in various public settings, including organizational meetings, restaurants and public transit. The most recent research also included Vietnamese workers and owners in Massachusetts and the San Francisco Bay Area.

The research design included ethnography at three kinds of salons (six sites) in New York City: (1) *nail spas* (Uptown Nails and Exclusive Nails) providing *pampering body labour,* upscale services, including massages, for predominantly white, middle- and upper-class customers; (2) *nail art salons* (Downtown Nails and Artistic Nails) providing *expressive body labour,* acrylic extensions and elaborate designs, for mostly black (African American and Caribbean) working- and lower-middle class customers; and (3) *discount nail salons* (Crosstown Nails and Convenient Nails) providing *routinized body labour,* quick, cheap and rudimentary manicuring services, for racially and socioeconomically mixed customers. This research design allowed for comparisons across different kinds of nail salons while also exploring variation within each category.

Racialized sexualization of nail salon work

Asian manicurists and the body labour they perform are easy targets for racialized sexualization because of the embodied intimacy of the work combined with projections of racialized sexual desire and antipathies onto Asian women by both men and women customers. As more and more men patronize nail salons, the potential for sexualized encounters based on heterosexual norms increases. At the same time, women customers can also imbue these interactions with homoerotic undertones.

Asian women, especially those raised with more traditional gender socialization, often experience discomfort and stress in their embodied service interactions with men and attempt to downplay or ignore any sexual meanings. Jinny, the manager at a nail art salon, when asked what she regards as the most difficult thing about her work, answered, 'I don't like to [serve men]. Sometime when I finish the manicure, I have to massage their hands and I don't like that. I don't like that feeling. I hate it... [Some men come here] just because they want to hold a woman's hand. Yeah, sometimes I feel that's what they like to do... I don't say anything, I just ignore it.' Jinny told me about one particularly challenging instance in which a man suggestively rubbed her hand and asked her to go home with him. 'I just told him he can go right away, because in front of my store, there always is a police car.' Her reference to the police car revealed her assessment of this customer's overtures as both uncomfortable and threatening. Although she had no problem speaking up to customers in other situations such as negotiations over fees, queues or quality of services, Jinny, consistent with the behaviour of other manicurists, refrained from confronting customers who engaged in sexual behaviour and instead simply tried to quell or overlook it.

Although Jinny does not explicitly attribute this kind of forward behaviour by men to the fact that she is an Asian woman, other respondents regarded such encounters as stemming from widespread stereotyping of Asian women as highly sexual and sexually available. One manicurist connected these perceptions to the US military presence in South Korea, starting with the Korean War in 1950 to 1953 and extending to the present ongoing tensions with North Korea. Military camptowns around the US bases have spawned an expansive growth in commercialized sexual services. She explained, 'Some think that we're easy, like bar girls. They've seen movies, or some may have been GIs in Korea and visited the camptowns.' Thus, the sexualization of Asian women in service interactions has deep historical roots in US-South Korean relations and complex military and business ties (Moon, 1997; Sturdevant and Stoltzfus, 1993; Yu, 2002). This larger context fosters racial and sexual associations in which certain customers come to sexualize manicurists and bring expectations of sexual services into the manicuring exchange.

In order to avoid such sexualized encounters, some salons limit services in attempts to discourage such expectations. An owner of a discount salon that opened in the mid-1980s explains:

We don't have many problems now, but in the beginning when people were not so familiar with nail salons, sometimes we got men who came in and looked around. They acted like something else was going on here besides manicures! That's why we decided not to do hair waxing here, because you had to go alone with the customer to a back room and that gave some men the wrong idea.

Although many other salons profitably offer waxing services, this owner instead curtailed her business opportunities in order to avoid potentially sexualized encounters, particularly with male customers.

Yet even when manicurists avoid secluded, one-on-one interactions with customers, they are still subjected to encounters in which the customer sexualizes the service, the service provider, or both. One salon owner, Cara Park, said that there is a higher turnover of manicurists when there are many men customers: 'Even though most men are good customers, if a worker has one bad experience, she feels really bad and doesn't want to come back. Most Korean women never touched another man's hand except their husband's.' I came across two salons in my research that regularly refuse services to men in an attempt to minimize the potential for sexualized interactions driven by racial perceptions of Asian women as easy and willing sexual targets.

Consistent with this owner's description of most men as 'good customers' the bulk of customer interactions with men that I observed were appropriate and respectful. However, the few times that services did take on sexual overtones loomed large for owners and workers and created an atmosphere of suspicion or discomfort when men entered the salons. These encounters played out in both similar and distinct ways with black and white men, revealing ways that race, class and gender simultaneously shape sexualized body labour.

At the upscale Uptown Nails, I observed an older white man in business attire exchange light-hearted yet still provocative banter with one of the manicurists: 'Don't you want to marry me? I bet I'm richer and better looking than your husband.' The manicurist laughed nervously and ignored him and the scene did not escalate. While fairly benign, this interaction nonetheless dramatized the proprietary assumptions of the customer in introducing romantic overtones to the provision of body labour, as well as the vulnerability of the manicurist to being objectified in this manner.

In another instance, I watched as a young black man came into Downtown Nails and insisted on being attended by one particularly attractive young manicurist. The owner responded that the desired manicurist was serving another customer in a lengthy acrylic application and pointed him toward another manicurist – a middle-aged woman. The customer surveyed the proposed manicurist disdainfully and scoffed, 'I can do better at another salon', then left abruptly. His demeanour suggested both his sense of entitlement in judging and refusing a woman who did not meet his standards, not based on her ability to provide a skilful manicure but because of her inability to fulfil his eroticized desire for receiving the attentions of an attractive manicurist.

Contrary to media and popular discourse that characterizes men who get manicures as gay or effeminate, many black men frame their visits to nail salons as increasing their desirability to women. When I asked another black male customer what his male friends or co-workers would think if they saw him getting his nails done, he responded, 'They'd think I was a player.' Far from fearing that he would be mocked or diminished in the eyes of other men, this customer regarded his practice of regular nail care as increasing his sexual reputation as a 'player.' I was not able to ask follow-up questions to discern the precise reasoning behind his comments, but I can infer that it hinged upon both his enhanced physical appearance as a result of the nail services and, perhaps, his involvement in an intimate embodied interaction with an Asian woman in the course of this service exchange.

Such interactions reveal that a small but significant minority of men might frequent nail salons not only for manicuring services but also for gratification of unspoken desires based on perceptions of Asian women as sexually desirable service providers. Legal scholar Sumi K. Cho argues that these presumptions increase the vulnerability of these women to both subtle and overt forms of 'racialized sexual harassment', which she defines as 'the particular set of injuries' that derive from the unique configuration of power relations shaping the position in the workplace of Asian Pacific American women and other women of colour (Cho, 1997: 165). She documents how the converging racial and sexual stereotypes of Asian women as, on the one hand, the passive and submissive model minority and, on the other hand, as exotic and erotic 'Suzie Wongs', combine to fuel harassers' beliefs that these women will be receptive to, or at least not reject, their advances. Furthermore, Cho shows how these converging forces foster an environment in which recourse to take action against these unwanted advances is unavailable or discouraged. None of the women in this study recounted any instances where they directly confronted a customer about offending behaviour, nor did they describe this behaviour as sexual harassment. In addition, while some owners seemed sympathetic to their plight, not a single owner could claim that she intervened in an uncomfortable sexualized exchange, nor did I witness any such efforts. Even usually assertive and vocal workers, like the manager Jinny, who had no problem confronting women customers regularly with regard to problematic demands or demeanor, instead assumed a passive stance towards unwanted advances from men, even as she professed her 'hate' for such sexualized interactions.

While Cho focuses on injuries based on racialized sexual harassment, the concept of racialized sexualization developed in this article more broadly addresses instances where sexual and racial meanings infuse interactions even if overt sexual victimization does not occur. This sexualized discourse further complicates the body labour that Asian manicurists already must negotiate in tending to the needs of the various customers they serve, and plays itself out in particular ways, both in actual interactions with women customers and in representations of the service relationship.

'Me love you long time': Sexualized representations of Asian women

In a blog posting entitled 'Asian Nail Salon Rudeness', the author, Jaime, who described herself as a stay-at-home mom living in 'Redneckville, United States', complained about an incident in which the owner of an Asian-owned nail salon treated her suspiciously when she wanted to buy some nail polish. Jaime not only attributed this 'rudeness' to the owner's Asian identity, but she also confessed her desire to retort with a sexualized racial slur. Jaime mocks the way that the receptionist told her the price of the nail polish ('8 dolla') and says she had to 'refrain from asking, "Me love you long time?" and instead reach into my pocket book and pull out the money and hand it to her. Even then she stands staring at me.... This isn't the first time this has happened. I don't know what it is about asian [sic] nail salons.' After several readers criticized her comments, the author responded: 'The "Me Love you Long Time" thing was thought in my mind, as a JOKE [emphasis in original].... In the end, this is my avenue to blog and to be honest, I don't think I've been hateful or rude in any of my reflections in regards to any race or nationality. Being ill treated as a consumer, irregardless [sic] of a person race or creed is just plain wrong in my opinion' (http://momaroundtheclock.blog-spot.com/2007/11/nail-salon-rudeness.html, November 21, 2007).

Jaime's comments on receiving service that she deemed rude reveal several rhetorical processes that situate nail salon interactions within a racialized sexual discourse, although she denies doing so. Indeed, Jaime may not know that the line 'me love you long time' references a well-known example of objectionable sexualized portrayals of Asian women in film, in this case, the words spoken by a Vietnamese prostitute in Stanley Kubrick's *Full Metal Jacket*. As performance artist Allison Roh Park comments in an interview with MTV, the 'me love you long time' phrase has permeated popular culture in ways that backlash against Asian women. 'That phrase is so loaded. People don't understand the history behind that... Asian women get exotified and hyper-sexualized to the point where it really affects our day-to-day life' (Vineyard and Kim, 2008). However, instead of acknowledging that she has used such a triggering phrase, intentionally or not, Jaime appeals to her position as an 'ill-treated' consumer to justify her reaction. By invoking the service ideology of 'the customer is always right' to sanction racist sexual remarks, Jaime demonstrates the almost unconscious ways that sexualized representations of Asian women are projected onto actual service interactions in the body labour sector. Even when the service interactions themselves are not sexualized, the fact that they occur in a site where body labour is performed by Asian women allows for easy slippage into prevailing racially sexualized frames.

These kinds of racialized sexual comments on the web unfortunately were expressed not only by random customers but also by purportedly more informed commentators. Surfing the internet for nail-related articles, I stumbled upon the following piece, and was immediately disturbed by its jarring depiction of Asian manicurists as simultaneously exoticized sexual objects and maternal caregivers. One moment, the author described being sexually aroused by her manicurist, the next she regressed into an infantilized state of passivity. Even more astounding is her insistence that this exchange somehow qualifies as a feminist exchange simply because it occurs between women. I was ready to dismiss this piece as the unfortunate ranting of some adolescent blogger, when I noticed the name of the author. Jennifer Baumgardner, who penned this reflection on her nail salon experiences, is widely recognized as a feminist author and leader in the Third Wave feminist movement. Baumgardner wrote:

> But finances and love aside, long, well-tended nails are sexy. And, the process that gets them that way has a nice sensual intimacy that is rare in a $6 service...The manicurist kneads your palm and slides her fingers up and down on the fleshy nook in between your pointer finger and thumb. As she pulls on your hand and wrist, your fingers splayed open, arm vertical, palm toward her, you rock slightly in your chair from the force of her rubbing...When it's over, if it's cold out, your manicurist has to help you into your coat. Standing in front of you, she zips or buttons you in, and wraps your scarf around your neck like she's your mom and you're suddenly six again...A big reason that the manicure transaction works the way it does – as safe, inexpensive carnality – is because it is a relationship among women...I'd be lying if I didn't note that there is a class and race overtone to the New York manicure experience: the manicurists are small ladies who speak loudly in Korean to one another; the clients are yuppyish, mainly white, and talk too loudly into cell phones to other yuppyish, mainly white people. (http://www.spoonbenders.com/nails. htm. This link is no longer active).

Unfortunately, Baumgardner's stature as a prominent feminist thinker stands in stark contrast to her sexual objectification of the Korean immigrant woman who performs her manicure. While she conceded that the exchange is shaped by race and class inequalities, this concession did not lead her to consider the manicurist's perspective on this exchange and what it means for her. Instead, she commended herself for turning the supposedly un-feminist obsession with her nails into what she sees as an empowering act. Baumgardner further congratulated herself for confronting an Asian male manicurist for groping her and her mother, while confessing, 'I didn't really want him to stop-I just didn't want him to go further.' Rather than owning her sexual objectification of both Asian men and women who serve as manicurists, she positioned herself as the hapless victim. In so doing, she discounted her own participation in this unequal exchange, and her reinscription of stereotypical representations of Asian service providers as exoticized others, even in ostensibly non-sexual services.

These blog comments are much more extreme than those voiced by participants in this study (which most likely was influenced by my Korean ethnicity and the hesitancy of customers to express such views directly to me). Nonetheless, these comments are consistent with processes which were observed at the research sites, such as customers' strong reactions to embodied exchanges, the underlying themes of cultural otherness that shaped performance of body labour and the sexual meanings given to these exchanges.

Discussion

A key link in the racialized sexualization of body labour performed by Asian women is the historical and ongoing construction of Asian women themselves as erotic and taboo objects of desire. The mix of fear and desire which fuelled the discourse of the 'yellow peril' over a century ago now fuels a new, contemporary version. Focusing her attention on Hollywood depictions, film studies scholar Gina Marchetti writes that 'the yellow peril combines racist terror of alien countries, sexual anxieties, and the belief that the West will be overpowered and enveloped by the irresistible, dark, occult forces of the East... [T]his formulation necessarily rests on a fantasy that projects Euroamerican desires and dreads onto the alien other' (Marchetti, 1993: 2). In this fantasy, which is often linked to fears and desires of miscegenation in relationships between Asian women and white men, Asian women are rendered as the spoils of war, trophies that symbolize the triumph of white, civilized men over a heathen, disease-ridden and threatening Asia (Chan, 1991; Lowe, 1996; Peffer, 1999; Yung, 1995).

The gender, racial and sexual subtexts of the yellow peril play themselves out in intimate labour relations even apart from the sexualization imputed to the relations between white men and Asian women. Views of Asian-owned nail salons that reveal the ongoing discourse of the yellow peril in contemporary sites of social interaction are also evident in the relations between women of different racial, class and citizenship status, as previously indicated, and in the wider anxieties connecting Asian-owned nail salons and the spread of disease that may be expressed by women customers. Current discourses targeting the health risks of nail salons easily trigger yellow peril fears of Asians as contaminants. A number of news shows and articles have spotlighted concerns about Asian-owned salons as spreading disease (Ahrens, 2000; Greenhouse, 2007; Rost, 2008). Fuelled by this flurry of negative media attention, the framing of Asian discount nail salons as the new yellow peril thus combines fears of physical contamination, cultural pollution and economic threat. These fears of contamination in these salons tap into deeply rooted historical beliefs that physical contact with Asian women's bodies breeds disease and degradation.

Contemporary debates about Asian discount nail salons reflect new 'yellow peril' stereotypes that are redolent of the virulently anti-Asian sentiments of a century ago, but are rewritten to reflect the contemporary economic, political and social position of Asian Americans. Nayan Shah, in his book *Contagious Divides: Epidemics and Race in San Francisco's Chinatown*, documents historical depictions of Asian bodies as dangerous and impure. He writes, '[T]he journey from menace to model minority followed a deep undercurrent of ideas about citizenship, conduct and health...At the turn of the century, "health" and "cleanliness" were embraced as integral aspects of American identity; and those who were perceived to be "unhealthy," such as Chinese men and women, were considered dangerous and inadmissible to the American nation' (Shah, 2001: 12). While Shah focuses on Chinese immigrants, these representations have repercussions for all Asian Americans. These depictions of Asian-owned nail salons as health threats have deep historical roots in fears of Asian women as sexually immoral disease carriers. From the passage in the late nineteenth century of the first exclusionary immigration laws in the US, single Chinese immigrant women entering as labourers were immediately labelled simultaneously as prostitutes and disease carriers, a conflation between sex work, disease and racial contamination that persists today. As Sucheng Chan demonstrates, prominent court battles in California argued that 'allowing the alleged Chinese prostitutes to enter would be akin to allowing persons with contagious diseases to enter' (Chan, 1991: 101). Similarly, in 1875 the US Congress passed the Page Law, one of the first in a series of Asian exclusion laws that barred not only felons and contract labourers from China and Japan, but also targeted Asian women, who were again assumed to be disease-carrying prostitutes. Lubheid (2002) documents how medical advances of the late nineteenth century which linked hygiene to disease reflected and fuelled racial fears of contamination through commercialized, inter-racial, sexual intercourse. By singling out Chinese women for sexually amoral behaviour (while ignoring the much larger problem of prostitution by white women), these laws laid the groundwork for the persistent perception of Asian women as both sexually and racially suspect bodies.

Conclusion

Exacerbated by a harsh and pervasive anti-immigrant climate, Asian women's performance of body labour easily slips into popular perceptions as sexualized work. Such perceptions then fuel processes in which certain customers expect and create sexualized service interactions predicated on racial discourses, a process which I refer to as racialized sexualization. The imposition of sexual meanings on manicuring provision, or even the potential for such elisions, reflects the conflation of Asian women with sexual commerce through the processes of embodied work, migration and racialized sexual discourses.

How do the actors in these exchanges negotiate the racialized sexualization of body labour? The manager, Jinny, and other women cited share experiences that underscore the ways that racial discourses combine with gendered service provision to make certain women more vulnerable to particular kinds of sexualization. The psychological and physical toll of managing racialized sexualization is wearing. In addition, the dynamics of working in the body labour sector, with its expectation of physical and emotional attentiveness, also increase these women's susceptibility to racialized sexualization. Although the majority of men who patronize nail salons are respectful customers, the few who engage in racialized sexualization, even in the form of 'playful' innuendo, make it necessary for women to keep up their guard. Furthermore, women customers can also sexualize these exchanges through same-sex desire or projections of longing for maternal care. Thus, nail salon employment illuminates an often invisible dimension of body labour – the racialized sexual dynamics that casts a shadow over the already demanding work which manicurists perform.

Taking up the dynamics of racialized sexualization in nail salons suggests that body labour cannot be fully understood without bringing migration and racist constructions into the equation. It is not simply that particular types of worker-customer relations are typical of the labour processes that salon work involves, but that body labour seems to be deeply permeated by racialized and sexualized constructions of the meaning of ministering to the body for pay. In Asian-owned nail salons, the context of longstanding processes of racialized sexualization shapes and permeates the relations between workers and customers. It is ironic that although manicurists seek to distinguish what they do from sex work, we could learn something from the wider scholarship on sex work, along with studies of gender, migration and labour, in seeking to upgrade this work. The lessons include the need to consider the laws, policies and larger social and economic concerns that stigmatize migrant women, including manicurists, sex workers and other body labourers, and make them vulnerable to racialized sexualization, further complicating their efforts to upgrade this work. Thus, workplace issues like wages, working hours and toxic exposures interconnect with the racialized sexualization of body labour to heighten the potential for stress, insecurity and exploitation in these jobs.

Note

1 All names used for individuals and salons are pseudonyms. Sections of this chapter appeared in *The Managed Hand: Race, Gender and the Body in Beauty Service Work* (University of California Press) and are reprinted here with permission.

REFERENCES

Ahrens, T. (2000). Nail Enhancements Increasing, So Are Risks. *(Kankakee, IL) Daily Journal.* Accessed 25 August at http://www.beautytech.com/articles/nailrisks.pdf.

Aradau, C. (2008). *Rethinking Trafficking in Women: Politics Out of Security.* London: Palgrave Macmillan.

Bernstein, E. (2007). *Temporarily Yours: Intimacy, Authenticity, and the Commerce of Sex.* Chicago: University of Chicago Press.

Chan, S. (1991). *Asian Americans: An Interpretive History.* Boston: Twayne.

Cho, S.K. (1997). *Asian Pacific American Women and Racialized Sexual Harassment.* Boston: Beacon.

Greenhouse, S. (2007). At Nail Salons, Beauty Treatments Can Have a Distinctly Unglamourous Side. *New York Times,* 19 August: A22.

Hochschild, A. (1983). *The Managed Heart: The Commercialization of Human Feeling.* Berkeley: University of California Press.

Kang, M. (2003). The Managed Hand: The Commercialization of Bodies and Emotions in Korean Immigrant-Owned Nail Salons. *Gender and Society* 17(6): 820–39.

———(2010). *The Managed Hand: Race, Gender, and the Body in Beauty Service Work.* Berkeley: University of California Press.

Kempadoo, K. (2004). *Sexing the Caribbean: Gender, Race and Sexual Labor.* Boston: Routledge.

Lowe, L. (1996). *Immigrant Acts: On Asian American Cultural Politics.* Durham: Duke University Press.

Luibheid, E. (2002). *Entry Denied: Controlling Sexuality at the Border.* Minneapolis: University of Minnesota Press.

Marchetti, G. (1993). *Romance and the 'Yellow Peril': Race, Sex, and Discursive Strategies in Hollywood Fiction.* Berkeley: University of California Press.

Martin, P. (2010). Nail Salons Veil Human Trafficking in Boston Area. Accessed 8 July at http://wwe.wgbh.org/897/sex_and_labor_trafficking_in_new_england_part_one.cfm.

McDowell, L. (2009). *Working Bodies: Interactive Service Employment and Workplace Identities.* New Jersey: Wiley-Blackwell.

Moon, K. (1997). *Sex among Allies: Military Prostitution and U.S.-Korea Relations.* New York: Columbia University Press.

Parreñas, R. (2011). *Illicit Flirtations: Labor, Migration, and Sex Trafficking in Tokyo.* Stanford: Stanford University Press.

Peffer, G. (1999). *If They Don't Bring Their Women Here: Chinese Female Immigration Before Exclusion.* Champagne-Urbana: University of Illinois Press.

Rost, A. (May 2008). Ripped from the Headlines. Nailpro.

Shah, S. (2011). Producing the Spectacle of Kamathipura: The Politics of Red Light Visibility in Mumbai. *Cultural Dynamics* 18(3): 269–92.

Sturdevant, S.P. and Stoltzfus, B. (1993). *Let the Good Times Roll: Prostitution and the U.S. Military in Asia.* New York: New Press.

▶

US State Department (2010). Press release for 10th Annual Trafficking in Persons Report. Accessed 14 June at http://www.state.gov/j/tip/rls/rm/2010/143107.htm.

Vineyard, J. and Kim, A. (2008). Mariah Carey, Fergie Promise to 'Love You Long Time' – But Is the Promise Empowering or Insensitive? MTV.com. Accessed 26 January 2012 at http://www.mtv.com/news/articles/1591868/20080730/story.jhtml..

Wolkowitz, C. (2006). *Bodies at Work*. London: Sage.

Yu, J.-Y. (2002). *Beyond the Shadow of Camptown: Korean Military Brides in America*. New York: New York University Press.

Yung, J. (1995). *Unbound Feet: A Social History of Chinese Women in San Francisco*. Berkeley and Los Angeles: University of California Press.

Touch in Holistic Massage: Ambiguities and Boundaries

11

Carrie Purcell

Introduction

Holistic Massage sits at the intersection of bodies, touch, sexualities and work. Unique issues accompany Holistic Massage and other practices which involve 'body work', not least because the intimate contact involved in such work may 'violate' everyday touching norms (Twigg et al., 2011; Wolkowitz, 2006). This chapter argues that touch is strongly implicated in the devaluation of such work and in its interpretation as 'sexual'. Powerful cultural narratives conflate massage work with sex and sex work; moreover, the organization of massage and sex work overlap, in that they take place in seclusion and one-on-one (Oerton, 2004; Twigg et al., 2011). Existing research on massage addresses the persistent links with sex work and the discursive tools used by practitioners to distinguish themselves from sex workers (Oerton, 2004; Oerton and Phoenix, 2001). There is also research on massage training (Wainwright, et al., 2010); the limited occupational structures (Marks, 2010); and attempts to codify 'nebulous' practices (Lea, 2009). In this chapter, ambiguities around this work are unpacked and problematic assumptions about the intertwining of touch and sex are addressed in a specific material context. This chapter draws out the central significance of touch to the conceptual slippage between massage and sex work, and argues that Holistic Massage is particularly open to misinterpretation because it employs intuitive, non-systematized touching. Practitioners thus have to construct boundaries on an ongoing basis.

This chapter draws on interviews with ten women who do Holistic Massage in a paid capacity. A deliberately small sample allowed for detailed analysis of the form and content of interviews. The sample includes the majority of practitioners of Holistic Massage in one Scottish city. That the interviewees were all female was not deliberate – two men were contacted but declined to participate – but it does reflect the gendering of the field.

The practitioners were aged from their late twenties to late fifties and had been practising for between six months and 19 years, thus offering a spread in experience. The sample approximates the general picture of health-oriented massage in that all participants had come to Holistic Massage as a career change. This chapter first outlines Holistic Massage as a form of work and unpacks some of the ambiguities around touch and its commodification. It then addresses the feminized character of Holistic Massage work and the significance of space and place in shaping constructions of it. An exploration of the physical and verbal strategies that practitioners use to disambiguate Holistic Massage from sex work concludes this chapter.

Holistic Massage as a profession

The majority of massage practiced in the UK is based on the practice formalized in nineteenth century Sweden by Per Henrik Ling, hence the familiar generic term 'Swedish Massage'. The first professional body for massage in the UK – the Society of Trained Masseuses (STM) – was established in 1894 as a direct result of a growing number of female practitioners, and their desire to differentiate themselves from sex workers (Barclay, 1994). However, the STM moved away from massage towards the systematized and technologized practice of Physiotherapy (having since morphed into the Chartered Society of Physiotherapists). Massage increased in popularity in the latter half of the twentieth century alongside other kinds of complementary and alternative medicines (CAM) stemming from the countercultural movements of the 1960s and 1970s, and a range of health-oriented massage sub-disciplines such as Sports and Aromatherapy Massage began to appear. While it has no fixed starting point, Holistic Massage developed as a response to practices such as Physiotherapy and Sports Massage, which are seen to compartmentalize or disembody people in a similar fashion to mainstream biomedicine. While it employs some of the same techniques for stroking and kneading the body, as well as using 'holds' (still touching with the whole hand), and movements of limbs around joints, Holistic Massage is constructed by practitioners as offering more than a basic Swedish Massage, taking a 'holistic' approach to bodily, mental and emotional/spiritual well-being, rather than concentrating on physical aches and pains alone.

Holistic Massage also rejects a structured routine, focusing instead on touching intuitively and employing 'awareness' and 'presence'. These practitioners also distinguish between health-oriented and beauty-oriented types of massage, distancing themselves from cosmetic and relaxation treatments (such as 'skin firming' and 'moisturizing' massages) offered in high street or hotel spas. To some extent this distinction between Holistic Massage and what I term, for the sake of brevity, 'Beauty Massage' is tangible, with the latter typically involving very gentle, surface-level touching or stroking, and a focus on applying products to the skin; in contrast 'health massage' – including holistic massage – typically also involves a more intensive kneading or manipulation of the muscles and joints. The distinction is also mobilized as a form of boundary work in order to enhance practitioners' status and, given that the boundary with beauty massage is of key significance to practitioners, I employ it here as a foil in sketching what Holistic Massage encompasses.

Generally speaking, Holistic Massage practitioners are usually trained to diploma level, self-employed and most often work in CAM clinics, other health-related venues such as yoga centres, or from home. As with other CAMs, practitioners often come to massage training as a career change and slightly later in life (Sharma, 1992). In the UK, they typically charge between £40 and £70 for a one hour session. Practitioners of beauty massage on the other hand are more often employees of spas, salons or hotels. The fee paid by the client for Beauty Massage may be somewhat higher, at anything from £50 to upwards of £200, but a significantly lower portion of this goes to the practitioner as an hourly wage. The higher cost to the client seems to be justified by the supposedly more luxurious surroundings of the spa or salon, and perhaps also the brand-named products used; the lower financial reward to workers in part reflects also these employees' training, which is less elaborate and costly. While beauty therapists may emphasize the physical and emotional work they do to make clients 'feel better' (Sharma and Black, 2001), Holistic Massage practitioners stress that what *they* do is more involved and challenging than 'mindless' and routinized beauty massage.

Because Holistic Massage is physically labour-intensive and can also be emotionally draining, practitioners typically work part-time. Where a spa worker may see numerous clients back-to-back on a daily basis, Holistic Massage practitioners limit both the number of massages per day (usually to between four and six) and the number of days worked in order to preserve their own physical and emotional well-being. This clearly places significant limitations on their earning capacity, and they may supplement their income by practising other less physically demanding CAM therapies (such as Hopi ear candling or Reiki), teaching massage, or engaging in unrelated employment such as administrative work.

Establishing precise (or even approximate) numbers of massage practitioners in the UK is difficult as there is no UK-wide register and no statutory licencing, meaning the regulation of massage operates on a voluntary basis. Practitioners need only register with professional associations if they want to obtain the public liability insurance required to work in a CAM centre and other spaces in which health-oriented massage is now available, such as the gym, yoga studio or integrated medical centres which (current economic conditions aside) have proliferated in the UK since the 1980s. Such registers do not include the many practitioners working from home or in the homes of clients. As some indication of the Holistic Massage field, its main professional association – the Massage Training Institute – currently has 380 registered members. Little can be known for certain about socio-economic characteristics of this occupational group; however, CAM in general has been found to be both female-dominated as a field of work (Marks, 2010; Sharma, 1992) and as a space of consumption (Sointu, 2011). More recent research in the Canadian context (which is quite similar to the UK in terms of CAM) found that of a sample of over 791 massage practitioners over 90 per cent were women (Porcino et al., 2011).

Holistic Massage training and skills

While standards of training for massage remain uneven, the more recently qualified practitioners interviewed had all trained to diploma level. A Holistic Massage diploma course typically involves 160 hours of training, spread over one weekend every month over nine months to a year, on courses that cost a total of £1300 to £2100. The longer qualified masseurs had less systematic training, but now teach these diplomas. Training for massage involves learning 'bodywork' skills of touching and manipulation, as well as a component of academic learning, primarily about anatomy and physiology. The latter is considered an underlying framework for what practitioners do, but not the substance of it. Although a certain level of competency in anatomy and physiology is a requirement for a diploma, the main focus of training is the development of a keen sense of touch, and on skills in awareness in tailoring their practice to individuals and being 'present'. Touching skills are developed through alternately working on or being worked on by a fellow student; other abilities are developed by incorporating body practices such as Tai Chi or Yoga and aspects of 'talking therapies', such as counselling. All skills are honed over a further 300 hours of self-study, including 40 hours of giving and 10 hours of receiving massage.

Training for massage also involves disciplining the appearance of practitioner bodies and appropriate coverage of the body is emphasized (no low-cut tops or low-slung trousers). Interestingly, however, despite advantages offered to CAM practitioners by the 'white coat effect' (Turner et al., 2007), Holistic Massage practitioners, unlike beauty therapists, do not usually wear a tunic or uniform, with Holistic Massage practitioners usually preferring loose-fitting casual clothes. In part, this stems from a desire for freedom of movement, but it may also be another means of differentiating from beauty massage. Because a uniform acts as an immediately visible 'social marker' of professionalism, 'seriousness' and 'distance from sexualisation' (Oerton, 2004), the choice not to utilize this is interesting, and ultimately means that practitioners are highly dependent on their demeanour to convey professionalism.

The grounding of Holistic Massage competencies in embodied, largely tacit, know-how raises the question of whether they can be considered acquired skills at all, or whether they are better understood as inherent abilities. This tension was typified by one practitioner, who explained the situation:

> I'm not saying I'm *special* with this I'm just saying that I'm *lucky,* cos that's how it is in my body, y'know what's his name,Nadal [Rafael, tennis player] is lucky that he has a tremendous ability to play tennis I am lucky that that's where my, my gift you could call it is [...] it just so happens I've worked in that and developed whatever my special gift is. (Kath)

In her fifties and with 19 years' experience, Kath is ambivalent as to whether the touching she does is an innate 'gift' or an acquired ability. She ultimately framed it as 'something everybody has', perhaps so that Holistic Massage might be viewed as a more serious and less esoteric or mystical practice. When pressed on whether a propensity for this kind of tactual ability is necessary, Kath responded emphatically that she has '*absolutely* no doubt that *every* single person on this planet could learn it'. Overall, her perspective suggests, somewhat dissonantly, that aspects of both gift and skill are at play.

The issue remains, however, that intuitive and attentive touching is not highly socially valued as a work skill. Furthermore, the amount of work which students are expected to do on their own bodies – ranging from maintaining short fingernails and avoiding foods that might cause bad breath, to caring for their own muscle and joints, and adopting practices which help develop intuition and awareness such as meditation or Tai Chi – arguably amounts to acquiring an entirely new embodied way of *being*, rather than simply a job-specific skill set. But this highly attuned way of being and of working suffers from falling into the category of 'women's ways of knowing' and, because these are generally devalued (Belenky et al., 1986), this way of working is not highly valued. It struggles to attain significant economic reward because it so closely parallels a kind of caring which women have in the past done 'for free' in the home (Boris and Parreñas, 2010; Hochschild, 2003). While Holistic Massage work may not be as poorly financially rewarded as some other types of body work (such as care work), neither is it afforded similar status to the practices of mainstream medicine which, broadly speaking, rely on less intuitive, less touch-centred and more codified epistemologies.

Contemporary understandings of touch

Touch may be the most problematic of the human senses for the social sciences to understand. Not only are the meanings attributed to touching historically and culturally specific (Classen, 2005), touch is also physiologically ambiguous, given its close associations with both pleasure and pain (Gilman, 1993). The 'undifferentiated' nature of touch receptors in the human body mean that it is at once powerful in its immediacy (Thayer, 1982) and open to a vast array of interpretations. It may be understood as aggression, an invasion of personal space and bodily security (Finnegan, 2002), or a means to well-being when illness has left the mind and body at odds (Leder and Krucoff, 2008). Touch can be caring and supportive; for example, a 'nurturing' tactile relationship between mother and baby is commonly awarded great significance in a child's development (Barnett, 2005; Montagu, 1971). It can be sexual, and pleasant or unpleasant, as in the caress of a lover or the unwanted touch of an abuser. That touch is perhaps more closely constrained and monitored than many other kinds of human behaviour is due – as well as to fears regarding the potential for physical harm – to its literal and symbolic power to pollute, as social order is maintained through normative behaviour and taboos (Douglas, 1966). The prohibitive 'Don't touch!' command instils a profound sense of taboo in children (Bosanquet, 2006), while the 'untouchable' label has throughout history been applied to those with the socially unacceptable contagion of the time, be it tuberculosis, HIV/AIDS or cancer (Gilman, 1993; Sontag, 1990).

In relation to healthcare, touch tends to be understood dualistically as either 'expressive' or 'instrumental'; 'affective' or 'procedural'; 'active' or 'passive' (Estabrooks and Morse, 1992; Routasalo, 1998). The mainstream medical encounter is characterized either by 'objectifying' touch or by its absence altogether (Leder and Krucoff, 2008). It is arguably 'the threat of the surreptitious slippage from one code to another' – that is, from the professional to the sexual – which leaves medical encounters 'so subject to the anarchy of the double entendre' (Porter, 1993: 196). Healthcare practitioners regularly employ 'desexualization' strategies to 'diffuse the [potentially] sexual meanings of the physical exam' (Atkinson et al., 2010; Giuffre and Williams, 2000: 470). While techniques may differ, Holistic Massage is in this respect no different (although the recognition of 'communicative' aspects of touch marks a significant difference between Holistic Massage and other CAM practices and more mainstream healthcare [Barcan, 2011]). However, while such dualistic categorizations go some way to describing different understandings of touch, clear-cut distinctions between categories are difficult to maintain. The meanings attributed to touch are shaped by context and, to some extent, by the intention of the toucher and the attitude of the 'touchee'. Moreover, one category of touch can beget another. In a practice like Holistic Massage affective touching may also have instrumental effects, becoming a means to an end, the end being an altered physical and emotional state. It is crucial to see touch as a multi-dimensional field, and to consider the ways in which touch and forms of work that incorporate it are shaped by prevailing social norms.

Ambiguities around touch may also reflect the inadequacies of language to articulate touch and embodied experience more broadly (Fortune and Gillespie, 2010; Scheper-Hughes and Lock, 1987). However, it is perhaps not so much a lack of appropriate language, but the assumedly solipsistic character of embodied, sensory experience that creates difficulty in articulating touch. Touch parallels pain, commonly positioned as the least communicable of human experiences; in the way pain relies on imprecise language, it can simultaneously underscore the inadequacy of words and obliterate language altogether (Scarry, 1985). There is a tendency to assume that touch is similarly ineffable, whereas, given that massage practitioners do in fact try to articulate the meaning, significance and experience of the touching that they do, it seems that it is to a great extent an assumption, rather than actual unspeakability, that is at issue in articulating Holistic Massage (Purcell, 2011).

Touch is also highly gendered, with men and women living 'different tactile lives' from early childhood (Synnot, 1993). Broadly speaking, men are aligned with ('rational') mind and thought and women with ('instinctual') body and feeling (Grosz, 1995). The result is that women are constructed as 'naturally' more available to both touch and be touched (Henley, 1973; Jourard, 1966). However, women also experience being touched on certain body parts – thighs, lips, chest – as sexual, whereas men perceived the same as 'friendly, warm and affectionate' (Field, 2003: 27). These ambiguities of interpretation are crucial to understanding the ways in which work that is primarily accomplished through touch is subject to specific challenges regarding its status and intent.

The feminized character of Holistic Massage work

One of the defining characteristics of Holistic Massage and other body work is that it utilizes abilities typically coded as 'feminine', such as care and attentiveness (McDowell, 2009). The ability to effectively do body work is discursively linked to 'women's bodily lives' (Twigg, 2000a: 407), particularly their role as mothers. While the reduction of women to their bodies is highly problematic, Holistic Massage practitioners are able to capitalize on the stereotyping of their work by staking claim to the gendered skills of nurturing and caring. This is evident in the ways they draw on tropes of motherhood. For example Eve, now in her fifties, and a practitioner of 18 years said:

> Nobody's touched you like that apart from your mother really y'know, your naked body y'know, your lover doesn't touch you the same way, y'know there's nobody but your mother that touches you in that sort of completely sort of judgemental un-expecting anything back [...] so it brings up a lot of kid feelings. (Eve)

Without expressly saying that women are better suited than men to this touching, Eve repeated this metaphor, characterizing the ideal massage practitioner as 'the perfect mother'. This is an evocative analogy when considered alongside the 'hypersymbolization of the mother' in the contemporary west, where an idealized mother figure is given increasing symbolic weight at the same time as the traditional role of the mother is being 'eroded' (Hochschild, 2003).The ideal Holistic Massage practitioner parallels this symbolic figure who offers the 'haven' where 'we imagine ourselves to be safe, comforted and healed' (Hochschild, 2003: 39).

This non-judgemental 'motherly' touch, however, sits to one side of a taxonomic binary which – while largely absent from the literature on touch previously considered – emerged from practitioners' constructions of their work. A nurturing/sexual dichotomy of touch maps onto the 'Madonna / whore' dualism – that is, the dichotomization of women as either mothers or sex objects, and nothing else in between – which continues to influence constructions of femininity in the contemporary west. Touch has the potential to slip relatively easily from one side of this dichotomy to the other, particularly for male clients, as Kath explains:

> The part [of touch] that um...a lot of *men* in particular get very caught into is they relate touch with being *sexual*...so anything around y'know what you call, um, caring touch sort of immediately becomes something that goes off in a sexual area. (Kath)

Kath's comment presents a highly gendered perspective on touch that resonates with Twigg's contention that touch is 'increasingly confined to erotic relations' and that men, especially, 'live in a world that is largely atactile except for sex' (2000b: 47).

Gendered constraints on who may acceptably touch whom, when and where only exacerbate the dichotomization of touch as either nurturing or sexual. Massage practitioners engage in close bodily interaction 'outside a narrowly circumscribed set of contexts (namely, with one man, in private and as an expression of desire)', which 'risk[s] imputations of disreputability and immorality' (Oerton and Phoenix, 2001: 387). Paid massage is thus inherently at odds with prevailing social norms because it is done with numerous different people and for money. The available picture of the massage field suggests that the majority of both clients and practitioners are female (Marks, 2010; Porcino et al., 2011), meaning the average massage interaction involves a woman working on a woman. However, massage is persistently both heterosexualized and conflated with sex work. Practitioners are acutely aware of this, as Sarah (in her late twenties with 18 months experience of practice) conveyed in relation to what she discusses in 'supervision' sessions with more experienced practitioners:

> Like issues with money as well as like what it feels like to be paid for your massage and how much you should be paying and [...] how people give you money [...] how you respond to it. [...] Everyone has different relationships with money and, like, I was brought up with it being slightly degrading and I guess I thought it almost felt like prostitution [...] and also, how much I was worth, what does it feel like for somebody to charge y'know £40 am I really worth that much, y'know, issues of self-esteem. (Sarah)

While Sarah initially situates her attitude as particular to her and her 'upbringing', the connection she draws between massage and 'prostitution' goes well beyond her individual experience and speaks directly to the assumed 'degradation' of intimate relationships by economic activity and vice versa (Boris and Parreñas, 2010; Zelizer, 2007). Her comment is suggestive of the way in which questions around taking money for touching, and the exact nature of this practice, bubble under the surface. Sarah's reservations stem directly from the question of what it is that she is paid for, and are tied closely to her sense of self-identity and self-worth.

Constructing their work in terms of 'mothering-not-sex', practitioners do not attempt to challenge binary thinking about touch as *either* sexual *or* nurturing, but instead reproduce it, situating themselves to one (respectable) side of the divide. This in some ways limits the possibilities for Holistic Massage, because it locates practitioner knowledge in the sphere of 'naturally' given feminine attributes, rather than learned technical skills. Therefore, while this enables practitioners to claim an occupational space, the power/status gained here at a micro-level also reinforces restrictive gender stereotypes typical of body work.

Massage is of course not an exclusively female occupation, and the question arises as to whether male practitioners are faced with the same challenges of sexual ambiguity. Research on male practitioners suggests that their main challenge is to efface the stigma of doing 'women's work' (Purcell, 2009). Nevertheless, although men say that the sexualization of massage is not an issue for them, but for their female colleagues, they do recount occasions where clients have clearly been expecting sexual services, and where they have had to 'turf out' clients or threaten to call the police. In light of this, these men either do not feel as vulnerable as female practitioners may, or else they are playing down the issue in order to efface homosexualization. A male practitioner also changes the dynamic of the massage interaction. In a society where male touch is sexualized, often in a way that makes it inherently risky or threatening (Harding et al., 2008 focuses on male nurses), it may be that men are just as vulnerable to accusations of sexual impropriety. Such assumptions about male touch and about their motivations for doing feminized work deter men from doing massage in the first place, or steer them into more 'masculinized' areas such as Sports Massage (Purcell, 2009).

Significance of space and place

Despite the ongoing devaluation of their embodied competencies, the options available to Holistic Massage practitioners regarding where and how they can work have significantly broadened in recent years in line with the increasing popularity of CAM. The increase in dedicated spaces noted earlier in the chapter marks an overall change in attitudes and a shift toward the desexualization of massage. As Kath suggests:

> Things have changed since the nineties y'know when I first became a massage therapist y'know there [...] were *massage parlours* all over the place y'know people used to talk about extras all the time, they don't now. Holistic Massage is much more acceptable and there's many more therapy centres than there ever used to be. (Kath)

That there is now a clearer coding of places for health-oriented massage – '*therapy* centres' as opposed to 'massage parlours' or 'saunas' – is both cause and effect, and Kath's comment reflects a general sense amongst practitioners that both the conditions and perceptions of their work have improved. However, this change is bidirectional in that the creation of dedicated social spaces may have facilitated the establishment of massage as a (relatively) legitimate practice and knowledge form, while increasing acceptance of 'alternative' perspectives on the body and health have enabled the creation of more 'legitimate' spaces.

For practitioners, the coding of places as 'heath-oriented' is primarily aimed at male clients. Many work from a dedicated room in their homes as well as in a CAM centre. Whereas women clients happily attend either, men tend to prefer the latter. Lisa (in her thirties with 15 months of experience at the time) suggested that she *'definitely* get[s] a lot more blokes' when working in a CAM centre:

> I think that's probably partly because if guys want a massage they don't want to go see go anywhere *dodgy* [laughs] they're probably looking for a clinic setting em cos a few of them have said that, em, I think they're worried in case they get like a massage parlour y'know some of them have said that they found it quite difficult to find somewhere but this looked all above board. (Lisa)

In a sense, then, place both symbolizes and engenders the legitimacy – that is, the non-sexual nature – of the interaction. That clients may have trouble finding a place that is 'above board' is also indicative of the use of 'massage' as a euphemism by indoor sex work establishments, and of the fact that some men who present themselves to massage practitioners are in fact seeking a sexual encounter.

Even when working in a clinic, however, female practitioners often will not work alone, or at least will not take new male clients without a colleague in the building, due to the blurred boundary with sex work and the perceived potential threat of male aggression or inappropriateness. But clinic working certainly goes some way to limit potential stigma, whereas working from home in some ways magnifies it. Doing body work from home or in clients' homes 'undermines' the professional, social and spatial boundaries required to differentiate work from non-work or pleasure (Cohen, 2010). Spatial (and thus professional) boundaries must, therefore, be reinforced through techniques such as escorting the client quickly into the massage room (rather than allowing them to linger in a living space), having a separate entrance where possible and creating a space that directly imitates a more clinical setting. However, these are not the only strategies practitioners use to bound their work, as the remainder of this chapter explores.

Maintaining boundaries and effacing stigma

The strong association between massage and sex work meant that masseurs developed physical and verbal strategies to maintain the health-oriented and non-sexual status of massage. One way in which Kath dealt with clients' potential confusion as to the nature of the interaction was to address it directly, and in a way which enforces boundaries of space/place: 'I just used to say to them that this massage is absolutely a massage and if you're looking for anything else you need to *go* somewhere else' (Kath). But raising this verbally can also create an issue, as Carol explained:

> When I started I made a really very conscious point of emphasising to any clients but particularly male clients um that what I did was strictly non-sexual et cetera [but] I very quickly felt really awkward because it was almost like, as soon as I'd said it, I'd like flagged up the possibility that something else could be the case. (Carol)

Interestingly, as Carol's experience grew, she began to feel that verbally 'flagging' that sex was not on offer was an inappropriate approach and she found it easier and less embarrassing to instead perform the boundaries of her practice tacitly and tactilely:

> I think there was one instance working with a male client... where there was perhaps a little question on his part of what he was expecting to get out of this session, and just by placing the hand... on... his shoulders it was like giving that message that this is strictly a non-sexual thing.

The underlying threat of male sexual aggression is most clearly evident in a particular story from Kath in which she recounts an encounter with a male client whom she treated in her home. This client had at first lingered in her living room, picking up and examining her possessions, which for Kath was 'not okay'; this was because it violated the boundaries necessary for home-based working. This man proceeded to make her very uneasy for the duration of the encounter:

> I knew it was something about this guy's sexuality and did not want to go near it. So I massaged his lower legs and I massaged his chest and his arms and I missed out his abdomen and I finished the massage and its very rare I've ever done that, normally I massage the whole body [...] and he said well... why wouldn't you massage my stomach and I said... because I said I feel like, to be honest, there's something not clear around your sexuality and I'm not qualified to deal with that, and he didn't like what I said to him.

Kath's simultaneous use of 'sexuality' to denote not only the client's personality and desires, but also clearly his genitals, is interesting: she literally avoids his 'sexuality' by refusing to touch his abdomen. This is suggestive of the intuitive and fluid way in which in/appropriate touching is defined in massage. This particular client responded angrily to Kath's refusal, which only served to vindicate her sense of discomfort.

Conclusion

The role of touch in holistic massage leaves it open to misinterpretation and it is beset by a number of ambiguities over its status and nature (Oerton, 2004). While maintaining the non-sexual status of Holistic Massage is not practitioners' only concern, it is a significant aspect of their day-to-day work. It may well be the case that health-oriented massage *is* less sexualized than in previous decades and, if this is so, it points to a significant change in the field. This shift may in part be due to the new prevalence of dedicated spaces, the plethora of types of massage available, the growth of CAM and/or popular ideas about the 'importance' of touch. Practitioners' claims can also be read as an effacement strategy, as an attempt to constitute Holistic Massage as non-sexual, thus evading the potential stigma of body work noted by others (Wolkowitz, 2006). By constructing their work as non-sexualized practitioners make it so, albeit in a tentative and unstable way requiring ongoing boundary work. The desire to efface stigma and to make legitimacy claims for their work shapes how practitioners talk about touching, while their emphasis on discursive links with motherhood serves to situate the ideal massage practitioner away from the stigmatized realm of the sexual and firmly in the field of nurturing and caring. This is not to deny practitioners' claims that massage is less sexualized today; rather, it is to highlight the specific problems associated with the feminized character of the work and the fact that it utilizes a kind of touching that is unclearly bounded and guided by intuition.

Acknowledgements

I would like to thank the ESRC, who funded this research via a PhD studentship. I would also like to thank the editors for their helpful comments on earlier drafts of this chapter.

REFERENCES

Atkinson, S., McNaughton, J., Saunders, C. and Evans, M. (2010). Cool Intimacies of Care for Contemporary Clinical Practice. *The Lancet* 376(9754): 1732–33.

Barcan, R. (2011). *Complementary and Alternative Medicine: Bodies, Therapies, Senses.* Oxford: Berg.

Barnett, L. (2005). Keep in Touch: The Importance of Touch in Infant Development. *Infant Observation* 8(2): 115–23.

▶

Boris, E. and Parreñas, R.S. (2010). Introduction. *In* E. Boris and R.S. Parreñas (Eds) *Intimate Labors: Cultures, Technologies and the Politics of Care*. Stanford: Stanford University Press.

Bosanquet, C. (2006). Symbolic Understanding of Tactile Communication in Psychotherapy. *In* G. Galton (Ed.) *Touch Papers: Dialogues on Touch in the Psychoanalytic Space*. London: Karnac. Pp. 29–48.

Classen, C. (2005). *The Book of Touch*. Oxford: Berg.

Cohen, R.L. (2010). Rethinking 'Mobile Work': Boundaries of Space, Time and Social Relation in the Working Lives of Mobile Hairstylists. *Work, Employment & Society* 24(1): 65–84.

———(2011). Time, Space and Touch at Work: Body Work and Labour Process (Re)organisation. *Sociology of Health & Illness* 33(2): 189–205.

Douglas, M. (1966). *Purity and Danger*. London: Routledge.

Estabrooks, C.A. and Morse, J.M. (1992). Toward a Theory of Touch: The Touching Process and Acquiring a Touching Style. *Journal of Advanced Nursing* 17(4): 448–56.

Field, T. (2003). *Touch*. London: MIT Press.

Finnegan, R. (2002). *Communication: The Multiple Modes of Human Interconnection*. London: Routledge.

Fortune, L. and Gillespie, E. (2010). The Influence of Practice Standards on Massage Therapists' Work Experience: A Phenomenological Pilot Study. *International Journal of Therapeutic Massage Bodywork* 3(3): 5–11.

Gilman, S. (1993). Touch, Sexuality and Disease. *In* W.F. Bynum and R. Porter (Eds) *Medicine and the Five Senses*. Cambridge: Cambridge University Press. Pp. 198–224.

Giuffre, P.A. and Williams, C.L. (2000). Not Just Bodies: Strategies for Desexualizing the Physical Examination of Patients. *Gender and Society* 14(3): 457–82.

Grosz, E. (1995). *Volatile Bodies: Toward a Corporeal Feminism*. Indianapolis: Indiana University Press.

Henley, N.M. (1973). Status and Sex: Some Touching Observations. *Bulletin of the Psychonomic Society* 2: 91–93.

Hochschild, A.R. (2003). *The Commercialization of Intimate Life*. Berkeley: University of California Press.

———(2012). *The Outsourced Self: Intimate Life in Market Times*. New York: Metropolitan Books.

Jourard, S.M. (1966). An Exploratory Study of Body-Accessibility. *British Journal of Social and Clinical Psychology* 5: 221–31.

Lea, J. (2009). Becoming Skilled: The Cultural and Corporeal Geographies of Teaching and Learning Thai Yoga Massage. *Geoforum* 40(3): 465–74.

Leder, D. and Krukoff, M.W. (2008). The Touch That Heals: The Uses and Meanings of Touch in the Clinical Encounter. *Journal of Alternative and Complementary Medicine* 14(3): 321–27.

Marks, A. (2010). The Professional Status of Massage Therapists: Experience, Employability and Evolution. *Journal of Human Resource Costing and Accounting* 14(2): 129–50.

Massage Training Institute (2007). *Code of Ethics for Registered Practitioners*. Available at http://www.massagetraining.co.uk/index.php.

Montagu, A. (1971). *Touching: The Human Significance of the Skin*. New York: Columbia University Press.

Oerton, S. (2004). Bodywork Boundaries: Power, Politics and Professionalism in Therapeutic Massage. *Gender, Work & Organisation* 11(5): 544–65.

Oerton, S. and Phoenix, J. (2001). Sex/Bodywork: Discourses and Practices. *Sexualities* 4(4): 387–412.

Porcino, A., Boon, H., Page, S.A. and Verhoef, M.J. (2011). 'Meaning and Challenges in the Practice of Multiple Therapeutic Massage Modalities: A Combined Methods Study. *BMC Complementary and Alternative Medicine* 11(75). Available at http://www.biomedcentral.com/1472–6882/11/75.

Porter, R. (1993). The Rise of Physical Examination. *In* W.F. Bynum and R. Porter (Eds) *Medicine and the Five Senses*. Cambridge: Cambridge University Press. Pp. 179–97.

Purcell, C. (2009). Men Doing Massage: Body Work through a Narrative Lens. Edinburgh Working Papers in Sociology, No. 35, University of Edinburgh. Available at http://www.sociology.ed.ac.uk/working_papers/show_paper?result_page=35.

———(2011). *Touching Work: A Narratively Informed Sociological Phenomenology of Holistic Massage*. Unpublished PhD thesis, University of Edinburgh.

Routasalo, P. (1998). Physical Touch in Nursing Studies: A Literature Review. *Journal of Advanced Nursing* 30(4): 843–50.

Scheper-Hughes, N. and Lock, M. (1987). The Mindful Body: A Prolegomenon to Future Work in Medical Anthropology. *Medical Anthropology Quarterly* 1(1): 6–41.

Sharma, U. (1992). *Complementary Medicine Today: Practitioners and Patients*. London: Tavistock.

Sointu, E. (2011). Detraditionalisation, Gender and Alternative and Complementary Medicines. *Sociology of Health & Illness* 33(3): 356–71.

Sontag, S. (1990). *AIDS and Its Metaphors*. London: Penguin.

Synnot, A. (1993). *The Body Social: Symbolism, Self and Society*. London: Routledge.

Thayer, S. (1982). Social Touching. *In* W. Schiff and E. Foulke (Eds) *Tactual Perception: A Sourcebook*. New York: Cambridge University Press. Pp. 263–304.

Turner, R.N., Leach, J. and Robinson, D. (2007). First Impressions in Complementary Practice: The Importance of Environment, Dress and Address to the Therapeutic Relationship. *Complementary Therapies in Clinical Practice* 13(2): 102–9.

Twigg, J. (2000a). Carework as a Form of Bodywork. *Ageing and Society* 20: 389–411.

———(2000b). *Bathing – The Body and Community Care*. London: Routledge.

▶

Twigg, J., Wolkowitz, C., Cohen, R.L. and Nettleton, S. (2011). Conceptualising Body Work in Health and Social Care. *Sociology of Health & Illness* 33(2): 171–88.

Wainwright, E., Marandet, E., Smith, F. and Rizvi, S. (2010). The Microgeographies of Learning Bodies and Emotions in the 'Classroom-Salon'. *Emotion, Space and Society* 3(2): 80–89.

Wolkowitz, C. (2006). *Bodies at Work*. London: Sage.

Zelizer, V. (2007). *The Purchase of Intimacy*. Princeton University Press.

Disciplining and Resistant Bodies

Racing Bodies   **12**

Janet Miller

Introduction

This chapter explores the body work undertaken in racing stables where thoroughbred horses are trained; it thus addresses body work on/with animals, an aspect of body work which so far has been under-reported. Racing stables employ around 4000 stable staff (British Horseracing Authority [BHA], 2011a) whose job it is to give care to the horses, to exercise them daily and to transport them to race meetings. During two periods spent with stable staff and some of the horses, either at racing stables or at the racecourse (Miller, 2010), it was found that there is a common labour process that involves body work by their human caregivers on both the racehorses and themselves.

I conceptualize body work in racing as paid work on and with racehorses, where the human body is the primary tool of production in a labour process that is labour intensive and cannot be mechanized and where there is huge reliance on lightweight and athletic human bodies to accomplish the production of fit and competitive racehorses. In this chapter, therefore, we are concerned with the production of a human body that displays physical characteristics specific to the labour process, namely athleticism and weight restriction. These workers also 'produce' the horse body, which itself is expected to reach levels of fitness and athleticism in order to compete in races.

This chapter draws on my qualitative study of the racing labour process and employment relations in racing stables (Miller, 2010). Over the period 2000 to 2004, qualitative research was conducted with stable staff, trainers and key industry figures in order to locate the labour process and associated employment relations in their widest industry and historical context. I conducted interviews with 90 stable staff and observation of their work. Fifty staff (26 men and 24 women) were interviewed at their primary workplace, the racing stable (14 stables in total), with a further 40 stable staff (22 men and 18 women) who were interviewed at their secondary workplace, the racecourse (11 in total). In the first phase, access to staff was gained through their employers, racehorse trainers, whereas in the second phase access was negotiated through the racecourses. This sample was opportunistic in nature, which is regarded by Buchanan et al. (1988) as a realistic approach to the difficulties surrounding access. The nature of opportunistic sampling gives no guarantee of numbers of interviewees or types of employee and some types of employee are under-represented, particularly women and first-line supervisory staff (head lad/lasses).

This chapter is structured as follows. First, I provide some contextual information about the stable staff labour force, the industry in which they are employed and their terms and conditions of work. I then analyse how the labour process requires the performance of several types of body work which overlap with each other: body work on the bodies of the workers and with and on the horses. Both aspects involve gender as a central dimension.

Stable staff in the racing industry

The jobs of stable staff are the bottom rung of a large and complex industry. Theirs is a low paid but 'skilled bodily craft' (Cassidy, 2002: 106) in which horse (wo)manship is embodied in stable staff (Game, 2001).

The racing industry is regulated by the British Horseracing Authority (BHA). Membership of the Authority's management committees is drawn from thirteen interest groups, representing trainers, owners, breeders and racecourse owners in particular. The BHA is the licensing authority for trainers and jockeys, holding the power to discipline members of both groups, including withdrawing or denying a license. Prior to 2007, these functions were the preserve of the Jockey Club, a private members' club which evolved as a sporting body for men and into which 'the integration of women remains problematic' (Velija and Flynn, 2010: 304). The Jockey Club continues to run the National Stud, supports and promotes the charity Racing Welfare and is a major landowner, including owning several racecourses.

Horses are trained in 573 small firms (BHA, 2011a), racing yards or stables, located in mainly rural areas throughout the United Kingdom, with two racing centres, Newmarket and Lambourn, where larger numbers of stables are concentrated. Newmarket is associated with Flat racing and Lambourn with National Hunt racing. Taken together, racing stables employ 3966 stable staff of which 57 per cent are men, 43 per cent women (BHS, 2011a). At the basic grade, stable staff are predominantly young workers. The

British Horseracing Authority (BHA, 2011) employment statistics show that in 2010, 40 per cent of stable staff are aged between 16 and 30.

The industry has wrestled for some time with a change of name for stable staff but seems unable to move beyond the gender-specific labels of 'stable lad' and 'stable lass' when referring to the workers who have daily responsibility for the care and well-being of racehorses in training. Their continued use underlines the subordinate role of stable staff in the racing labour process.

In a report compiled for the BHA on the economic impact of racing (BHA, 2009), Deloitte records that the racing industry employs 18,600 core employees, of which the largest proportion are to be found in the production and training of racehorses, which encompasses the thoroughbred breeding industry as well as staff employed in racing stables. However, when one focuses on the training of racehorses, it is clear that stable staff and their body work on and with racehorses are crucial to the production of racehorses. It is a labour-intensive process in which horses must be cared for and exercised daily, year-round, and where there is no possibility of machines being substituted for human labour.

Skill is a contentious issue in racing, with 93 per cent of stable staff saying that their work was a 'skilled profession' (Miller, 2010), whereas some trainers asserted that 'anyone' can do the work of a stable lad. While it is true that mucking out, once accomplished to the standard required, is repetitious work, as I show in the following paragraphs there is skill involved in understanding horse behaviour and in communicating with horses and skill in riding racehorses. But, it is not quantified or measured and recognized through a formal qualification, a fact that contributes to the low wages received by stable staff. While the stable staff role in winning may be recognized by prize money, 'presents' from the horse's owner, or the 'best turned out' prize on a race day, this is variable pay and not guaranteed as part of the wage-effort bargain.

Part of the problem is that the embodied skills required of stable staff – represented by weight, youthfulness, riding skills, sensory skills, communication skills and deference – are not formally quantified or rewarded through the wage-effort nexus. They are all essential elements in the labour process, without which the task of training racehorses could not work in its current form. Similarly, Fine (2005) also points to issues of the manual nature of work, skill and gender as arbiters of the status of care work with humans.

As already observed, the work of stable staff is manual and physical and contains elements of 'dirty work', itself an arbiter of low wages and status (Ashforth and Kreiner, 1999; Sanders, 2010; Twigg, 2000). In racing, despite the varied nature of the work and the level of skill involved, stable staff remain in low paid, low status employment; as one stable lad put it, 'we are looking after valuable animals but we're paid a pittance'. Stable staff were quite clear that they had to resort to overtime working to improve pay, 75 per cent of those surveyed saying that they needed to do overtime to improve pay. Stable staff enjoy the lowest status and pay of any worker in the racing labour process. The national wage rates for stable staff are only slightly higher than the National Minimum Wage, and very close to agricultural wages. Although there has been national wage bargaining machinery since 1975, stable staff are represented by a weakly organized staff association, the Stable Lads' Association, which lacked the resources and bargaining nous to press home their undoubted strengths in the labour process.

The low status of stable staff in the racing hierarchy is further evidenced by the canteen and overnight accommodation facilities at UK racecourses. The poor quality of some provision was much commented upon by stable staff, some 93 per cent of respondents saying that racecourses should improve staff facilities (Miller, 2010).

Body work in the racing labour process

In racing stables, the labour process reflects the three 'simple elements' of Marx's (1976: 284) description, namely, purposeful activity; the object on which that work is performed; and the instruments of work. In racing, these are respectively the exercising, care, transportation and racing of racehorses; the racehorse itself; and the equipment and physical environment of the stable and racecourse. From my earlier study of this labour process (Miller, 2010), it was clear that two bodies were being produced: that of the stable lad and that of the horse. However, the concept of body work, paid or unpaid, has largely been associated with the work that women (and some men) do on their own bodies or on the bodies of other women and men (Gimlin, 2007; Sanders, 2008; Wolkowitz, 2006) in occupations such as nursing, beauty therapy, hairdressing and sex work. As of yet, there have been fewer attempts to encompass the body work undertaken by humans on animals, such as by veterinarians or farm labourers. Therefore, the rest of this chapter discusses the categories of body work I identified as part of 'purposeful activity', namely body production of both the workers' and horses' bodies, including as part of the latter care work and communication work with the horses.

The purposeful activity of stable work

The workplace in racing is generally referred to as a racing stable/yard in which horses are kept in individual boxes/stables. There are two forms of horseracing: Flat racing and National Hunt racing. Flat racing, as the name suggests, is conducted on racecourses without obstacles, whereas in National Hunt (or jumps) racing horses must also clear a series of high fences or rather lower hurdles. Trainers are more often licensed to train racehorses in both codes of racing, although they tend to be more associated with one code than the other. It should also be noted that we are looking at sports workers, rather than competing athletes. Nevertheless, the use of the body is essential to accomplishing the task of training a racehorse, whose body in turn can be regarded as an athletic body.

The job of a stable lad or girl is largely physical, involving the manual labour of mucking out, grooming and feeding, coupled with the skilled physical work of riding racehorses during the exercise routine. In addition, staff are responsible for the transportation of horses to and from race meetings. During the course of their working lives they develop skills around equine veterinary matters and, from being involved in associated care work, often detecting injury or illness. Their working day is arranged around these activities, year-round. For some, there is the additional work of breaking yearling horses, another skilled activity in which year-old horses are initially trained to accept saddle and rider. In the daily routine, stable staff are in close contact with at least three horses from early in the morning until early evening. They check on the health and general well-being of the horse, moving on to grooming and preparing it for exercise. They ride each horse, in turn, at the trainer's instruction, 'feeling' how it 'goes' when on the gallops and reporting back to the trainer. They then settle the horse back in its stable. It must be acknowledged that some duties require more than one form of body work so it is very difficult to completely separate tasks from each other into discrete types.

This purposeful activity involves a number of human capacities and skills, including the maintenance of the workers' own bodies in particular forms. It is argued by Mewett (2008) that horse care is predicated on human ways of caring, which have been discussed in the context of care-home workers (Fine, 2005; Twigg, 2000) and nursing (Shakespeare, 2003; Van Dongen and Elema, 2001). One of the problems highlighted in the literature is the fact that care work with humans often involves 'dirty work' of some variety (Twigg, 2000), 'dirty work' being defined by Ashforth and Kreiner (1999: 413) as 'tasks and occupations which are likely to be perceived as disgusting or degrading'. This in turn is often associated with low status because society stigmatizes this work and as Twigg (2000) points out dirty work attracts the double stigma of physical and moral 'dirtiness'. In looking at veterinary work, another form of work with animals, Sanders (2010) finds that although vets are closely involved with animal treatment, it is the veterinary technicians who do the dirty work of cleaning up faeces and blood. Therefore, it seemed likely that staff working closely with individual horses would experience the same division of labour; they would be the ones cleaning up after the horses, in the stables and in connection with injury or illness. Another part of the care work in racing involves sensory work, discussed by Hockey (2009) in his study of infantrymen in the British Army. Hockey identifies the sensory activities of working, particularly those using the senses of sight, hearing, touch and smell, and how these are deployed in the skilled work of infantry patrols in conflict situations.

The production of human bodies has been discussed in a range of ways, both in work situations (Wolkowitz, 2006) and as the subject of practices such as piercing and tattooing. Some of the discussion, such as that of Warhurst et al. (2000) and Wellington and Bryson (2001), is taken up with the different aesthetic reasons for producing a certain type of body. The athletic body has been the subject of research by Wacquant (1995), who studied the use of boxers' bodies as a means of production and the training methods used to produce a particular type of body. The making of the athletic body is also taken up by Brace-Govan (2002) in her study of women body builders, ballet dancers and weight lifters. She finds that a specific physicality is being sought in each case to meet the demands of the chosen discipline.

Stable staff are expected to produce their own bodies in certain ways (Gimlin, 2007) by undertaking three forms of body production work on themselves: first, the maintenance of a fit and athletic body; second, the restriction of body weight; and finally the presentation of a deferential body. With regard to athletic work, stable staff keep fit by riding every day and by mucking out, both very physical tasks. Women and men are equally expected to be tough and fit; otherwise, they will not be taken seriously as riders. However, their bodies are at risk of serious injury since horseracing is a dangerous sport, even for these support workers. Smartt and Chalmers (2008: 376) found that of different sports the 'death toll from horse racing is only exceeded by swimming and rugby and the hospitalisation rate exceeded only by rugby'. For those who are injured, there is a high risk of long-term or permanent disability, as described by one Newmarket stable lad who, at the age of 17, fell from his horse, fracturing his pelvis in five places. He was not expected to ride again, though made himself get back on a horse after twelve weeks out of work. In the racing labour process, the human body confronts the horse body, which may be privileged over the human. Evidence from stable staff was to the effect that human injuries might be overlooked or at least the expectation was that staff would return to work quickly in order to deal with 'their' horses.

Weight maintenance is essential in this job, further evidence of the primacy of horse over human found in the specificities of the labour market, where body type and youth are important factors. The British Racing School

(BRS), which conducts basic training for new stable staff, clearly stipulates the weight requirement of 60 kg on its website (BRS, 2011). Low body weight is particularly required in Flat racing where horses are raced as juveniles whose bodies are not fully developed. In order to avoid strain on the animal, workers are expected to keep to low weight thus transferring potential body stress to the worker, for example through dieting. In National Hunt stables, where horses are older and can carry higher weights, workers still have to keep their weight down.

As a result of the desired physicality of athletic forms (Brace-Govan, 2002), in several industries attaining different body weights forms an essential part of these bodily demands, for instance to meet the conditions set for boxing at different levels (Wacquant, 1995). In racing, the achievement of body weights has allowed women into the industry. In the specific context of racing, Tolich (1996) identifies the capacity of women to meet the strictures of body weight production amongst female jockeys, echoed by Velija and Flynn (2010) in a study of embodied female qualities in racing. Women make up 47 per cent of the basic grade of stable staff (BHA, 2011a), offering employers the prospect of meeting a 60 kg body weight restriction imposed by industry requirements that racehorses bear low weights when being ridden. Thus, there is evidence of the commodification of women's embodied capacity to restrict weight (Tolich, 1996).

The history of women's active involvement in racing reflects Pfister's view (2010: 234) that 'the gender of sport in the past was clearly and conspicuously masculine'. Racing was traditionally a male world, until the Sex Discrimination Act 1975 made it impossible to legally exclude women from the roles of trainer or jockey. It was not until the mid-1970s that women were finally 'allowed' to be jockeys – again it was the Jockey Club which stood in women's way by denying them a jockey's licence on the grounds that race riding was 'too dangerous' for women.

As early as 1919, women had worked as stable staff but for purely instrumental reasons – in order to break a strike by male stable staff at Epsom. But it was considered 'unsuitable' as a form of paid employment for women. Their bodies were to be protected from exposure to physical dirt in the stables and from the moral dirt of gambling, reflecting the commonly held belief that only 'certain types of sport and exercise were suitable for women' (Pfister, 2010: 234).

During the 1950s and 1960s, women started to occupy more jobs as stable staff and to become a significant presence in racing stables. Although there is no published evidence, it is not unreasonable to think that this is because of women's embodied capacity to be light in weight, reflecting to an extent Tolich's (1996) findings that women jockeys in New Zealand were only able to get more race riding when men started to become bigger and heavier in the second half of the 20th century. Women now make up nearly half the total of stable staff, offering employers the prospect of meeting the weight restriction stipulated in the industry, particularly in Flat racing. Women who enter their working lives in Flat racing stables also tend to stay there, suggesting that they find it easier to continue to meet this weight requirement throughout their working lives. However, owners and trainers, predominantly male (BHA, 2011a, 2011b), are still resistant to employing women jockeys, even arguing that horses can sense the gender of their rider, responding differently to women and men (Miller, 2010; Velija and Flynn, 2010).

There is some suggestion that the health and safety aspect of weight restriction in racing is gendered, but atypically in stables as compared to the wider society. Baum (2006) argues that horse racing is a high-risk sport for eating disorders in men, where there is a need to 'make the weight' (particularly, for jockeys, through sweating, skipping meals, vomiting, laxative abuse, cocaine and amphetamine use). Evidence from Racing Welfare suggests that young men working stables are more prone to eating disorders than young women and it was obvious from my earlier research (Miller, 2010) that levels of smoking cigarettes were high amongst stable staff, both men and women, possibly as part of the need to suppress appetite. While there have not yet been any studies of the dietary habits of stable staff, their union, the National Association of Stable Staff (NASS), has warned employers of the possible adverse effects of not eating properly, such as lack of concentration, illness and absenteeism, impact on health and safety, and poor physical strength (NASS, 2011).

Finally, the appearance of staff is also an issue. Staff are not expected to produce one particular image which would project the success of their employer's business, as discussed by Wellington and Bryson (2001) in their work on image consultancy. In fact, stable staff are expected to remain 'invisible' when in the public gaze. At the stables there is less emphasis on personal looks and turnout because of the practical requirements of horse management discussed in the following paragraphs. However, at the races, stable staff are expected to display a 'deferential body' by remaining in the background when in the public gaze, where all eyes are focused on the horse, its jockey and trainer. Part of the body production work involved here is to be neat and clean but not to stand out against the horse.

Working with racing horses

Working with racing horses requires embodied skills, including those of care, communication and skill. These all contribute to the production of the horse's body and value. Hockey (2009) argues that we need to look at practical experiences of embodiment, identifying a research gap which parallels Wolkowitz's (2006) concern that more empirical work is needed to extend our understanding of the embodiment of different labour processes.

In the particular circumstances of dealing with animals, a number of authors have discussed the use of the human body as a tool of communication. For example, Game (2001) considers the embodied skill of riding horses in the discipline of dressage, which is also taken up by Brandt (2005) in her study of the human-horse communication process. However, communication as a form of paid body work with animals remains undertheorized. In this section, attention is paid to the ways in which, given an absence of a common, spoken language between body workers and the recipient of their labour, stable staff use their bodies to bridge a gap in communication.

Stable staff are akin to Beardsworth and Bryman's (2001) zookeepers in that they are working with a live, but domesticated animal. They are coaxing the performance of certain 'tasks' out of the horse as part of the training process. This is not for daily consumption by the public as part of a regular daily display, as it would be in the captive surroundings of the zoo or theme park. Stable staff are, however, caregivers to a large and dependent animal towards which they already have a predisposition, if not feelings of love. The majority of stable staff come from a background with horses, as evidenced in my earlier research (Miller, 2010).

The financial value of the horse is related to its ability to generate earnings for the owner. In an historical account of animals in the industrial revolution, Hribal (2003) argues that horses are part of the working class because they contribute to the development of capitalism, while reaping none of the profit. He sees this as analogous with the social relationship between workers and employers. It could be argued that this applies to horseracing also, as the racehorse 'works' and will bring profits to at least some of its investors and its trainer. The value of a racehorse is vested in three sources: prize money, betting and breeding. The first two apply to all racehorses, whether on the Flat or National Hunt while the third applies in the main to stallions raced on the Flat. However, prize money is greater on the Flat, which in 2010 was more than double the prize money for National Hunt racing, £67,572,859 as against £31,389,808 (British Horseracing Authority, 2011b).

There is a strong relationship between racing thoroughbred horses and breeding from them. The most profitable part of the industry is breeding, specifically stallions' fees at stud. This means that profitability is skewed in favour of Flat racing, because National Hunt horses run as mares or geldings, whereas Flat racing horses run as fillies or colts (i.e., young stallions).

Working with horses involves two kinds of work, care work and communication, and the relationships formed as a result both contribute to the success of the work as well as workers' job satisfaction.

Care work

Mewett (2008) finds that horse care is predicated on human ways of caring. As we know from the work of Twigg (2000: 407), 'bodywork is poorly regarded in terms of pay and employment esteem' (see also Fine, 2005). Therefore, it seems likely that the low status of dirty work has an adverse impact on wages for stable staff. Care work in racing stables involves dirty work and sensory work, both of which are essential to the care of horses. Stable staff clean up the dirt produced by horses by removing urine and manure soiled bedding from the stables as they muck out, from the horse lorry during transportation, and at the racecourse stables. Mucking out also brings them in contact with dust from clean straw and hay. They also have the job of cleaning muddy tack, rugs and other horse apparel. They groom horses and keep their bodies clean, which involves the genitals as well as the coat, mane and tail. They also deal with body fluids such as blood, pus or nasal fluid when dealing with a sick or injured horse, saliva when administering a worming compound. There are clearly parallels between stable staff and Sanders' veterinary technicians, as well as with the care workers whose dirty work was observed by Twigg (2000). We are discussing the nature of work in a specific labour process that makes particular demands on the bodies of stable staff. Nevertheless, the work of stable staff is often characterized by employers as 'a way of life' in which staff accept low wages for 'love of horses', neatly obscuring the real nature of the employment relationship (Miller, 2010).

Gender also enters into understandings of the production of horses' bodies, especially in care work. While employment rates of women and men are nearly equal in racing stables, the gendering of roles *within* racing yards 'provided further evidence of continuing gender inequalities within the racing figuration' (Velija and Flynn, 2010: 310). Here the assumption is that women are more caring, nurturing and domestic than men; thus sweeping the yard or plaiting horses' manes will be undertaken with more diligence. While there was some suggestion from my earlier research (Miller, 2010) that in some stables women might not be offered the difficult horses to ride during exercise, in others the reverse was true as women were regarded as more empathetic and emotionally engaged, thus better able to use their bodies to communicate with the recalcitrant horse.

Interestingly, gender is also believed to enter into the behaviour of horses as well as of those who care for them. Horse behaviour in racing is also often explained through applying gender stereotypes to horses. Fillies and mares behave in a skittish fashion because they are female, are generally less successful in the racehorse stakes for the same reason, and are seen as inferior to colts and stallions. Colts are seen as difficult, moody and uncooperative, rather like a teenage boy, while stallions and geldings are 'brave', 'fearless', and likened to (male) warriors. Therefore, it can be seen that all female bodies in racing are judged to be inferior in some way.

The other, equally important, part of the care work is in the form of olfactory, sight, hearing and touching work (Hockey, 2009), especially when checking horses for injury and illness. Horses cannot tell us when they are ill or hurting and rely on humans to interpret their bodily signs for evidence of problems. This may arise in the stables or when out on the gallops at exercise, often when looking for an explanation of why a horse has performed less well than normal or is playing up. One of the aspects of horse care that stable staff talked of was that of 'knowing your horse', as a result of daily and repeated contact with the animal as part of the process of 'producing' the racehorse.

Communication work

It is this category that marks out the racing labour process as inherently different from body work with humans. In some ways, it is the most difficult to capture because it deals with the embodied skill of communication with an animal. Little attention has been paid to the human/animal relationship where communication has to be organized on a different basis because the horse can only communicate through behaviours. The human, of necessity, fills in the blanks.

Game's (2001) research on the horse-human relationship helps us to understand this. She looked at the ways in which horse and rider interact with each other very closely in a successful riding partnership. In racing, as in other forms of equine sport, horses rely on the bodily instructions that are given by their riders to know whether to go forward and at what pace, or to stop, or to be prepared to take off over a jump. Humans have to tell the horse these things by using a combination of their body weight in or out of the saddle, the riding 'aids' of leg pressure and manipulation of the reins. As Cassidy (2002: 112) observes, 'Riding racehorses is conducted according to its own detailed set of rules that cannot be extrapolated from the technology alone, so must be learnt.'

Stable staff must also use their bodies to move a horse around the stable and out of the way when mucking out; to persuade a horse to load on to a horse lorry; and to stand still when being tacked up/untacked, or when 'legging up' a jockey into the saddle at the racecourse. Communication is essentially non-verbal, for lack of a common, spoken language, and is essential to successful performance of all these tasks (Brandt, 2005).

Horse-human relationship

It must be recognized that the horse body also provides moments of pleasure. There is the thrill of galloping and jumping; the pleasure to be gained from grooming and touching; the pride when 'your' horse wins; and the pride drawn from riding skill and communicating with 'your' horse. There is also the possibility of pain from loss of a horse or of fear of a difficult horse. Stable staff also exercise power with their bodies and power is embodied in them, especially when riding. A further, and important, aspect is the pleasure that workers derive from the highly physical and tactile tasks that make up the labour process. This complexity offers a striking set of reasons why stable staff have such a strong bond with horses. It does not solely derive from the love of horses, which staff undoubtedly have (Cassidy, 2002; Miller, 2010), but also from the practical need to avoid being kicked, bitten or thrown off a horse, all potential dangers inherent in the body work referred to previously. Consideration of the body work undertaken by stable staff showed that the reason why stable staff 'love' horses is bound up in the specificities of the particular labour process in racing stables. This reflects Wolkowitz's (2006) concern with the ways in which our bodies are implicated in particular labour processes.

Conclusion

This chapter identifies a group of workers, sports support workers, whose labour processes have, so far, been less theorized in the literature than those of sports (wo)men (Wacquant, 1995). In studying stable staff, we can see that some bodily practices, such as weight restriction, are passed on to them from other parts of the industry. We can also see that the demands of the production process require athleticism from the large numbers of young people who form the basic grade of stable lad/lass, as well as expecting them to be largely 'invisible' when at race meetings. Stable staff are also dependent on their bodies as a means of communicating with race horses, the other body involved in the labour process. The racing industry also relies on embodied capacities and attributes amongst stable staff which remain unquantified or rewarded in the wage-effort bargain.

The horse body is produced to meet the demands of the industry for fit and competitive racehorses; some horse bodies also go on to produce more horses through the breeding industry. The animal body has also been under-theorized, particularly in its form as a 'commercial' animal, 'working' in the racing labour process alongside its human companions. It is argued by Probyn (2000: 14) that 'in an obvious manner, sport highlights that bodies do something'. There is firm evidence that the bodies of stable staff make a significant contribution to the production of racehorses. While the success of the labour process in racing stables is highly dependent on a good relationship between horse and human, worker status is inextricably linked to body work. The work is skilled but low paid because the skilled element is in part embodied and in general goes unrecognized in a formal sense, as it is overlaid by the stigma of undertaking dirty work.

REFERENCES

Ashforth, B.E. and Kreiner, G.E. (1999). 'How Can You Do It?': Dirty Work and the Challenge of Constructing a Positive Identity. *Academy of Management Review* 24(3): 413–34.

Baum, A. (2006). Eating Disorders in the Male Athlete. *Sports Medicine* 36(1): 1–6.

Beardsworth, A. and Bryman, A.E. (2001). The Wild Animal in Late Modernity: The Case of the Disneyization of Zoos. *Tourist Studies* 1(1): 83–104.

Brace-Govan, J. (2002). Looking at Bodywork: Women and Three Physical Activities. *Journal of Sport and Social Issues* 26(4): 403–20.

Brandt, K.J. (2005). *Intelligent Bodies: Women's Embodiment and Subjectivity in the Human-Horse Communication Process*. Unpublished Phd thesis, University of Colorado at Boulder. Accessed February 2011 at http://gradworks.umi.com/31/78/3178342.html.

British Horseracing Authority (2009). The Economic Impact of Racing. London: BHA. Accessed April 2012 at http://www.britishhorseracing.com/resources/media/publications_and_reports/Economic_Impact_of_British_Racing_2009.pdf.

———(2011a). Annual Statistics: Training and Riding. London: BHA. Accessed January 2012 at http://www.britishhorseracing.com/resources/media/publications_and_reports.

———(2011b). Annual Statistics: Racing and Prize Money. London: BHA. Accessed January 2012 at http://www.britishhorseracing.com/resources/media/publications_and_reports.

British Racing School (2011). Careers in Racing for Stable Staff. Accessed March 2011 at http://www.brs.org.uk/Careers/Stable_Staff/.

Buchanan, D., Boddy, D. and McCalman, J. (1988). Getting In, Getting Out, and Getting Back. *In* A. Bryman (Ed.) *Doing Research in Organizations*. London: Routledge.

Cassidy, R. (2002). *The Sport of Kings: Kinship, Class and Thoroughbred Breeding in Newmarket*. Cambridge: Cambridge University Press.

Fine, M. (2005). Individualization, Risk and the Body: Sociology and Care. *Journal of Sociology* 41(3): 247–66.

Game, A. (2001). Riding: Embodying the Centaur. *Body and Society* 7(4): 1–12.

▶

Gimlin, D. (2007). What Is Bodywork? A Review of the Literature. *Sociology Compass* 1(1): 353–70.

Hockey, J. (2009). 'Switch On': Sensory Work in the Infantry. *Work, Employment & Society* 23(3): 477–93.

Hribal, J. (2003). Animals Are Part of the Working Class: A Challenge to Labor History. *Labor History* 44(4): 435–53.

Marx, K. (1976). *Capital*, vol. 1. London: Penguin.

Mewett, P. (2008). The Animal Other: Horse Training in Early Modernity. The Australian Sociological Association. Accessed January 2011 at http://www.tasa.org.au/uploads/2011/05/Mewett-Peter-Session-55-PDF2.pdf.

Miller, J. (2010). *How Does the Labour Process Impact on Employment Relations in the Small Firm? A Study of Racehorse Training Stables in the United Kingdom*. Unpublished doctoral thesis, London Metropolitan University.

National Association of Stable Staff (2011). Healthy Eating Advice for Stable and Stud Staff. Accessed 28 March 2011 at http://www.naoss.co.uk/feelgoodfodder/employers.php.

Pfister, G. (2010). Women in Sport – Gender Relations and Future Perspectives. *Sport in Society* 13(2): 234–348.

Probyn, E. (2000). Sporting Bodies: Dynamics of Shame and Pride. *Body and Society* 6(1): 13–28.

Sanders, C. (2010). Working Out Back: The Veterinary Technician and 'Dirty Work'. *Journal of Contemporary Ethnography* 39(3): 243–72.

Sanders, T.L.M. (2008). Selling Sex in the Shadow Economy. *International Journal of Social Economics* 35(10): 704–28.

Shakespeare, P. (2003). Nurses' Bodywork: Is There a Body of Work? *Nursing Inquiry* 10(1): 47–56.

Smartt, P. and Chalmers, D. (2008). A New Look at Horse-Related Sport and Recreational Injury in New Zealand. *Journal of Science and Medicine in Sport* 12: 376–82.

Tolich, M. (1996). Negotiated Turf: The Feminisation of the New Zealand Jockey Profession. *Journal of Sociology* 32(2): 50–60.

Twigg, J. (2000). Carework as a Form of Bodywork. *Ageing and Society* 20: 389–411.

Van Dongen, E. and Elema, R. (2001). The Art of Touching: The Culture of 'Body Work' in Nursing. *Anthropology and Medicine* 8(2): 149–62

Wacquant, L. (1995). Pugs at Work: Bodily Capital and Bodily Labour among Professional Boxers. *Body and Society* 1(1): 65–93.

Warhurst, C., Nickson, D., Witz, A. and Cullen, A.M. (2000). Aesthetic Labour in Interactive Service Work: Some Case Study Evidence from the 'New' Glasgow. *The Service Industries Journal* 20(3): 1–18.

Velija, P. and Flynn, L. (2010). Their Bottoms Are the Wrong Shape: Female Jockeys and the Theory of Established Outsider Relations. *Sociology of Sport Journal* 27: 301–15.

Wellington, C.A. and Bryson, J.R. (2001). At Face Value? Image Consultancy, Emotional Labour and Professional Work. *Sociology* 35(4): 933–46.

Wolkowitz, C. (2006). *Bodies at Work*. London: Sage.

Body Work and Ageing: The Biomedicalization of Nutrition Practices

Giulia Rodeschini

Introduction

In recent years, a number of changes have affected the reality of becoming old. Lengthening of life expectancy has led to an increase in the number of the very elderly and to a more complex management of late life, especially for the frail. If contemporary old age is often characterized by forms of 'active' and 'successful' ageing (Kahana et al., 2003), at the same time there are increasingly more elderly people who long persist in a state of reduced vitality, often defined by debilitating physical and/or psychological conditions. This is, in part, a consequence of medical and technological innovations coupled with highly effective geriatric clinical treatments and assistance that have radically changed late life and end-of-life in postmodern societies. Now more than ever, the processes of medicalization (Conrad, 2007) and biomedicalization[1] (Clarke et al., 2003, 2009) permeate old age, forcing us to ask new sociological questions about the meaning of care, medical treatments and death in the later phases of life. In these processes, bodies are the silent protagonists. They are the subjects and the objects of care and medical practices and are strongly affected by new forms of the 'biomedicalization of aging' (Estes and Binney, 1989) that promote the notion that ageing is not inevitable and can be held in abeyance by employing restorative and replacement procedures (Kaufman et al., 2004).

This chapter intends to explore organizational changes in the setting of care for older people, and the influences of these changes on recipients' and providers' bodies, by studying the geriatric care and medical practices enacted by health care professionals.

Health and social care work is conceptualized as 'body work' (Gimlin, 2007; Twigg, 2000b; Wolkowitz, 2002, 2006): 'employment that takes the body as its immediate site of labour, involving intimate, messy contact with the (frequently supine or naked) body, its orifices or products through touch or close proximity' (Wolkowitz, 2006: 147).

The concept of closeness/distance between professionals' and residents' bodies is relevant to this chapter. Proximity to or distance from bodies lead to significant hierarchies among professionals: more proximity to bodies-worked-upon traditionally means a lower professional social status (Twigg, 2001). At the same time, the ageing body lives a kind of stigmatization related to the cultural conception of oldness, as 'old age represents a piling up of undischarged remnants of a lifetime of eating and drinking and is dirtier than youth' (Widding Isaksen, 2002: 143). Therefore, ageing bodies are usually more problematic to relate to than are younger bodies, and proximity to them lowers professional status even more. In health care facilities, the proximity between residents' and professionals' bodies is subjected to many transformations because of technological innovations and new care practices related to processes of reorganization. But these changes need to be critically analysed. As suggested by Cohen (2011: 189), we are witnessing the 'emergence of a new political mantra: the realization of "efficiency savings" in health and social care without degradation of frontline services'. She identifies in body work three constraints on labour process organization and reorganization connected to the rigidity in the ratio of workers to bodies-worked-upon, to the requirement of co-presence despite temporal unpredictability in demand for body work, and to the nature of bodies as material of production (Cohen, 2011: 191). Although these constraints are also found in body work for older people, this chapter aims to investigate some of the organizational strategies that are used to try to overcome them. These strategies comprise new forms of care practices that transform bodies and relations between residents and professionals, with the aim of achieving standardized and rationalized labour.

This chapter first focuses on the physical and relational transformations of bodies produced by nutrition work. Second, I deal with the perception of bodies as *bodies at risk* and as *risky bodies*. In this section a discussion of three organizational strategies put into practice by professionals is presented: (a) the creation of a boundary between inside and outside of the body; (b) the creation of (symbolic) barriers between bodies; and (c) attempts to create immunity from choices. The conclusion focuses on the different meanings of the processes of medicalization inside facilities for the elderly, on the apparently rational solutions offered by new forms of nutrition and on the 'securitarian' character of risk management by professionals.

Methodology

My analysis draws from fieldwork research conducted in a care home and in a nursing home in northern Italy. Care and nursing homes have recently been subjected to more rapid organizational transformations than have other settings of care (Trabucchi et al., 2002). In contrast to the past, today only those older people whose care needs cannot be met in any other way have access to a care or nursing home. Therefore, most of those who move into a care or nursing home are in advanced old age, sick, and frail (Österlijng et al., 2011). As residents' average age, their physical and mental problems, and their dependence on others have increased, organizations and professionals have adapted by modifying working practices and creating innovative medical strategies, often based on new kinds of tools and technologies.

Both facilities I studied are part of the Italian National Health Care System. They house 60 elderly residents each. I used 'theoretical sampling' (Glaser and Strauss, 1969) to select facilities, selecting two facilities that offer different kinds of assistance. The care home is characterized by relatively few doctors and nurses, whereas the nursing home constantly has medical staff present. With regard to the processes of nutrition, on which this chapter focuses, in the care home 6 patients were tube-fed and 10 were fed with pureed food, whereas in the nursing home 11 were tube-fed and 19 were fed with pureed food. The remaining residents ate solid food through their mouths.

Data was collected during 4 months of participant observation and shadowing (June and July 2010 and April and May 2011). During this period, I also conducted in-depth interviews with 12 key facility personnel (nurses, care assistants and doctors). The focus of my observation was nutrition work: nutrition practices performed by professionals. In particular, I collected data on mealtime and decision-making processes. Data was collected and analyzed following grounded theory methodology (Charmaz, 2006; Glaser and Strauss, 1967), and using the NVivo8 program. To respect the privacy of participants, I do not provide their real names, instead adopting medicinal herbs and plants as pseudonyms.

Feeding as a key practice of body work

In workplaces of care for the elderly, nutrition work is important because it has undergone a number of significant transformations in the last few years. Now more than ever, both medical and non-medical health care professionals consider nutrition a fundamental practice in the care of the elderly. The care assistant coordinator of the care home, Ginestra, suggested:

> The fundamental things for the well-being of older people are: nutrition, hydration, and good management of posture. In particular, it is very important to manage how much residents eat and drink. (Ginestra)

This position is also strongly confirmed by a geriatrician, who emphasized:

> (…) well-being is strongly conditioned by food (…) malnutrition has to be considered an illness within other illnesses. (Doctor Giaciglio)

Consequently, in recent years changes in the practice of nutrition have been developed: the personalization of each resident's diet, and the use of pureed food, food supplements and water gels and artificial nutrition[2]. These processes lead to a sort of reversal in the division of labour between health professionals (doctors and nurses) and care assistants: doctors and nurses increasingly become protagonists of nutrition work, whereas in the past feeding involved only non-medical professionals, such as aides, food assistants and caregivers. The shift of nutrition towards the medical sphere of care results in significant changes in the management of the last phase of geriatric life. In the past, when older people began refusing to eat (because they were very frail and generally close to death), a common response from care and nursing home professionals was to guarantee assistance and to help the person with drips, as a means of accompanying them toward a quiet and 'natural' death. Today, the use of food supplements and, in particular, the insertion of a gastrostomy tube (G tube or PEG tube) or a nasogastric tube (NG tube) for artificial nutrition has completely changed the management of the last phase of life.

The process of nutrition highlights important analytic questions related to the practices of care work as body work. During my fieldwork, two principal issues emerged: on one hand, the complex transformations of bodies as a consequence of particular (and often new) care practices. On the other hand, the relation between bodies and risks, and the central role that the concept of risk plays in body work in a care setting.

Feeding as a means of transforming bodies

Because of the nutrition work, bodies are subjected to transformations. I observed different kinds of interconnected physical and relational transformations. The first involved the penetration of bodies by tubes; the second had to do with the fact that bodies can benefit or suffer because of artificial nutrition. The third was that bodies undergoing artificial nutrition were often isolated and excluded from typical relational dynamics.

During the process of artificial nutrition, bodies are *penetrated* by NG or PEG tubes. The NG tube enters the body from the nose, whereas the PEG tube is inserted directly into the stomach. These transformations are of a peculiar type: definitive, endless and eternal. Whereas artificial nutrition is often a temporary situation for the non-elderly (e.g., after a surgery), when a feeding tube is used for older people it almost always becomes a definitive tool, one that remains inside the body until the person dies. According to medical protocols, NG tubes can be used only for three or four months, while the PEG tube has no formal time limit, though for any number of reasons it is better not to excessively prolong its use. Despite these protocols, I observed several cases of people using NG tube or PEG tubes for many months (or years), usually until their death. As confirmed by the physiotherapist of the care home:

> When doctors insert an NG tube, they say this kind of practice can go on for two, three or four months...But here, we have patients who have been using NG tubes for years. (Guaiaco)

This usually happens because artificial nutrition is the only way to feed people. The PEG tube may, however, remain inside the body even when patients restart autonomous oral feeding, because they need the PEG tube for hydration or because it is considered useful in case of future emergency. For example, once while I was in the dining room of the care home helping assistants with the distribution of food, I saw a woman eating by mouth. I was surprised because I knew that she had a PEG tube:

> I ask Echinacea [the care assistant coordinator] about the woman who is sitting close to the door. I imagine that doctors have removed the PEG tube (...). But Echinacea tells me that she still has a PEG tube inserted in her stomach. And she adds: 'she had an ictus and has problems with dysphagia. Now she is much better. We rehabilitated her and she eats autonomously, but when she doesn't eat enough we still use the PEG tube.' (Ethnographic notes)

I heard of a similar case from the psychologist of the nursing home. An elderly woman with a PEG tube restarted oral nutrition, but the doctors did not want to remove the tube because they thought it might be useful in the future. In the end, the woman ripped the tube out, with obvious consequences. Doctors had to do an emergency operation to stop the bleeding.

The definitive character of tube feeding is due, first of all, to the fact that during old age, and in the presence of important pathologies, it is very difficult to re-obtain the capacity of taking in food, especially fluids, orally. But, beyond this, the prolonged use of artificial nutrition is also conditioned by its organizational advantages compared with the normal process of nutrition. The care assistant coordinator of the care home, after having strongly criticized the excessive use of the artificial nutrition, acknowledged that, according to her:

> (...) it is easier to manage a PEG tube than to reaccustom older people to eating by mouth... it is much easier. Honestly, it's also easier for us, because you position the bottle [of artificial food], turn on the pump and, consequently, they are fed and you are at peace with yourself because the food is balanced, and you know they aren't missing anything. Actually, they find all the elements they need inside the bottle. (Echinacea)

Thus, artificial feeding becomes a convenient tool for managing difficult situations with more organizational security. Thus, the penetration of bodies remains a typically definitive characteristic.

Artificial nutrition also transforms the nature and severity of patients' physical wellness and suffering. They can both benefit thanks to the artificial nutrition and suffer because of it. On the one hand, bodies reap physical benefits, not only at the metabolic level, but also in the resolution of other problems, such as the disappearance or reduction of bedsores:

> Good artificial feeding also heals bedsores, eh! Because the feeding gives all the nutritional supplements... it is so effective! A 102 year old person stayed for two years in bed with a PEG tube and... she didn't have any bedsores. It was incredible! It also depends on the elasticity of the skin, but the process of feeding is the fundamental step. (Echinacea)

On the other hand, the insertion of feeding tubes can create or increase corporeal suffering. The internal sores caused by NG tubes and rejection of the PEG tube by residents' bodies are two clear examples. For instance, the nursing coordinator at the care home explained the pain that NG tube use can create:

> I should change the NG tube every month. But it creates a lot of pain for the patient. So I decided to change the tube once every three or four months, because it's a torment to insert a tube into a body, especially in the case of elderly and uncooperative patients. (Melissa)

The third kind of transformation is related to the social/relational lives of people using artificial nutrition. As a consequence of the different working practices adopted by professionals during the process of artificial nutrition, residents fed by PEG and NG tubes live a sort of isolation and exclusion from organizational life. As the daughter of an elderly patient explains:

> When you feed your mother through the mouth, you touch and caress her (...). But when you feed someone through a tube it's a very mechanical thing, it's a...it's not nice, it's no longer human, it's no longer a human thing. When professionals feed through the PEG tube, they should be...they should touch the patients, speak to them, caress them, but usually a person with a PEG tube becomes an abandoned person. This is what I feel when I see my mother. Professionals ensure that the PEG system works correctly, but they're not really interested in the patient.

This 'mechanization' of the process of feeding has important consequences for the relationship between recipients and providers of care, as it does for that between residents and their families. Compared to people who feed by mouth, those with a PEG or an NG tube no longer enjoy the moment of the meal, which plays an important role in social-relational dynamics, particularly in settings such as care and nursing homes. Whereas families are normally able to substitute the relational contact connected to the practices of nutrition with other forms of contact, many professionals cannot do that. Even if many professionals pay attention to the relationship with residents, the physical and social contact is no longer joined with the process of feeding. The relationship is no longer a prerogative of feeding because bodies can be fed without any physical and relational contact. Moreover, in many cases, artificial nutrition leads to the exclusion of the resident from the spaces and moments of socialization during meals. Though there is always an attempt to imitate the 'normal' meal, giving artificial feeding at the same time and in the same space of 'normal' meals, this is almost never possible – for physiological and/or organizational reasons – and so people with PEG or NG tubes live in an 'excluded' organization of space and time completely different from that of the other residents.

As such, working practices connected to the process of artificial nutrition influence in different ways the sensitivity of bodies and their physical and relational life inside the facilities. Professionals are involved in innovative practices of body work that radically transform bodies and, at the same time, create new distances between bodies.

In the next section, I discuss the development of these distances, starting from an analysis of how risk was conceptualized inside the two facilities studied.

Bodies at risk and risky bodies: Managing the risk on the residents' bodies

In the facilities, different attitudes of protection towards bodies emerged. Bodies are considered simultaneously or alternately as *bodies at risk*, because they are debilitated (and then at risk of infection), and *risky bodies*, because they represent a space of risk for professionals (as a source of infection and as a field of error in the medical decision-making).

I identified three organizational strategies put into practice to manage these risks, all connected to the idea of sanitizing care settings. The first strategy is the creation of a boundary between inside and outside as a response to the risk that bodies are subjected to. The second is the use of physical (and symbolic) barriers to protect some bodies from other 'risky' bodies. Both of these strategies were part of the professionalization of feeding. The third organizational strategy, which I call 'immunity from situational decision', occurs because bodies represent a difficult space of medical decision-making.

'Professionalism of feeding': The creation of boundaries and barriers between bodies

Because of their frailty and debility, residents in care and nursing homes are generally considered by professionals to be physically *at risk*. This representation leads to a sort of obsessive sanitization of the setting of care and is aimed at protecting residents from various, in particular, external dangers. Even in this case, the process of nutrition is a good example of the development of this organizational tendency. Food is considered as both important, but also dangerous for residents. The care assistant coordinator explains that residents in the care home cannot eat anything that comes from outside:

> (...) we have to give our residents only food cooked inside our structure, we cannot give them food that comes from the outside. Things from outside can be used only if they are packaged and dated. But food prepared by relatives... not at all! Because once something happens, we have all the responsibility. Some infections come from outside... it's better to always be really careful. (Echinacea)

Therefore, even residents who still eat normal food cannot eat food prepared by their relatives or friends. In this way, the organizational setting imposes a distance between residents and their relatives that exacerbates the distance already forced on the older person by institutionalization. Eliminating the possibility for relatives to prepare food for residents means removing one of the most important roles that relatives can have in 'caring for' their parents or relatives or loved ones. This organizational practice is a kind of 'professionalism of feeding', similar to the dynamics engendered by the process of artificial nutrition. It falls within the general process of the 'medicalization of feeding'. This organizational behaviour is justified by the dangers related to sanitization, but is contradicted by daily care practices, which demonstrate that the closeness of families and friends (and all symbols connected to them, such as the food) represents a source of wellness for residents. An example is the behaviour of a care assistant with a very ill resident, Mrs. Damiana, to whom her son brought some special tomatoes for lunch:

> The care assistant says to the son that it would be forbidden to bring in food from outside, but than adds: 'Mrs. Damiana, if you look at me with those eyes...you seem healed by the sight of your son's tomatoes.' And she tells the son that he can give some tomatoes to the mother, but only this once. (Ethnographic notes)

Food is recognized as an important vehicle of care, but instead of focusing on its value as a means of 'caring' at the organizational level it is managed by following the medical standard of 'curing', which hides the social and symbolic aspects of food.

Beyond protection from external risks, a parallel dynamic develops. Here ageing bodies are (implicitly or explicitly) considered a risk to professionals. Mealtime is characterized by a strong attention to hygiene and sanitation, and by a consequent use of protections against contamination. In particular, in the care home all professionals who have any kind of contact with food and/or with residents have to wear, in addition to the usual uniform, an apron, a cap and, during some practices, latex gloves. The use of protective clothing is represented, first of all, as a safeguard for the residents, considered (as previously described) at risk:

> We always, always, use gloves. Everything we do, we use gloves; in particular when we do something on them [residents]. We are very careful about the hygienic protection, it is very important for our residents. (Echinacea)

At the same time their use is considered a protection for the workers:

> The use of gloves, like the use of the white coat, the mask, and of the accident prevention shoes, is a tool of individual protection. Normally, we use them when it's more necessary, for example, with residents who have some particular pathology, such as hepatitis. (Echinacea)

> The use of gloves protects both us and the residents. (Gladiola)

Beyond the important aspects of physical protection, these objects also seem to embody other meanings. From the first day of my fieldwork, I noticed that all care assistants and nurses who collaborated on the distribution of food consistently wore all the available kinds of protective gear. The rule was so strict that:

> While I feed a resident, I see the nursing coordinator, Centella, who is approaching me. When she is close to me, she says with a strict tone: 'Please, put on your cap immediately, it's really important'. (Ethnographic notes)

But on the following days, I observed the following:

> In the dining room there are 26 residents, 5 assistants, 1 volunteer, and 2 relatives. The assistants and the volunteer wear an apron, a cap and, in some instances, latex gloves, while the relatives don't wear anything protective. They feed their relatives, but they also help other residents eat, cutting food, giving them water (…). (Ethnographic notes)

And then:

> During the distribution of food, all care assistants and nurses wear their caps, but many of them don't cover the entire head. They are simply placed on the head, leaving a lot of exposed hair. Some care assistants wear the cap as a part of their look, being careful not to damage their hairdos. (Ethnographic notes)

If relatives can enact the same practices as professionals – for example, feeding residents – without wearing any kind of protective clothing, and if professionals can wear caps without covering their hair, these protective measures do not seem necessary for ensuring hygiene or for protecting residents and assistants. The practices are the same whoever performs them, but the distance between bodies increases in the relationship between residents and professionals. As already suggested by Twigg (2000a), gloves and instruments of protection have symbolic meanings which go beyond the rationale of hygiene. In particular, they are an example of the processes explored by Douglas (1966) in relation to food avoidance, whereby scientific explanations in terms of hygiene are used to explain practices that have their roots in social categories and symbolism. Professionals' bodies are symbolically distant from those of the residents. These protective objects assume a role that Twigg (2000a: 151) defines as 'barriers of professionalism between the client and the worker'. A similar symbolic process is typical of much body work, in which physical protections often assume a wider role of 'barrier'. In relation to the main theme of this book, it is worth noting the link to how sex workers use condoms and wear separate working clothes to manage risks connected to their profession. Condoms are generally presented as health prevention tools, but can also be read as a psychological and symbolic 'protection strategy' (Sanders, 2001) aimed at creating a barrier between sex workers and clients.

In the case of health and social care, the use of barriers represents another symptom of the process of medicalization affecting this workplace, through a sort of imitation of medical habits. Their role is not only related to medical needs, rather the proximity to ageing bodies is perceived as risky even when there is no epidemiologic risk. This organizational behaviour depends on the symbolic perception conditioned by the representation of oldness. Old bodies represent decline, putridity, infection and, consequently, something to avoid and from which to protect oneself. Notably care assistants often wear more protection than doctors. Historically, doctors have dressed in uniforms and protective clothing, but now, especially in the care home, doctors do not use a uniform, and often do not wear gloves during visits involving contact between bodies. This is partly explained by the fact that fewer and fewer doctors actually touch the bodies they are caring for (and so are better able to avoid this stigmatized contact), but I also noted that on some occasions it is a consequence of a greater awareness of the low real risk of infection due to contact with the resident's skin:

> (...) during the examination, the doctor touches [resident] Mr. Guaiaco's skin without gloves. He doesn't wear a uniform. (...) When he leaves the room, the nursing coordinator tells him that it would be better if he washes his hands. He goes to the kitchen to wash his hands, but I note that he doesn't consider it necessary. (Ethnographic notes)

Conversely, many care assistants fear getting infected even in situations in which infections cannot occur, as these notes show:

> (...) a resident affected by HIV is left alone in the corner of the living room. (...) During the care assistants' weekly meeting, many workers request additional protective clothing (in particular, long gloves, a mask, and an additional apron) to avoid infections. The coordinator explains to them that there is no risk of infection (as they have to feed her but not enter into contact with her blood), but they insist, claiming that, as protective measure, it is their right. (Ethnographic notes)

In this behaviour, it is possible to read a desire to adopt medical symbolism, an attempt to embody higher social status as a means of claiming recognition for social assistance in the hierarchy of the medical professions.

Risky choices on bodies: Immunity from choices

In the third organizational strategy I outline, the body is perceived as a source of risk not only in relation to its infectious potentialities, but also as a place of choice and of the risk of error for professionals.

Professionals make many decisions (and assess risks) regarding the kind of care and treatment to offer to their elderly patients, and in the last few years the process of decision-making has became increasingly more complex and articulated. The process of nutrition is affected by innovative treatments that give professionals a new form of control over the bodies and lives of elderly patients, in particular regarding longevity. This control does not only relate to the effectiveness of medical practices, it is also related to ethical and deontological questions.

During my observations, a number of professionals criticized the use of artificial nutrition for the very elderly because every day they see, beyond some medical benefit, the complex and sad consequences of this practice on the whole life of the person. As underlined by the nursing coordinator of the nursing home:

> For these people [with artificial nutrition]...is it a dignified life? Because they don't understand, they're not living, and their life is terrible. And it's even more terrible for their relatives. How can families live like this? It's an awful life (...). (Melissa)

Notwithstanding this, as soon as a patient has serious problems regarding nutrition, professionals propose to the family the insertion of PEG or NG tubes, as in the case of Mr. Ginepro, a resident who had not eaten for one week:

> I am with Melissa in Mr. Ginepro's room. She tells him that if he does not start eating, they have to insert a PEG or NG tube. He shakes his head [he cannot speak but he can communicate with a tablet] and writes 'no' on the tablet. (...) When we leave the room, Melissa says to the doctor that if he refuses to eat and refuses the PEG tube, they will have to insert an NG tube. (Ethnographic notes)

This behaviour is connected to the fear of legal consequences. Patients and their relatives are currently more aware of, and increasingly protagonists in, the setting of care than they were in the past. In care and nursing homes in particular, relatives have become new subjects of 'control' for professionals, and often represent the threat of legal action. As a result, professionals want to be sure that relatives make choices, and assume responsibility for their decisions, as evidenced in this talk between a doctor and the daughter of a very old and ill patient who cannot eat:

DOCTOR: I can't tell you what to do, you have to choose. I only can tell you that if we don't do anything, your mother could starve. I cannot assume responsibility for this choice.
DAUGHTER   But doctor, what would you do if she were your mother?
DOCTOR: I have to speak as a doctor. But, if I could speak personally, not as a doctor...I don't know. It's very difficult. (Ethnographic notes)

In this very typical situation, the professional avoids making a decision, and leaves relatives in an extremely difficult position: deciding to not intervene would mean starving their loved ones. Only professionals can drive the difficult choice of non-intervention, but driving this choice would be risky because it could lead to moral and legal charges of starving their patients. The contemporary health care system seems to misappropriate categories for facing the complexity of these situations and technologies and medical innovations have assumed a very relevant role in this. As suggested by Kaufman et al. (2004: 732), a new ethical field is emerging, 'characterized by the difficulty or impossibility of saying "no" to life-extending interventions'. Professionals thereby attempt to immunize themselves from the risks connected to choice. This reaction on the part of professionals highlights how working practices of body work are strongly conditioned by the presence of bodies as objects of work: the efficient management of nutrition answers the problems of bodies without resolving the problem of management of end-of-life decision-making. It simply prolongs the time of non-choice, and hides the moment of choice.

Conclusion

The analysis of the working practices enacted by health and social care professionals highlights how organizational and management changes directly involve residents' and professionals' bodies. In particular, this study has highlighted three principal analytic issues.

First, the level of medicalization inside facilities for the elderly is on the rise. Both in care and nursing homes, this process increasingly involves body work. This was investigated in the context of nutritional practices, showing how the process of nutrition – which in the past was not related to medical care – is moving toward the medical field of care in two ways. On one hand, the medical practice of artificial nutrition is rapidly increasing; on the other, the current process of nutrition involves a variety of professionals, including medical ones. Consequently in this process, other elements emerged: the medicalization of social care professions and the 'socialization' of medical professions. Professional roles, which until few years ago were relegated to the context of social care, have now assumed a more clearly defined and recognizable medical aura. This 'medicalization of nutrition' modifies the relationships between bodies in the setting of care and creates a new form of distance between bodies, in particular between professionals' and residents' bodies. At the same time, doctors – who traditionally only took part in planned procedures, such as surgery, or those considered emergency interventions – are now involved in a wider concept of care. Nutrition work represents a field in which traditional hierarchy can be challenged.

Secondly, the new forms of nutrition, particularly artificial nutrition, would seem to permit a new means of rationalization and standardization of body work. Contrary to what Cohen's (2011) analysis suggests, these new forms of nutrition would seemingly allow care facilities to increase capital-labour ratios, to avoid the need for co-presence and temporal unpredictability and to change the nature of bodies, transforming them into a new kind of material of production that can be assimilated into a capitalist logic of standardization and rationalization. As such artificial nutrition appears to be a 'rational solution' (Cohen, 2011), both economical and easy to manage. My analysis, however, shows this to be only apparently rational. In fact, artificial nutrition strongly affects residents' bodies and their lives as a whole in a complex way: it can be a means of prolonging life, but is used without appropriate reflection on the relationships between ageing, illness, death and quality of life. And this increases long-term costs of care, both economic and the social/human costs.

Finally, this chapter highlights the important role of bodies as spaces of risk and choice. Professionals who protect themselves through a kind of 'immunity from choices' (perhaps unintentionally) put into practice a sort of 'securitarian policy of care'. This behaviour is reminiscent of the more general 'securitarian policy' presented in many social contexts, such as urban and migration policies. In the contemporary society of uncertainty, a number of things are considered a risk and the answer to this risk is often expressed in short-term solutions aimed at risk avoidance. However, my analysis reveals ways in which risk is not considered in its entirety, and is faced by making as few choices as possible. Doctors insert PEG and NG tubes as definitive tools because by doing so they avoid assuming responsibilities for end-of-life decision-making. In this process, doctors' traditional power of choice in medical settings becomes a painful and sad power, as many of them feel compelled to enact innovative strategies of care (as artificial nutrition) even when they personally disagree. At the same time, social care professionals have to accept this policy and act so these strategies work day by day. This 'securitarian policy' becomes internalized even if all professionals try to resist it. As a result, the medical context tends to create the possibility of significantly delaying the moment of death without finding ethical and professional sense in this process. Therefore, the choice of artificial nutrition often does not represent a true choice. Insertion of PEG or NG tubes simply offers the choice of bypassing the choice.

Notes

1 'Biomedicalization' is 'the increasingly complex, multisited, multidirectional processes of medicalization that today are being both extended and reconstituted through the emergent social forms and practices of a highly and increasingly technoscientific biomedicine' (Clarke et al., 2003: 162).
2 Artificial nutrition (also known as tube feeding) is defined as receiving nutrition in any form other than the taking in of food and fluid through the mouth (orally). This can be achieved through a nasogastric tube (NG tube), a gastrostomy tube (G tube or PEG tube), or through total parenteral nutrition (TPN).

REFERENCES

Charmaz, K. (2006). *Constructing Grounded Theory: A Practical Guide through Qualitative Analysis*. London: Sage.
Clarke, A.E., Mamo, L., Fosket, J.R., Fishman, J.R. and Shim, J.K. (2009). *Biomedicalization: Technoscience and Transformations of Health and Illness in the U.S.* Durham: Duke University Press.
Cohen, R.L. (2011). Time, Space and Touch at Work: Body Work and Labour Process (Re)organisation. *Sociology of Health & Illness* 33(2): 189–205.
Conrad, P. (2007). *The Medicalization of Society: On the Transformation of Human Conditions into Treatable Disorders*. Baltimore: Johns Hopkins University Press.
Douglas, M. (1966). *Purity and Danger: An Analysis of the Concepts of Pollution and Taboo*. London: Routledge and Kegan Paul.
Estes, C.L. and Binney, E.A. (1989). The Biomedicalization of Aging: Dangers and Dilemmas. *The Gerontologist* 29: 587–597.
Gimlin, D. (2007). What Is 'Body Work'? A Review of the Literature. *Sociology Compass* 1(1): 353–70.
Glaser, B.G. and Strauss, A.L. (1967). *The Discovery of Grounded Theory: Strategies for Qualitative Research*. Chicago: Aldine.
Kahana, E., Kahana, B. and Kercher, K. (2003). Emerging Lifestyles and Proactive Options for Successful Ageing. *Ageing International* 28(2): 155–80.

▶

Kaufman, S.R., Shim, J.K. and Russ, A.J. (2004). Revisiting the Biomedicalization of Aging: Clinical Trends and Ethical Challenges. *Gerontologist* 44(6): 731–8.

Österlijng, J., Hansebo, G., Andersson, J., Ternestedt, B.M. and Hellstrom, I. (2011). A Discourse of Silence: Professional Carers Reasoning about Death and Dying in Nursing Homes. *Ageing and Society* 31: 529–44.

Sanders, T. (2001). Female Street Sex Workers, Sexual Violence, and Protection Strategies. *Journal of Sexual Aggression* 7(1): 5–18.

Trabucchi, M., Brizioli, E. and Pesaresi, F. (2002). *Residenze sanitarie per anziani* [Nursing Homes for Older People]. Bologna: Il Mulino, Fondazione Smith Kline.

Twigg, J. (2000a). *Bathing – The Body and Community Care*. London and New York: Routledge.

———(2000b). Carework as a Form of Bodywork. *Ageing and Society* 20: 389–411.

Widding Isaksen, L. (2002). Masculine Dignity and the Dirty Body. *NORA – Nordic Journal of Feminist and Gender Research* 10(3): 137–46.

Wolkowitz, C. (2002). The Social Relations of Body Work. *Work, Employment & Society* 16(3): 497–510.

———(2006). *Bodies at Work*. London: SAGE.

Getting the Bodies of **14**
the Workers to the Bodies of
the Clients: The Role of Rotas
in Domiciliary Care

Gemma Wibberley

We are paid only for the houses that we are in...*I'm not paid for the time it takes to get there*...[so] if I'm working *8 hours in a day*...I've probably worked *9 and a half* [hours] *unpaid*. (Sarah, Domiciliary)

Getting the bodies of the workers to the bodies of the clients, can be a logistical challenge in any sector. In domiciliary care, however, as Sarah highlights, problems are compounded by the lack of remuneration for domiciliaries' travel time, and therefore the extensive unpaid work they are expected to perform. The quotation is drawn from a wider research project[1] that examined domiciliaries' labour process, and argued that this is largely determined by rotas. Therefore it is the role of rotas in the organization of body work that this chapter addresses.

Domiciliaries are paid workers who travel to the homes of older people whose physical or mental health restricts their ability to go about their daily routine. The 'rota' is a document created by domiciliary care managers. It determines the place, duration and timing of each care visit and ensures the right client and domiciliary bodies are in position. Rotas are not, however, merely an administrative tool, but are a key source of work-related problems.

Rotas are of vital importance because of their ability to shape the time and resources available for care, and domiciliaries' pay and working conditions, yet there is little research into rotas. Meanwhile, in policy there appears to be a move to increase the 'efficiency' of rotas (Campbell, 2008). This chapter addresses these issues by asking the following questions: What shapes rotas? What impact do rotas have on domiciliaries? And what actions do domiciliaries take to overcome rota problems? The chapter begins by examining research on domiciliary care (DC) and other mobile work, then presents the methods used in empirical research highlighting the issues raised by rotas.

Literature

Domiciliary Care (DC) overview

Since the introduction of the *NHS and Community Care Act* 1990, the provision of formal care[2] for older people in the UK has been transformed. Previously, there was 'home help' for assistance with domestic tasks, or residential care for those with more severe needs, and local authorities provided most of these services. The Act created a twin shift towards care in the community for older people, even those with high-level needs, and privatization. Domiciliaries increasingly undertook tasks such as bathing, dressing, and health-care activities, with less emphasis on housework. Service provision also increased. Many clients have serious physical and/or mental health problems (McClimont and Grove, 2004) and, therefore, require support several times a day, everyday (Sinclair et al., 2000). The privatization of care, which was part of the Act, was introduced in the belief that it would reduce costs and increase efficiency (Carey, 2008). Competitive tendering, based on 'value for money' services, encourages private DC organizations to submit low-cost tenders, something that they achieve by decreasing provision and/ or staff pay and benefits (Young, 1999). These private organizations now provide the majority of DC (Eborall et al., 2010).

There, is however, a purchaser-provider split, as much DC is procured from private DC organizations by Social Services on the behalf of older people. Social Services then tightly prescribe the terms of DC provision (Patmore, 2003). However, most clients are also expected to contribute financially, and only those who are deemed unable to care for themselves independently are likely to be eligible for Social Services support (Milligan, 2009). For all clients, based upon their assessed needs, a 'care plan' is drawn up in conjunction with the client, provider and purchaser(s). This care plan then informs the organization and the domiciliaries of what work is to be done and funded (Sinclair et al., 2000).

Although the work has significantly intensified, domiciliaries' reward and recognition has not (Eborall et al., 2010). In part, this is because of the lack of acknowledgement of what DC actually involves, and the invisibility of much of their labour from official documents such as rotas. These mostly female workers are generally paid little above minimum wage and are often on zero-hour contracts in the private sector, with only basic employment rights (Aronson and Neysmith, 2006).

Body work

Issues of under-recognition apply to many 'body workers' (Wolkowitz, 2006). Wolkowitz defines body workers as those who work on bodies with their own bodies as an inherent part of their labour process. This is particularly relevant for DC, as the clients' bodies require care and domiciliaries bodies are necessary to provide it (England and Dyck, 2011; Twigg, 2000).

Twigg et al. (2011) argue that the role played by the bodies of clients and how it affects the work and the workers are often neglected aspects in care. Particularly under-acknowledged are the difficulties in coordinating the needs of clients' bodies with the availability of staff; because 'body work requires co-presence...they must be in the same place at the same time' (Twigg et al., 2011: 176). These problems are compounded when profitability rationalizes staffing. Similarly problematic is the government agenda of increasing efficiency in care. Cohen (2011) highlights the difficulties in achieving this rationalization without decreasing quality because in body work neither the number of workers nor their time can easily be decreased, and the variation in, and between, client bodies reduces opportunities for standardization.

Rotas in DC

In DC, a rota organizes body work. In terms of what shapes the design and application of rotas, studies have highlighted: insufficient time allocated for care (England and Dyck, 2011); poor rota design, particularly the lack of travel time (Cuban, forthcoming); difficulties in scheduling due to the unpredictability of the time clients and their bodies need (England and Dyck, 2011); government efficiency drives (Campbell, 2008); and clients receiving shorter and less frequent visits (McClimont and Grove, 2004). Domiciliaries' time must also be spent travelling between clients, typically unpaid, yet this aspect of their work is rarely the focus of the literature. Rubery and Urwin (2011) provide a notable exception, describing the tensions between Social Services and private DC organizations over responsibility for paying domiciliaries for their travel time, with both parties blaming the other for not funding this. All the aforementioned issues constrain managers when organizing rotas (Patmore, 2003).

Unsurprisingly, the literature reveals that rotas have mostly negative impacts upon domiciliaries, such as stress (Cuban, forthcoming) and deterioration in their conditions and experiences due to rationalization (Campbell, 2008). Many studies focus on the time pressure that workers are under during visits, which makes 'caring' difficult (Denton et al., 2002). Despite these challenges, domiciliaries still try to provide the care required (Meintel et al., 2006), often giving their own time and resources. Studies of DC organizations' perspective on the provision of unpaid work include some contradictory findings. In some studies, it appears that providing unpaid work is endorsed (Rasmussen, 2004), while Patmore (2003) shows it could lead to disciplinary actions. In addition, while less frequently commented upon, domiciliaries are generally not remunerated for their travel time or expenses. Cuban's (forthcoming) much needed account reveals the stressful and costly nature of travel. One way in which rotas can benefit domiciliaries is through allocating regular clients thus enabling relationship building; however, frequent interactions with the same client can also be challenging (Campbell, 2008). There is insufficient research into the action domiciliaries take to overcome these rota problems, except for acknowledging that many are working unpaid to ensure that their clients' needs are met (Robison, 2003).

Mobile workers

Because of the lack of research into domiciliaries' mobility, I briefly examine some of the issues faced by other 'mobile workers' – those for whom travel is recognized as an extensive part of their job. Mobile workers' travel has received more attention in literature (Brown and O'Hara, 2003; Hislop and Axtell, 2007; Holley et al., 2008; Laurier, 2001), although these authors also argue that all forms of mobile work are under-researched. The travel of mobile workers is shaped by the need to be in the right place, at the right time, to meet the right person; however, this co-ordination of activities and people can prove challenging (Brown and O'Hara, 2003). Travel time can be productive as workers do tasks during the journey or use it to recharge (Holley et al., 2008). Laurier (2001) shows that relying on travel, communications and company infrastructures can be either supportive or unsupportive for staff. Nevertheless he and Brown and O'Hara (2003) argue that mobile workers typically have control over their own schedules and location.

In general, the impacts of mobile work on workers depend upon: the level of discretion over their work; duration and timing of hours worked; boundaries between work and personal life; amount of travel involved; and client interaction (Hislop and Axtell, 2007). Alternatively, Laurier (2001) does not present mobile working as stressful. Furthermore he reports that although disruptions to mobile working are frequent, they are not deemed to be problematic. In addition, although their temporary workplaces can constrict the performance of planned activities, problems can be reduced by adapting the work or workplace to the mobile worker (Brown and O'Hara, 2003).

These studies have, however, typically focused on 'knowledge workers'. Cohen (2010, 2011) provides a noteworthy exception, arguing that for body workers mobility may be even more important because of the need for physical co-presence with clients. Cohen's (2010) typology of mobile workers highlights the differences between the common representation of professional teleworkers, whom she describes as 'working while mobile', and those who are engaged in 'mobility for work', who are travelling to get to the variety of places required by the job, and uses mobile hairstylists as an example. Most importantly Cohen argues that knowledge workers are likely to have more choice in their mobility and work than other groups of mobile workers. Domiciliaries are undoubtedly 'mobile workers', as they must travel between each client, but potentially the body work they perform differentiates them from the stereotypical portrayal, so Cohen's typology is a useful framework for understanding domiciliaries' work.

This review has highlighted an intensification of DC, which has had a direct effect on rotas, reducing funded time for carework, and thus increasing pressures upon domiciliaries. Nonetheless, insufficient attention has been paid to workers' strategies to manage these stresses, and this is what this chapter aims to address. Furthermore, because domiciliaries' travel is under-researched, theories on other mobile workers are drawn upon when examining the findings.

Method

The data for this chapter comes from my PhD. I interviewed 47 participants from across the DC sector in England, including domiciliaries, managers and stakeholders, in both the public and private sector. In the course of these interviews, respondents often commented that the best way to understand the work would be to either become a domiciliary or to watch how it was performed. Recognizing that I do not possess the relevant skills to perform DC and undertake 'participant observation', I decided that 'shadowing' would be a more appropriate method (McDonald, 2005). I arranged shadowing with two private DC organizations, and I was able to shadow domiciliaries, office staff and managers as they went about their day-to-day work, for around 60 hours. A comprehensive picture of DC emerged as I followed staff in and out of offices, clients' homes, cars and their own homes.

Findings

Joanna's day

From this shadowing, I compiled an example of a day in the life of a domiciliary, Joanna[3]. However, all of these events did not all happen to one domiciliary, nor on one day; 'Joanna's' experience is a composite of common experiences in DC work. These visits have been slotted into an anonymized real rota (Table 14.1), so that the distances travelled and the duration of the visits are based on one day of a domiciliary's work. Normally, when domiciliaries' receive their rota it would show clients' addresses; however, I have replaced this with the distances between clients. That Joanna is scheduled to leave one client and arrive at the next one at the same time has not been fabricated.

Visit 1. Joanna gets to her client earlier than scheduled, as her company advises, in order to get a good start on the day. This client, Bob, no longer has the use of his lower body, so Joanna has to physically undertake much of his personal care. This includes cleaning Bob's catheter, assisting him with a bed bath and then maneuvering him out of bed via the use of hospital-style equipment.

Visit 2. This is a new client, so Joanna has to work out how to get to and enter the house, and how best to work with this client. It appears that the client, John, is able to maneuvre and communicate, but it seems that he either gets confused easily or that he chooses to make inaccurate comments; for example, John says that he has brushed his teeth, when his relative argues that he has not. Joanna has to negotiate between the two and decide the best course of action for John, whom she has never met before. We leave just before the scheduled time of 9.30 am, but somehow need to arrive at the next client before 9.30 am.

Visit 3. Unsurprisingly we are now running late. Here Joanna knows the client Beryl, and this knowledge enables Joanna to realize that a very different type of care is needed to the one described on the care plan. While Joanna is making breakfast, it appears that Beryl is unwell. Joanna rings the

Table 14.1 Joanna's rota for the day

Client	From	To	Hours	Location (miles apart)
Bob	7.30 am	8.30 am	1	0.2
John	8.30 am	9.30 am	1	1
Beryl	9.30 am	10.30 am	1	3
Esther	10.30 am	11.30 am	1	9
Catherine and Rachel	11.30 am	12.00 noon	0.5	5.5
Fred	1.00 pm	1.30 pm	0.5	3
Margret and Arthur	1.30 pm	2.00 pm	0.5	10
Sue	2.00 pm	3.00 pm	1	3
Bob	5.00 pm	5.30 pm	0.5	n/a

office to ask her manager to call the doctor. In the middle of all of this, the toast gets burnt. Joanna is concerned as to how long the doctor will take to arrive and whether Beryl will be OK on her own, but Joanna can't stay, as she has other clients to see. We leave at 10.30 (as scheduled).

Visit 4. We are running late again, to a visit where yet again Joanna is required to perform unscheduled care. Although she is supposed to be here to help Esther perform her morning routine, Joanna frequently has to squeeze in time between all her other tasks to hunt for lost items. Today is no exception as Esther had lost her teeth, and Joanna has to find them, along with the tools required for the task; i.e., to clean her client's false teeth Joanna has to find the teeth, a toothbrush and toothpaste. This means that all the tasks take much longer than scheduled.

Visit 5. It is 11.50 am by the time Joanna gets to her fifth visit, 20 minutes later than scheduled, because of hunting for items and the nine mile drive between the clients. Two clients live here. Catherine appears to have mental health problems and, therefore, needs advice on what tasks to do and how, whereas Rachel's main problems appear to be physical, meaning that the domiciliaries need to undertake the tasks for her. Another domiciliary is also working here, yet, even with two careworkers, supporting the two clients differently but holistically is time consuming and we are now running 30 minutes behind schedule. By the time we have driven for another 20 minutes to get to the next client's house, Joanna's one hour unpaid break is reduced to only 10 minutes. During this 'break' Joanna grabs a sandwich from the corner shop and eats it in her car, while ringing the office to discuss her concerns about Esther. Joanna then continues with the rest of her visits.

The Rota: An impossible framework?

During the fieldwork it was noted that the rota's purpose is to ensure that client care is provided at the right place and time, by the right domiciliary(ies) and, from the employer's perspective, efficiently. The timings of visits are linked to clients' assessed care needs and are negotiated with them. Typically, support is needed at meal and bed times, creating peaks of demands around those times, and troughs in the afternoons. The high levels of demand for DC also means that numerous clients are visited each day by each domiciliary.

Comparing Joanna's scheduled rota, in Table 14.1, with the actual time of visits in Table 14.2 reveals significant disparities. Table 14.2 demonstrates that Joanna worked for at least 7 hours and 55 minutes, rather than the 7 hours her given rota had suggested.

So why is there such divergence from rotas? The fieldwork uncovered multiple and interrelated reasons. The key problem is the lack of funding,

Table 14.2 Joanna's real rota

Client	From	REAL From	To	REAL To	Hours	REAL Hours	Location (miles apart)	TRAVEL TIME (mins)
Bob	7.30 am	7.25 am	8.30 am	8.25 am	1	1	0.2	5
John	8.30 am	8.30 am	9.30 am	9.30 am	1	1	1	5
Beryl	9.30 am	9.35 am	10.30 am	10.30 am	1	55 min	3	5
Esther	10.30 am	10.35 am	11.30 am	11.40 am	1	1 hr 5 min	9	10
Catherine and Rachel	11.30 am	11.50 am	12.00 noon	12.30 pm	30 min	40 min	5.5	20 (10 min lunch)
Fred	1.00 pm	1.00 pm	1.30 pm	1.25 pm	30 min	25 min	3	5
Margret and Arthur	1.30 pm	1.30 pm	2.00 pm	1.55 pm	30 min	25 min	10	25
Sue	2.00 pm	2.20 pm	3.00 pm	3.05 pm	1	45 min	3	5
Bob	5.00 pm	5.00 pm	5.30 pm	5.30 pm	30 min	30 min	n/a	n/a

because Social Services only pay private DC organizations for the time domiciliaries spend in clients' homes, and that is based on the strict time allocated for their care needs. Therefore, private DC organizations base their rotas only on this funded time. Yet, Joanna's day revealed the significant underestimation of the work to be performed and the time this takes as well as the time it takes to travel to and between clients.

Another major difficulty for rotas is the constantly changing needs of clients and their bodies. This includes changes in the terms of care and the time that an individual client needs, as well as in the total number of clients needing care. Unfortunately, many clients' conditions deteriorate, thereby increasing their care requirements. Alternatively, some clients only require short-term DC, for instance upon leaving hospital, before then regaining their independence. Death unfortunately is also a regular, but rarely predictable, variable in DC:

> Clients are up and down all the time … you might have had an influx of [new] clients coming out of hospital, … or then come the winter months you might have them dropping off. (Jen, Domiciliary)

Lack of staffing was another significant problem. This increased the challenges in rearranging rotas. Furthermore, the needs of domiciliaries and clients clash frequently. For example, clients may want visits late at night to go to bed, but domiciliaries may find this too tiring to combine with the early starts necessary to provide assistance in getting out of bed (Patmore, 2003). These factors highlight the inherent challenges presented by the fragility and unpredictability of client and staff bodies.

In addition, badly designed rotas made sticking to the prescribed times almost impossible. For instance, in some organizations different clients may be scheduled at the same time, that is, both Mr. Smith and Mrs. Jones have a 9.00 am appointment on the same domiciliary's rota. These scheduling flaws placed extra pressure on domiciliaries:

> You finish at ten to eight, first client, then you move onto your next one for 8 o'clock...it can get a bit stressful...moving from a to b...10 minutes driving time, and you get stuck in't traffic...or you're just running late...therefore the caring side can suffer, cos you can't give it all...you're not relaxed in your job. (Jen, Domiciliary)

From a manager's perspective, rotas are incredibly difficult to organize, and they spent a considerable amount of time and energy trying to ensure that they matched clients' needs with domiciliaries' availability. It was unacceptable that clients would not be visited, and in many cases there was little flexibility with the timing of the visits because of clients' condition or medication needs: the requirements of the body dictated scheduling. These rota problems show similarities with Patmore's (2003) study, and are the opposite to the typical portrayal of a mobile worker who has autonomy over their schedule. This reinforces Cohen's (2010) argument that there are wide variations in the capacity mobile workers have to control their work.

Time pressures

The majority of respondents argued that rotas imposed tight time constraints, and this was seen as one of the key pressures within DC. Domiciliaries' work has also intensified in recent years and now they are expected to do more work in less time. Often, there was insufficient time in the rota to undertake all the activities required, as domiciliaries Nicola and Marie explained:

> NICOLA: You have half an hour, you go into in a job, you're supposed to read the (care plan), find out what's been happening...to that person...by the time you've got through the door, you've

said hello to the person, ... *10 minutes is at least gone* ... and then you're supposed to ... shower them, dress 'em, feed 'em, medication, make the bed, *well* ... with all the will in the world.

MARIE: ... in some cases it's not physically possible.

Fieldwork revealed that certain tasks, such as cleaning, have been removed from many care plans to officially reduce the time a visit should take. Other official tasks have been modified, again allegedly to save time, for example, microwaving 'ready meals' rather than cooking. Nevertheless, I found that domiciliaries often try to fit tasks back into the visit, and are also under pressure to undertake extra unscheduled tasks, each of which exacerbates the time pressure they experience (Meintel et al., 2006). In order to try to fulfil as many of these tasks as possible, domiciliaries have to work at speed. This gives them little opportunity to deal with any problems:

We started at half seven and finished at half one ... bang, bang, bang, bang ... if we had problems, there was *no room for you to sorta sit down and think 'Ohh'*. (Robyn, Domiciliary)

Emergency situations did arise, as described in Joanna's third visit, and under tight time constraints domiciliaries struggle to deal with them without impacting upon other clients' care. They have to juggle the needs of different clients, prioritize their work tasks and deal with the repercussions of their decisions:

If you find somebody on the floor ... you can get delayed and you're worried about the next person waiting for you and it's very difficult and some clients are ... not very understanding. (Katie, Manager)

Domiciliaries described various strategies for dealing with time pressures. For instance, they develop efficiencies which enable them to 'catch up' on rota. In the homes of regular clients they learnt the location of resources and how to perform tasks quicker. Any 'spare time' in client visits, through a fluctuation in clients' needs, was also utilized, an upside of the changing nature of bodies. Workers would also prioritize activities, for example ignoring or minimizing paperwork. Sometimes I noted that domiciliaries did not work in the procedurally correct manner, similarly to Lopez's (2007) residential care-workers, as efficiencies had to be found, regardless of the potential risks.

Unsurprisingly, this time pressure and intensive working caused considerable strain, a contrast to Laurier's (2001) presentation of mobile work as not stressful. Additionally, body work took a considerable toll on domiciliaries' bodies. Some described time-off as 'dead time' as they were too tired to do anything and several felt exhausted after work:

> It was really intense...you were really, really tired, you used to get home and you were like that (pulls face of exhaustion) (laughs)...it was *just too much for us*. (Suzanne, Domiciliary)

Rotas, which included lots of calls, also caused stress (Denton et al, 2002) because domiciliaries were often unable to concentrate on their current client, because of an awareness of the many others:

> I had 24 visits...on one day...when you have that many, your mind's on the next client...Thinking are you going to get there on time and...sometimes you...get talking and you say 'Look I'm sorry but I'll just...have to do, what I've got to do for ya, and I can't stay, I must go'. (Alice, Domiciliary)

Lack of travel time

These time pressures are exacerbated by the lack of travel time allocated on rotas, particularly in the private sector. It is impossible to visit clients without travelling, and, as Joanna's day shows, travelling can be considerable: between her first and last client she spent almost an hour and a half driving, covering almost 35 miles.

It is very difficult to reduce the amount of time travelling and, therefore, domiciliaries have to save time elsewhere. Cutting short client's time typically enables domiciliaries employed by private organizations to be paid for some of the time they spend travelling. This corresponds with Robison's (2003) findings, but I would add that managers may also encourage domiciliaries to use client time for travelling, but not all domiciliaries can do this. Furthermore, taking time from a client forces domiciliaries to choose between their own and their clients' needs. Lastly, even when domiciliaries are able to leave clients early they may still not have sufficient time for travelling, as Table 14.2 demonstrates.

Domiciliaries complained that the lack of travel time pay, in the private sector, further decreases their low wages to 'pretty...*minimal wage*', which is exacerbated by insufficient mileage payments. Journey times may be unexpectedly increased by traffic problems and if late for visits domiciliaries risked complaints from all stakeholders. All of these factors seemed to encourage domiciliaries to drive fast and forcefully.

This stressful presentation of travel concurs with Denton et al. (2002), while lending no support for Leppanen (2008), who describes travel time as a 'break' for domiciliaries, during which they 'recharge', despite describing domiciliaries utilizing travelling as an opportunity to reflect on their last client and 'prepare' for their next. My findings also contrast with descriptions of travel for mobile workers (Holley et al., 2008; Laurier, 2001). This may be because the mobile workers featured in previous studies were presumably paid for their travel time and, therefore, did not experience the same tensions, nor have such concerns about being late for clients as the DC workers in this study. In general, domiciliaries can be classified as mobile workers who use 'mobility for work' (Cohen, 2010), and similarities emerged between them and Cohen's mobile hairdressers. For example, both groups suffer from 'deadtime' of not earning between clients. Yet interestingly, dependent clients did not seem to give domiciliaries' control over their own schedules, unlike the hairdresser in Cohen's study. In addition, I would argue that domiciliaries are also 'working while mobile', such as making phone calls, an intensification of work more commonly expected of professionals.

Overcoming the rota

Most domiciliaries attempted to overcome rota problems by giving 'their own time', as Joanna did. She started early, worked through her break, and gave almost an hour unpaid. It is widely recognized that domiciliaries perform care tasks outside of their working hours, whether 'voluntarily' for clients (Robison, 2003) or as a sign of resistance (Stone, 2000). Nevertheless, I argue that domiciliaries do not always feel that they have much choice about giving this extra time to clients who desperately need it, especially when bodies require attention off schedule:

> As I was leaving, [the client] said…'Oh I really need to go to the toilet, I think I've had an accident'…you stay…help her to get…cleaned up and re-dressed. (Freda, Domiciliary)

There are also substantial expectations that 'good' careworkers provide the time that clients require (Robison, 2003), and not doing so 'highlights…the care giver's inadequacy' (Stone, 2000: 102), rather than, as I would argue, the rota's inadequacy. Nevertheless, providing extra care may also cause tensions between domiciliaries and managers, or their colleagues, as Nicola and Marie (domiciliaries) described:

> NICOLA: (Clients) get *less and less* time…so we get less and less time…but being the type of job where you're working with people if you've got a *conscience* you end up giving a *lot* of your own time…the company don't really want you to do it.

MARIE: (Nicola) runs late *all the time*...she *irritates* the (domiciliaries) that (she)'s working with...but she *can't leave* a job *half way through*...cos of the demands on it...I mean I find it very difficult, but I have *got better*...at walking away, because I work *so* many hours.

NICOLA: I just find it too stressful to [walk away].

Managers' expectations regarding extra care appeared contradictory. They seemed to want domiciliaries to fulfil clients' care needs and were aware this could take longer than allocated. Equally they did not want domiciliaries to be late for their next client, and risk generating complaints. Therefore, it was beneficial when domiciliaries gave their own time, outside of work, and some organizations encouraged this (Sinclair et al., 2000).

Conclusion

This chapter provides insights into rotas, demonstrating the challenges for domiciliaries to get their bodies to clients on time. This is because of the many factors that shape rotas. These include: underfunding; instability of bodies; clashes between the needs of domiciliaries' and clients' bodies; efficiency drives; insufficient staffing; increasing client needs; poor rota management; insufficient time allocated for care; and declassification of tasks, especially travel. These factors typically lead to domiciliaries' labour expanding outside of their scheduled time, which has negative implications for them financially, physically and mentally, particularly because of the lack of extra reward for this time.

The findings explore domiciliaries' methods for dealing with these pressures and their strategies for developing efficiencies, including working at speed and reappropriating time. Yet these cannot counter-balance rota inadequacies. Therefore, the burden of making rotas work rests upon domiciliaries, who give substantial amounts of unpaid time travelling and providing care. Highlighting this unofficial work time is important in order to recognize the reality of domiciliaries' work and reward, and the inadequacies of the social care system.

Lopez (2007) argues that residential careworkers' acceptance, and ability to deliver care under extreme time pressure, provides a disincentive for resource increases. Potentially, this also applies to DC, as it has and continues to face severe cuts. Social Services threaten to remove support for clients with 'substantial' needs, who are unable to undertake their own personal care, moving to only support those with 'critical' needs whose life is at risk. Meanwhile, further cuts are proposed to social care funding for providers and staff pay (Samuel, 2011). The concept of 'care' in DC policies seems continually diluted, focusing on only the essential tasks a body, rather than a person, requires. Policies pursue 'efficiencies', yet this chapter demonstrates that DC cannot stand any further cuts without negative impacts upon clients and domiciliaries.

Notes

1 The author's ESRC funded PhD.
2 Informal care by friends or family has always provided the majority of eldercare but is outside of the remit of this discussion of paid carework.
3 All names in the paper are pseudonyms.

REFERENCES

Aronson, J. and Neysmith, S. (2006). Obscuring the Costs of Home Care: Restructuring at Work. *Work, Employment & Society* 20(1): 27–45.

Brown, B. and O'Hara, K. (2003) Place as a Practical Concern of Mobile Workers. *Environment and Planning A* 35(9): 1565–87.

Campbell, M. (2008). (Dis)continuity of Care: Explicating the Ruling Relations of Home Support. *In* M. DeVault (Ed.) *People at Work: Life Power, and Social Inclusion in the New Economy.* New York: NYU Press.

Carey, M. (2008). Everything Must Go? The Privatisation of State Social Work. *British Journal of Social Work* 38(5): 918–35.

Cohen, R. (2010). Rethinking 'Mobile Work': Boundaries of Space, Time and Social Relation in the Working Lives of Mobile Hairdressers. *Work, Employment & Society* 24(1): 65–84.

———(2011). Time, Space and Touch at Work: Body Work and Labour Process (Re)organisation. *Sociology of Health & Illness* 33(2): 189–205.

Cuban, S. (forthcoming). *Staffing the Global Care Industry: The Roles of Professional Migrant Women.* Basingstoke: Palgrave Macmillan.

Denton, M., Zeytinoglu, I., Davies, S. and Lian, J. (2002). Job Stress and Job Dissatisfaction of Home Care Workers in the Context of Health Care Restructuring. *International Journal of Health Services* 32(2): 327–57.

Eborall, C., Fenton, W. and Woodrow, S. (2010). *The State of the Adult Social Care Workforce in England, 2010: The Fourth Report of Skills for Care's Research and Analysis Units.* Skills for Care. Available at http://www.skillsforcare.org.uk/research/research_reports/annual_reports_SCW.aspx.

England, K. and Dyck, I. (2011). Managing the Body Work of Home Care. *Sociology of Health & Illness* 33(2): 206–19.

Hislop, D. and Axtell, C. (2007). The Neglect of Spatial Mobility in Contemporary Studies of Work: The Case of Telework. *New Technology, Work and Employment* 22(1): 34–51.

Holley, D., Jain, J. and Lyons, G. (2008). Understanding Business Travel Time and Its Place in the Working Day. *Time and Society* 17(27): 27–46.

▶

▶

Laurier, E. (2002). The Region as a Socio-Technical Accomplishment of Mobile Workers. *In* B. Brown, N. Green and R. Harper (Eds) *Wireless World.* London: Springer.

Leppänen, V. (2008). Coping with Troublesome Clients in Home Care. *Qualitative Health Research* 18(9): 1195–1205.

Lopez, S. (2007). Efficiency and the Fix Revisited: Informal Relations and Mock Routinization in a Nonprofit Nursing Home. *Qualitative Sociology* 30(3): 225–47.

McClimont, B. and Grove, K. (2004). *Who Cares Now? An Updated Profile of Independent Sector Home Care Providers and Their Workforce in England.* United Kingdom Home Care Association Limited. Available at http://www.ukhca.co.uk/pdfs/whocaresnow.pdf.

McDonald, S. (2005). Studying Actions in Context: A Qualitative Shadowing Method for Organizational Research. *Qualitative Research* 5(4): 455–73.

Meintel, D., Fortin, S. and Cognet, M. (2006). On the Road and on Their Own: Autonomy and Giving in Home Health Care in Quebec. *Gender, Place & Culture* 13(5): 563–80.

Milligan, C. (2009). *There's No Place Like Home: Place and Care in an Ageing Society.* Farnham: Ashgate.

Patmore, C. (2003). *Understanding Home Care Providers: Live Issues about Management Quality and Relationships with Social Services Providers.* York: Social Policy Research Unit, University of York. Available at http://www.york.ac.uk/inst/spru/research/summs/homecare.htm.

Rasmussen, B. (2004) Between Endless Needs and Limited Resources: The Gendered Construction of a Greedy Organization. *Gender, Work & Organization* 11(5): 506–25.

Robison, J. (2003). Consulting Home Carers: An Exploration of Views about Quality and Values, and the Status of Domiciliary Care. Southampton: The Quinn Centre. Available at http://www.thequinncentre.co.uk/Documents/homecarersreport.pdf+domiciliary+carers.

Rubery, J. and Urwin, P. (2011). Bringing the Employer Back In: Why Social Care Needs a Standard Employment Relationship. *Human Resource Management Journal* 21: 122–37.

Samuel, M. (2011). Top Five Victories against Social Care Cuts of 2011. Community Care. Available at http://www.communitycare.co.uk/Articles/21/12/2011/117890/Top-five-victories-against-social-care-cuts-of-2011.htm.

Sinclair, I., Gibbs, I. and Hicks, L. (2000). *The Management and Effectiveness of the Home Care Services.* Social Work Research and Development Unit, University of York. Available at http://www.york.ac.uk/inst/spru/research/summs/homecareservice.html.

Stone, D. (2000). Caring by the Book. *In* M. Harrington Meyer (Ed.) *Care Work: Gender, Class, and the Welfare State.* New York: Taylor & Francis.

Twigg, J. (2000). Carework as a Form of Bodywork. *Ageing and Society* 20: 389–411.

▶

Twigg, J., Wolkowitz, C., Cohen, R. and Nettleton, S. (2011). Conceptualising Body Work in Health and Social Care. *Sociology of Health & Illness* 3(2): 171–88.

Wolkowitz, C. (2006). *Bodies at Work*. London: Sage.

Young, R. (1999). Prospecting for New Jobs to Combat Social Exclusion: The Example of Home-Care Services. *European Urban and Regional Studies* 6(2): 99–113.

Saliva, Semen and Sanity: Flat-Working Women in Hong Kong and Bodily Management Strategies

Olive Cheung

Introduction

This chapter highlights the body's role in the understanding of sex work and more specifically workers' management of their bodies in what they understand to be 'risky' interactions with customers. Risk has been a major theme within social science research on sex work, with the focus tending to be on so-called 'occupational hazards' as a way of understanding any undesirable impacts on the physical and emotional health of the (mainly) women workers in this potentially 'risky business' (Sanders, 2005a). Because sex work mostly involves intimate physical contact and specific uses of female sex workers' bodies, bodies have been seen as the basis of the 'problem' for these women. This chapter, rather than challenging the conclusions of existing literature, argues that whereas the 'use' of individuals' bodies has long been linked to detrimental emotional consequences in sex work contexts, the resistance of individuals in these same contexts should not be ignored. By examining female sex workers' accounts of their embodied and emotional experiences at work in brothels in Hong Kong, this chapter explores how social and cultural factors influence individuals' interpretation and accounts. The sources of stress and difficulty in these women's lives are not solely due to their body in the exchange. Rather, they are shaped by material and other concerns, such as the feeling of shame and the pressure of working in secrecy.

Risks and prostitution

As previously noted, across disciplinary fields, including biology, medicine and psychology, the various occupational hazards faced by sex workers have been perceived as 'an inevitable feature of the clandestine activity' (Sanders, 2005a: 3). Central to these concerns has been a focus on the psychological harm and mental health consequences of selling sex (Connell and Hart, 2003; Day, 2007). These problems are reported to include 'the stress of living such complex lives and an abiding sense of injustice' (Day, 2007: 230; Day and Ward, 2004),with some sex workers describing emotions of guilt, disgust and shame as a consequence of selling sexual services (Sanders, 2005a). In this sense, the stress of sex work is argued to emerge from the specific 'use' of sex workers' bodies in the sex work exchange. For example, the epidemiological perspective has viewed (female) sex workers as an epidemiological 'core group' (Bloor, 1995), more popularly known as a 'risk group', because it is presumed that this group of women are likely to engage in 'risky behaviour' such as drug use and unprotected sex. It has also been argued that sex workers are at high risk of physical assault, rape and murder (Barnard et al., 2001; Kinnell, 2008; McKeganey and Barnard, 1996).

Moreover, because of the intimate physical contacts between the worker and the client, the sex worker's body has long been seen to be at the centre of those risks. Additionally, in Chinese patriarchal societies, including Hong Kong, non-reproductive and commodified sex is still marginalized. In these societies, sex workers internalize social views and experience unpleasant emotions relating to the 'whore' stigma through intimate physical contact with clients. As discussed further in the following section, when bodies are assumed to be the root of the 'problem' for women in sex work, women's agency appears to be ignored or goes unconsidered.

Methodology

This chapter draws on a research project that considers how female sex workers in Hong Kong experience and deal with risk. This study focused mainly on flat-based sex work: women working from a rented flat (apartment) or a flat of their own. As part of the indoor sex market, this group comprises only a subpopulation of all sex workers. Due to a lack of a comprehensive record of the number of flat-working women, this study used the number of advertisements for sexual services posted by flat-working women on two local adult entertainment web sites as an indicator of the number of flat-working women in Hong Kong. On this basis, the estimated population of flat-working women totalled approximately 1500 when this study was conducted in 2009.

The main sampling technique used was networking, which inevitably produces bias. Nevertheless, given the characteristics of this population, it proved the most effective – if not the only way – to gather a sample. In order to minimize bias, I negotiated access through different groups (an agency, sex work support group and individual women) and recruited participants from various ethnic groups.

Interviews were held and observational data collected mainly during a seven-month period. Thirty women were recruited and interviewed for this study. They were all Hong Kong residents with legal status but had differ-ent origins: 15 women were originally from Hong Kong; 15 women were from other cities in Mainland China. Pseudonyms were used in the research project in order to protect participants' anonymity. Most of the interviews were audio-taped using a digital recorder. All of the files were transcribed and were imported into NVIVO 7 for analysis.

Observational research was based on partial immersion. I spent a great deal of time taking part in the activities for sex workers organized by Sex Worker's Alliance of Hong Kong, stayed in women's working flats and hung out with women. I observed everything I could, but focused especially on occupational risks. The main focus of the observations were the ways in which women managed risk through spatial control or manipulating iden-tity; how women interacted with colleagues (at or outside work) and how they responded to information about occupational risk provided by the agency. The observational data were recorded in field notes. The follow-ing section begins by exploring sex workers' reactions to intimate physical contact.

Disgust as exposure to body fluid

The interactive nature of bodies within the sex work encounter produced a number of problems for sex workers. In particular, many respondents expe-rienced negative emotions when they had physical contact with clients, and specifically when they were exposed to clients' bodily emissions. Saliva, specifically, aroused their feelings of disgust. Therefore, most respondents avoided touching their clients' saliva and explained that this was the main reason why they did not kiss mouth-to-mouth (Kowlgi and Hugar, 2008; Ning, 2004). This may be explained by the fact that in the context of Hong Kong, the typical sexual encounter between a client and a flat-working woman included basic acts such as oral sex and sexual intercourse. The time of each session was limited (around 45 minutes), therefore, the encounter was unlikely to become a 'girlfriend experience': a session that 'might proceed much more like a non-paid encounter between two lovers', which 'may include a lengthy period of foreplay' and 'perhaps even kiss passionately' (Bernstein, 2007: 126). For example, Lisa explains her response to saliva:

> Sometimes the client, even if you didn't allow them to kiss you, they grabbed you when you refused to let them do so.... I'm a bit fearful of their saliva.... I felt very dirty! Yeah, very dirty. It's because you didn't have any feelings for him! It's very dirty and disgusting!...Apart from saliva, people may have things like...some people have bad breath.

Sanders (2005b) argues that retaining body exclusion zones is an important technique amongst sex workers. Kissing, for example, may be considered as a sexual act that is too intimate to be sold. For Lisa, kissing was an intimate act that she undertook only with intimate partners or someone she liked. In contrast, she found the physical experience of kissing someone with bad breath repellent. Lisa further explained her concerns about infection from clients:

> Moreover, some have mouth ulcers, or, they may have things such as tuberculosis. These are all infectious. Other than HIV, many diseases are infectious, aren't they? I want to be healthy.

Therefore, it was both the experience and the physical risk which made many women refuse to kiss clients. According to my field notes,

> Rose was among the few respondents who did kiss clients. But, like other respondents, she also said that the smell of saliva disgusted her. However, Rose believed that as a sex worker, she should do as much as she could to satisfy her clients' requests: 'One of my clients had an extraordinarily smelly mouth. The smell was... [laughing]. Anyway, I still needed to be passionate. I still kissed him.'

Interestingly, while many respondents reported that saliva disgusted them, only a few respondents (three out of 30 women) told me that they were disgusted by touching clients' semen. The use of condoms among flat-working women in Hong Kong was standard practice and, to a great extent, this practice protected sex workers from exposure to clients' sexual fluid during vaginal or anal intercourse. This may explain why respondents rarely described their feelings of exposure to semen and more often described their response to saliva (although this may also be attributable to a unwillingness to discuss semen). Nevertheless, some respondents were unexpectedly exposed to semen, because of condom failure. For example, as Crystal described:

> When we had sex, he suddenly tried to remove the condom. I stopped him but he just pushed my hands away. I shouted, 'No! No! Don't do this!' and started to cry. I told him if he really wanted to shoot his load, 'Don't shoot inside me. Shoot over my belly.' He did that and I sobbed. It's disgusting. I immediately used toilet paper to wipe the dirty thing off and scolded him.

While women often viewed bodily fluids as a source of disease, Crystal understood that in this case she was unlikely to be infected with anything

(Sanders, 2005a). Her negative feelings did not, therefore, come from fear of disease, but because her client's semen had come into contact with her body.

Apart from the case of condom failure, sex workers were most likely to be exposed to clients' semen when they offered clients hand relief or fellatio. Many respondents said that simply coming into contact with clients' semen in these contexts did not produce negative feelings. In contrast, some respondents did report being particularly repulsed by situations in which clients' semen *entered* their bodies. Joey, for example, said that once when she offered a client oral sex, he did not use a condom and he ejaculated in her mouth: 'I pushed him away, rushed to the bathroom and vomited. I rinsed my mouth a couple of times, but I could still sense the smell.'

Rose, in contrast, offered clients *ha-baau* (口爆, ejaculation into the mouth), but she was the only respondent in the study who reported to do so:

When I first did it I found that it was quite unpleasant. Men's thing down there, I mean the ball, that, the smell was very unpleasant. No matter how hard I washed it and it looked clean, I still felt very dirty. The smell of semen also made me sick. Sometimes I fear I'll get diseases. But I also feel this is my job. I need to get the job done.

In Hong Kong, flat-working women offer clients oral sex, but many do not offer *ha-baau*. This is identified as a kinky act and workers may charge a higher price for doing so.

Body emissions have long been identified as polluting (Meigs, 1978) and are perceived as a potential health threat (Curtis et al., 2004). Mary Douglas' *Purity and Danger* (2007/1966) suggests that bodily emissions are 'sources of impurity' (p. 41), in particular those which '[relate] to the bodily functions of digestion or procreation' (p. 35). Using the example of Indian caste structure, Douglas argues that sexual behaviour has a significant impact on preserving the purity of caste. Consequently, 'in higher castes, boundary pollution focuses particularly on sexuality' (p. 155). Sex workers experienced these boundary crossings as disturbing both to their bodies and selves. Therefore, it may be argued that pollution rules about bodily emissions related to procreation reflect individual anxieties about maintaining a social hierarchy. In the context of sex work, sex is separated from procreation as it is used as an economic means of production. Sex workers and their clients are not concerned to maintain the purity of the hierarchy. As such, women's negative feelings about being exposed to clients' bodily fluids may be attributed to their fear of diseases, in particular AIDS, but also, importantly, to issues of intimacy and selfhood.

Given that semen carries a higher HIV transmission risk, it is noteworthy that women felt less disgusted by semen than saliva. In order to understand this, the symbolic meanings attached to bodily emissions in the context of sex work should be taken into account. If we treat the bodily orifices as the symbolic exits and entrances to the human body, the client can apparently 'enter' the sex worker's body through intercourse and mouth-to-mouth kissing. In other words, both acts are associated with the symbolic crossing of body boundaries and, as such, threaten women's bodily integrity.

Establishing body exclusion zones during the commercial sexual encounter

Sex workers developed strategies to manage transgressions of self and body, and the development of a 'professional' identity was a key strategy for managing difficult bodily experiences, such as undressing:

> I didn't find it easy the first time I got undressed. It's just like what happens to a model the first time she gets undressed. [...] In our case, after a client enters the room, we start to get undressed. We see it as something natural but not something special. However, it doesn't mean that I can get undressed in front of my friends. I don't find it easy to get undressed in front of people when I am off work. (Fung)

By adopting the role of 'professional sex worker' during her sexual encounter with the client, Fung drew a boundary between her private self and her work self. She exposed her body in front of a client as a *sex worker*. By adopting the 'sex worker role', Fung's public self was separated from her true self. As a sex worker, the respondent believed that it was *her job* to display her body in front of a client. The meaning of clothing also changed. For a sex worker, clothing was not 'the outward sign of dignity' (as a woman). Rather, Fung relinquished her clothing as a personal front during her performance/sexual encounter, as a sex worker, with a client. As such, the client gets access to the sex worker's body, but the woman keeps control of her private self and her body.

Other strategies included excluding certain sex acts or limiting access to certain body parts during the commercial sexual encounter (Chapkis, 1997; Høigard and Finstad, 1992; Ning, 2004; Sanders, 2005a). These are seen as a coping mechanism which sex workers adopt to protect their 'true self' and 'true feelings':

> Prostituting yourself is providing something of value for money; [...] The vagina is rented out. But nothing more. You never get my thoughts. Not my mind, not my soul, not my mouth. There's something that is mine alone and that you'll never get hold of. I'm not really there. Prostitutes

have worked out an ingenious, complex system to protect 'the real me', the self, the personality from being invaded and destroyed by customers (Høigard and Finstad, 1992: 64).

During intercourse, a condom acts as a barrier which prevents flesh-to-flesh contact and protects women from exposure to the clients' bodily fluid. Therefore, even though the client apparently 'enters' a woman's body with his genitalia, a boundary between the two individual bodies is still maintained. However, when a client's bodily fluids enter a woman's body, such as with saliva, the boundary is blurred: the client's bodily fluid is now *inside* the sex worker's body and, therefore, has crossed the boundary to her *self*. Therefore, sex workers' disgust at bodily emissions may reflect individual anxieties about maintaining a boundary between their true selves and their work roles.

It is difficult, if not impossible, to maintain the body boundary in mouth-to-mouth kissing. Unlike sexual intercourse or oral sex, it is not easy for sex workers to adopt any physical, or psychological, barriers (such as condoms and dental dams) when they kiss their clients. In other words, whereas the use of condoms is viewed as symbolically separating work sex from private sex, it is relatively difficult to draw a boundary between a 'work kiss' and a 'private kiss'. This may explain why sex workers are less willing to kiss clients mouth-to-mouth.

Many respondents said that they did not allow clients to put their fingers into their vaginas. For them, although the vagina was rented out, this did not mean that clients could do whatever they liked with it. As Joey said:

If a client wanted to fuck me, that's fine. He paid me and I was prepared to do so. I didn't allow him touch me down there with his stinking hands. His hands were dirty and I didn't want him to touch me.

When the client puts his fingers inside the woman's body, the woman is inevitably touched by the flesh of the client. As Joey's account indicates, this client behaviour appeared to cross the symbolic boundary between the two parties. Therefore, for some respondents this act was never acceptable at work.

Some sex acts were also excluded because the negative cultural meanings attached to them were relatively universally recognized. For example, an interview with Mo-mo was conducted in her working flat while she was expecting clients. Like many other respondents, Mo-mo talked in a serious manner during the interview. The advent of a client, however, effected a dramatic change in her attitude. Before going to answer the door, Mo-mo asked me to hide myself in the kitchen. As the door of the kitchen did not close tightly, I could see what was happening in the living room, as this account from my fieldnotes reveals:

> A guy came to see Mo-mo in the middle of the interview. The man stepped in, lifted her skirt a little and looked at her bottom. Mo-mo slapped his hand and moved away from him...The guy asked if Mo-mo did anal, but she said no. The guy put his hand on her back, and asked what services she provided...She explained to him the prices for services in a friendly way...[she] stood still, smiled and asked what he thought...[he] said that the price was too expensive and left.

Like Mo-mo, many sex workers in this study said that they did not offer anal sex, although all women offered vaginal intercourse. Some women said that anal sex was 'dirty' and 'abnormal'. Many women in this research, including Lily, believed that 'only those girls who are really desperate and have no choice' would offer these services.

Pheterson (1993) argues that, in contrast to the popular discourse, sex workers do not necessarily see selling sex as shameful, but they have their own interpretation of dishonour. She notes that sex workers divide themselves into 'good whores' and 'bad whores', but have different ways of defining these two terms. In my research, many respondents said that they exclusively offered 'normal' sexual services (usually vaginal sex with protection). They refused to engage in 'abnormal' or 'unsafe' sexual practices, and appeared to find it degrading to be involved in so-called kinky sex.

Another way of being a 'good whore' was to dis-identify from the 'sex worker' identity and instead to assert lack of choice. Natalie was once interviewed by reporters who wanted to write an article on female sex workers. In the interview, she explained that she had been abandoned by her husband. As a single mother who had two young children to take care of, she said that she was desperate and felt miserable. I discussed this article with her during the interview. She said, however:

> In fact my life was not that miserable. If I was really desperate, I could definitely get help from the government. For us, say if we can have three clients, we will get HK$1000 [£82.40] daily. Roughly we earn HK$30000 [£2473.49] per month. It's not bad, is it?

The income that Natalie estimated was based on a worker having three clients a day and working 30 days a month. This may overestimate sex worker income, as most workers were unlikely to work every single day and few women in the study had as many as three clients daily. By the time of the interview, however, Natalie did not need to support her children, as both of them had finished school, and so faced considerably less hardship. Nevertheless, she still told her clients the 'miserable story' that she had reported to the newspaper, as she felt that 'people want to hear miserable stories. They think that we're miserable. So we pretend that we are.' She said this was important as it enabled people to sympathize with sex workers, even though it might not reflect the real situation of sex workers.

As Hochschild (1989/2003: 58) suggests, we 'receive rule reminders from others who ask us to *account* for what we feel' (original emphasis). Sex workers might describe 'miserable stories' when they provide accounts about their work because this was what they assumed others thought they should feel. These stories fit well with the widespread understanding of sex workers as 'victims': the usual social story about sex workers is not one of rational choice, or of people with agency over their decisions, but rather one of desperate, difficult and troubled lives. This might also explain why the majority of academic findings (and indeed questions) on sex work establish a relationship between undesired emotional consequences and selling sex.

Despite the fact that drawing a boundary between work sex and private sex is a universal practice among sex workers (Edwards, 1993; Sanders, 2005b), it is evident in this study that for some women the divide is not necessarily rigid (Brewis and Linstead, 2000). Four women in the present study said that they gained sexual pleasure from having sex with their clients, which echoes the findings of earlier work (Brewis and Linstead, 2000; Exner et al., 1977; McKeganey and Barnard, 1996; Sanders, 2005a). For example, Helen argued that it was natural 'for a woman to have feelings when a man laid his hand on her body'. She suggested that women lied about their feelings if they claimed that they 'felt nothing' or did not get sexually aroused during the sexual encounter with clients. Ying said that she heard that 'some' sex workers 'got turned on' when clients performed particular sex acts:

> Some clients like to eat abalone.[1] I know some girls let their clients do it to them. [...] Some clients really know how to lick you out.

In the preceding accounts, respondents used *others'* experience to illustrate that women might actually experience pleasure and intimacy during the encounter with clients. When I asked about *their* experiences, Helen and Ying smiled in an embarrassed way, gave short answers ('erm...yeah'; 'sometimes') and avoided provided further detail. Two respondents, however, explained exactly why they found the encounter enjoyable. Fong was in her late forties. She became a flat-working woman after she divorced her husband:

> People may think I'm insane. But I do love having sex with clients. [...] I know some women think that it's weird to enjoy sex at work. But what's wrong? You get paid and you can have fun.... Some of my clients are in their twenties or thirties. I don't think they will bother to look at me if we meet on the street. You know, I'm in my forties and I'm not really attractive. But now these handsome guys pay me and ask me to have sex with them. Think about it! [She laughs] I don't know why other girls always feel unhappy about what they're doing, but I do enjoy it.

Fong described her ex-husband as 'a decent man', but that she had 'felt bored' when she was with him. Sex became enjoyable only after she entered the business and she particularly enjoyed her sexual encounters with a few regular clients:

> I really love to do this [have sex]. Therefore I feel that I'm happy in my work. Maybe because of my sexual needs, I do love to do this. People pay me to do it...er, to be honest, among my clients, at least six, seven of them are in their 20s and 30. Some are over 40. Most of them are good. I am not satisfied with one or two clients. The sex was not satisfactory. But when I consider that they give me money...I am happy when I see the money. My happiness will be double if we have good sex.

In contrast to other respondents, these two women said that they did not fake their feelings towards their clients. They believed that clients 'knew whether it is *zan-cingzan-ji* [真情真意 means a genuine show of cordiality] or *heoi-cinggaa-ji* [虛情假意, meaning a hypocritical show of cordiality]' (Fong, Mainland China), and emphasized that they did have cheerful feelings during the encounter:

> I treat every single client well, no matter if he is a builder or a cleaner; or he has bad breath, his body stinks, or he is very dirty. I am enthusiastic and always treat them with passion. There were many clients, at least 70, 80 clients who said that they had the feeling of first love when they were with me. It's because I treated them from my heart. I did not fake it. (Rose)

Unlike other women in this study, Rose and Fong said that work sex was better than private sex. It was, however, not easy to feel passion with all clients. Rose admitted that bad breath and an unwashed or smelly man made her sick, but she felt that she *'should be* nice and passionate' and behave *as if* she 'loves the client very much'. She explained:

> Because I feel this is my job. Clients came to me and expected that they would enjoy themselves. I took HK$300 from them. My service should warrant HK$300. They arrived in high spirits, and I wanted them to leave satisfied. (Rose)

This account suggests that Rose felt ambivalent towards sex as work. She said that she had 'determined to be professional' since she entered the industry. Viewing herself as a 'professional sex worker' who was 'enthusiastic' in her work, Rose believed she *ought to feel* that she enjoyed sex with clients and *should* 'treat clients with passion' in every single encounter. But how could she express her *true* happiness in adverse conditions, for example when she found that a filthy client had bad breath or a smelly body?

In this situation, Rose needed to do emotion work to control the underlying feeling of nausea. Although she repeatedly emphasized that she did not pretend to have feelings, Rose described herself as an 'actor':

> Like an actor, you should act from deep in your heart. If you want the audience to be moved by what you do, you must do it from your heart. He will not be moved when he sees you pretending to cry. (Rose)

As detailed elsewhere (Cheung, 2011), the social front is institutionalized. When an actor takes on a social role, s/he presents a particular social front. The manner and appearance of an actor is expected to be consistent (Goffman, 1959). In fact, a social setting not only shapes how an individual acts, but also how *s/he should feel*. Accounts given by women in this study demonstrate how sex workers undertook either surface or deep acting to feel and display what they felt they were expected to in the sexual encounter.

Discussion

Sex working women's undesired emotions have been explained as reactions to the 'whore' stigma. In the last few decades, however, in parallel with the experiences of LGBT minorities, adult 'prostitutes' in Hong Kong, as elsewhere, seem to have become more socially accepted than they were in the past. Yet women supplying sexual services still feel stigma and the unpleasant emotions such as shame attributed to the 'whore' stigma (Scambler, 2007).

This chapter argues, however, that rather than seeing women working in the sex industries as necessarily suffering from the undesired emotional consequences of the specific 'use' of sex workers' bodies in the sex work exchange, the 'misery stories' provided by sex workers can themselves be viewed as a performance, or part of the front of sex work. In parallel, with the creation of the 'whore image', sex workers might adopt the 'victim role'. Both follow from stereotyped expectations and existing narratives about women involved in the sex industry.

Previous research has argued that creating geographical space between home and the working location is one strategy adopted by sex workers to manage information and consequently their stigmatized identities (Sanders, 2005a). Although geographical distance has been so core to sex workers strategies for managing their lives, the women in the current study, local sex workers in particular, found it hard to create space between home and their working location. This was partly because of the geography of Hong Kong, as a small city, and partly due to the seeping of one part of life into another. In his research on opportunist migrant sex workers in London, Scambler (2007: 1091) found that these workers were apparently 'able to switch sets of identities' easily; because these women '*were* and *were not* in the trade, so the stigma they experienced *was* and *was not* at the core of their self-identities' (italics in the original). For most women in the Hong Kong study, sex work was seemingly a permanent job (in terms of the length of time that they stayed in the business). They were, therefore, likely to find it difficult to 'switch sets of identities', and consequently felt stigma, which they experienced at the core of their self-identities. Moreover, where workers had children, being 'whores' (or 'bad girls') at work was sharply contrasted to being 'Madonnas' (or 'good girls') at home. All these factors are likely to contribute to women's feeling of stigma and consequently to their experiences of unpleasant emotions.

How can we understand the ambivalent emotional experiences of flat-working women in Hong Kong? This chapter argues that Everett Hughes' (1962) concept of 'dirty work' may shed light on this issue. In his work about the Holocaust, what concerns Hughes is the ways in which individuals conceptualize the 'dirty work' done in the concentration camp to Jews and others by ordinary Germans or 'good people'. What dirty workers did was broadly conceived as morally wrong. Hughes conceptualizes Germans' common silence on this issue as a ritual expression of their collective guilt. Nevertheless, Hughes (1962) argues that if a society is considered as a network of in-groups and out-groups, we may sacrifice the out-groups to uphold the well-being of the in-groups. In this sense, 'we do our own dirty work on those closest to us' (p. 8). In other words, the meaning of dirty work held by dirty workers are ambivalent: privately dirty workers do not necessarily perceive what they have done as wrong. Nevertheless, because the dirty work is widely recognized as morally wrong, they may express their 'guilt' rather than defend themselves.

Conclusion

Drawing on the findings of the research project on risks faced by sex workers, this chapter describes how women developed different mechanisms for commercializing their feelings and body (parts), without selling 'themselves' or turning themselves into an object. However, women recounted the difficulty they had in direct internal bodily contact with clients, particularly in managing bodily fluids such as saliva and semen, suggesting that many seemingly experienced unpleasant emotions.

It is perhaps more interesting to consider the ways in which the sex workers accounted for pleasurable emotions. Although many sex workers spoke of the unpleasant emotions that they experienced in the course of their work, a few of them also commented on their enjoyment of sex with their clients. Similar findings have been found in previous studies, but mostly commentators have treated these as the exceptions (Sanders, 2005a). Recent changes in the perceptions of female sexuality may explain why a few flat-working women described the sex with their clients as enjoyable, in the sense that women are now more likely to be able to enjoy the pleasure of sex rather than repress such feelings and are able to vocalize such feelings. Yet, women's unwillingness to discuss this issue (which was reflected in the fact that only a few women were willing to talk about it and some appeared to feel embarrassed in giving their accounts) perhaps also highlights the ongoing normalizing of women's marginalized sexuality in the Chinese context. In Hong Kong, traditional norms regarding women's sexuality still operate. It has been taken for granted that women's sexuality is about danger rather than pleasure (Chan, 2008), and that therefore it is 'inappropriate' for women to talk about their experiences of sexual pleasure, in the context of commercial sex in particular. For many sex workers who experience pleasure, denying it may be part of the symbolic boundary necessary to manage their stigmatized identity.

Note

1 In Cantonese slang, an 'abalone' refers to female genitals. 'Eating abalone' means performing oral sex on a woman. It is equivalent to 'eating pussy' in English slang.

REFERENCES

Barnard, M.A, Hart, G. and Church, S. (2001). *Client Violence against Prostitute Women Working from Street and Off-Street Locations: A Three City Comparison*. ESRC.

Bernstein, E. (2007). *Temporarily Yours: Intimacy, Authenticity, and the Commerce of Sex*. Chicago: University of Chicago Press.

Bloor, M. (1995). *The Sociology of HIV*. London and New Delhi: Sage.

Brewis, J. and Linstead, S. (2000). *Sex, Work and Sex Work: Eroticizing Organization*. New York: Routledge.

Chan, A.H.N. (2008). Talking about 'Good Sex': Hong Kong Women's Sexuality in the Twenty-First Century. *In* C. Jackson, J. Liu and J. Woo (Eds) *East Asian Sexualities*. London: Zed.

Chapkis, W. (1997). *Live Sex Acts: Women Performing Erotic Labour*. New York: Routledge.

Cheung, N.Y. (2011). *Accounting For and Managing Risk in Sex Work: A Study of Female Sex Workers in Hong Kong*. PhD Thesis, Royal Holloway, University of London.

Connell, J. and Hart, G. (2003). An Overview of Male Sex Work in Edinburgh and Glasgow: The Male Sex Work Perspective. MRC Social Public Health Sciences Unit, Occasional Paper, June. Accessed 15 August 2007 at http://www.sphsu.mrc.ac.uk.

Curtis, V., Aunger, R. and Rabie, T. (2004). Evidence That Disgust Evolved to Protect Us from Risk of Disease. *Biology Letters* 271: 131–33.

Day, S. (2007). *On the Game: Women and Sex Work*. London: Pluto.

Day, S. and Ward, H. (Eds) (2004). *Sex Work, Mobility and Health in Europe*. London: Kegan Paul.

Douglas, M. (2007/1966). *Purity and Danger: An Analysis of the Concepts of Pollution and Taboo*. London: Routledge.

Edwards, S. (1993). England and Wales. *In* G. Davis (Ed.) *Prostitution: An International Handbook on Trends, Problems and Policies*. Westport: Greenwood.

Goffman, E. (1963/1990). *Stigma: Notes on the Management of Spoiled Identity*. New Jersey: Penguin.

Hochschild, A.R. and Machung, A. (1989/2003). *The Second Shift*. New York: Penguin.

Høigard, C. and Finstad, L. (1992). *Backstreets: Prostitution, Money and Love*. Philadelphia: Penn State University Press.

Kinnell, H. (2008). *Violence and Sex Work in Britain*. Cullompton: Willan.

Kowlgi, A. and Hugar, V.K. (2008). Ethnographic Profile of Female Sex Workers of Dharwad, Karnataka. *In* R. Sahni, V.K. Shakkar and H. Apte (Eds) *Prostitution and Beyond: An Analysis of Sex Work in India*. New Delhi: Sage.

McKeganey, N. and Barnard, M. (1996). *Sex Work on the Streets: Prostitutes and Their Clients*. Buckingham: Open University Press.

Meigs, A. (1978). A Papuan Perspective on Pollution. *Man* 13: 304–18.

Ning, Y.B. (甯應斌) (2004). 《性工作與現代性》[Sex Work and Modernity]. 台灣: 中央大學性FF0F5225研究室 [Taiwan: The Centre for the Study of Sexualities].

▶

Pheterson, G. (1993). The Whore Stigma: Female Dishonour and Male Unworthiness. *Social Text* 37: 39–64.

Sanders, T. (2005a). *Sex Work: A Risky Business*. Cullompton: Willan.

——— (2005b). 'It's Just Acting': Sex Workers' Strategies for Capitalizing on Sexuality. *Gender, Work & Organization* 12(4): 319–41.

Scambler, G. (2007). Sex Work Stigma: Opportunist Migrants in London. *Sociology* 41(6): 1079–96.

Index

Abbott, S. A. 132, 136, 139, 140
aestheticizing services, 10, 15, 33, 38–9, 160–72
aesthetic labour, 47–8, 82, 112–15, 138–9, 142–3, 198–200
Agamben, G., 46
ageing bodies, 6, 15, 47, 207–8
  see also elderly
altporn, 130, 133–43
amateur pornography, 14, 130, 133–43
AMMAR-CTA, 53–4, 55
anal sex, 246
artificial nutrition, 12, 210–13, 218–20
Asian women, 160
  racialized sexualization of, 162, 164–72
Attwood, F., 130, 133, 137
authenticity, in DIY porn, 141–2
autonomy, 15, 32, 34–7, 46

Baerenholdt, J., 30
Barton, B., 112, 130, 131, 132
Baumgardner, J., 169
beauty industry, 6
beauty massage, 176–7
beauty services, 6, 15, 33, 38–9, 160–72
biomedicalization, 207–21
Blackstone Capital, 93, 98
bodily fluids, 241–4, 245
body/bodies
  ageing, 6, 15, 207–8
  autonomy of, 34–7
  desexualization of, 10–12, 112, 180–4
  corporeal relations between 118–120, 208

emotional labour and, 78–80, 81
essentialized, 43, 45–6
female, 77, 114
as materials of production, 4–5, 14, 61
proximity between, 110, 208
of racehorses, 196–204
at risk, 208, 214–19, 220–1
sexualization of, 10–12, 114, 77–8
of sex workers, 43, 45–6
social meanings of, 9, 32–9
sovereignty and, 31–2
worked upon, 5,7,10, 12–14,16, 19, 40
workers' own, 112, 115, 121, 197–200, 214–7
body capital, 150
body care/maintenance work, 33, 34–7
body exclusion zones, 244–9
body labour, 48, 82, 110, 161, 162–3
body politics, 52–6
body practices, 86–9, 178
body/sex work
  commodification of, 12–18
  conceptualizing, 7–10
  introduction to, 3–5
  social organization of, 12–15
  and socio-economic structures, 6–7
  standardization of, 12, 13, 130, 139
body studies, 9
body technologies, 21, 129–32, 135–38, 141–3
body work
  ageing and, 207–21
  and animals, 201
  commodification of, 12–18

body work – *continued*
  concept of, 3, 7–11, 29, 48, 78-9, 95–6, 207
  with horses, 202–3
  controlling body work, 3, 28, 33, 37–38
  co-presence in, 13, 14, 96, 208, 220, 225–7
  efficiency in, 95–6
  and feeding, 209–213
  gendered, 77–8, 79
  interactions in, 28–41
  interactive, 84–6, 118–120
  legal constructions of, 61–74
  male workers in, 11, 204
  marginalization of, 7–8
  multiple dimensions of, 81
  power relationships in, 16, 19, 72–3
  prevalence of, 3–4
  in racing labour process, 196
  rationalization of, 94, 100, 220, 225
  recipients of, 19, *see also* customers/ clients, care recipients, worked-upon bodies
  self-employment, 110–23
  standardization of, 22, 94, 220, 225
  types of, 3, 32–9, 77
  without bodies, 13
bouncers, 37–8
boundaries, 185–6, 244–9
Bourdieu, P., 9
breast augmentation, 132
British Horseracing Authority (BHA), 194–5
British Medical Association (BMA), 19
brothels, 78–90, 239–51
Butler, J., 152

Campbell, C., 30
capital, 54
  erotic, 146–7, 158
capitalism, 6
care
  domiciliary 223–37
  familial, 6, 68–73, 236
  residential 93–109, 207–221, 235
care recipients, 72, 74, 93–4
care work, 7
  commodification of, 12, 94, 95
  cost-cutting in, 95–6, 100–4, 208
  of elders, 92–109, 207–21, 223–38
  evolution of social/community care law and policy, 70–2
  informal, 71

legal regulation of, 67–72
  negligence in, 93–4
  nutrition in, *see* feeding
  privatization of, 94–6, 104–6
  of racehorses, 202–3
  standardization of, 94–5, 223–36
care workers, 15, 70–1
  unpaid, 71–3, 74
caring practices, in sex work, 86–7
Chan, S.. 171
class, *see* social class
clients/customers, 65, 69–71
  bodies of, 12, 230
  dangerous, 68–9
  high-end, 13
  interactions with, 239–51
  relations with workers, 15–18
  sovereignty, 28–32, 37, 38–9
Cohen, R.L., 90, 96, 220, 225, 226–7
Colosi, R., 111, 112, 115, 120
commercial sex, 43, 44, 61
  see also sex work
commodification, 12, 46, 54, 56, 94, 95, 142
common law, 62
communication work, 203–4
condoms, 245
consent, 18–20
consumption, 30
  organization of, 29
content analysis, 134–6
controlling body work, 33, 37–8
Coopersmith, J., 133
corporeal identity, 150
corporeal labour, 118–20
cosmetic surgery, 6, 131–2
cosmetic surgery tourism, 14
counterfeit intimacy, 132
criminalization, 66–7
Crossley, N., 49–50, 51
Cuban, S. 226
customer sovereignty, 28–32, 37, 38–9
cyber-sex, 149
cynical performance, 116–7

Davies, K., 100
De Certeau, M., 154
decriminalization, 54
deferential body, 200
De Rode Draad, 53
desexualization, 11–12, 110, *see also* body work
diagnostic work, 14

Diamond, Timothy, 94–5
discursive practices, 146–158
dignity, 28–41
'dirty work', 18, 79, 86–7, 197, 250–1
disgust, 241–4, 245
do-it-yourself (DIY) pornography, 130,
   133–43
domestic work/workers, 68–9
domiciliary care (DC), 223–36
Donne, John, 32
Douglas, M., 243

efficiency, 95–6, 208
Egan, D., 111, 123, 129, 130, 132
elderly, 70, 72, 73
   biomedicalization of nutrition and,
      207–21
   abuse of, 73, 93, 94, 100–5
   care of, 4, 5, 6, 11, 12, 18, 93–107,
      209–38
   domiciliary care, 223–36
embodied labour, 4, 8–10, 46–7, 90
embodied sexuality, 140–1
embodied skills, 201–4
emotional work/labour, 7, 35, 46, 78–80,
   83–4, 115–18
employers, 53
   dangerous, 68–9
employment relationship, 62–3, 65, 66,
   70–2, 74, 116, 121–2
employment rights 18, 61–76
empowerment, 69
enchantment, concept of, 30
erotic capital, 22, 146–7, 158
erotic dancers, 4, 17, 47–9, 110–23,
   130–1
erotic knowledge, 157
erotic looking glass, 141
escort services, 47
ethnography, 34, 94, 99–100, 133,
   136–7

Falk, P. 32
family law, 71
family members, as care providers, 71–3,
   see also care, familial
fantasy production, 132–3
feeding
   as key practice of body work, 209–10
   as means of transforming bodies,
     210–13
   professionalism of, 214–19
   tubes, 210–13, 218–19
female body, 77

female sexuality, 11
femininity, 151, 152, 154, 181–4
feminism, 62
   critical, 129–30
   cultural, 129–30
   material, 55
   radical, 45–6, 53
flexibility, 8, 63, 121
Folbre, N., 94, 95, 106
Fordist model, 62–3
Foucault, M., 9, 32, 141
Fraser, N., 51

gender
   and body work, 77–8, 79
   exploitation, 142
   of horses, 202–3
   inequality, 130, 142
   and labour law, 62–3
   narratives, 86, 87
   repertoires, 48, 153–7
   in racing , 199–200, 202–3
   and the social body, 151–2
   stereotypes, 152–5
gentlemen's clubs, 6
geriatric medicine, 15
Goffman, E., 99, 132, 249
government funding, 19

hairstyling, 8, 13, 38–9, 110–23, 137
Hakim, C., 146, 157
Hardy, K., 10, 48, 120
health care, 6, 8, 17, 34–7
health and safety, workers', 18, 161,
   170–1, 200, 225
Held, V., 94, 96
Hillyer, M., 133, 141
HIV/AIDS, 243–4
Hochschild, A., 78, 247
Hockey, J., 198, 200, 203
hoists, 13, 102–3, 228
Holistic Massage, 175–87
   feminized character of, 181–4
   maintaining boundaries in, 185–6
   as profession, 176–8
   space and place for, 184–5
   stigma and, 185–6
   touch and, 180–1
   training and skills, 178–9
home care aides, 34
home, as site of work, 67, 73, 147, 149
Hong Kong, sex workers in, 239–51
horse breeding, 200
horse racing industry, 193–205

hospitality industry, 65
Huebner, L., 35–6
Hughes, E. C., 250
human rights, 64, 66, 68, 73
hustling, 115–18

incontinence care, 12, 103–4
independent contractors, 49, 80, 111–23
industrialization, 6
informal care, 71
institutional care, 94–5
interactive sexual labour, 48–9, 81, 84–6
intercorporeality, 44, 49–51, 54, 55
International Union of Sex Workers (IUSW), 53
internet, 14
intimacy, 16, 17
   commodification of, 6
   counterfeit, 132
   in DIY porn, 141–2
   professional, 35–6
Isaksen, Widding, 32
Italy, 149, 208
IUSW-GMB, 53

Jameson, J., 140
Jeffreys, S., 45
Jenkins, D., 30

Kang, M., 39
Kaufman, S.R., 207, 219
kissing, 245
knowledge workers, 64
Korea, 165
Korczynski, M., 30–1
Kubrick, Stanley, 168

labour
   aesthetic, 47–8, 81, 82, 112–15, 142–3
   body, 48, 82, 110, 162–3
   commodification of, 46
   corporeal, 118–20, 139–41
   embodied, 46–7, 90
   embodiment of, 4, 8, 9–10
   emotional, 35, 46, 78–80, 83–4, 115–18
   non-human, 13–14
   physical, 81–2, 197
   sexual, 43–4, 46–51, 77–9, 132
   sexuality in, 10–12
labour force, women in, 6, 62–3
labour laws, 61–9, 71, 73–4

labour market, 55, 56, 62, 63, 95, 110, 123, 198
labour process, 4–5, 13, 19–20, 53, 77, 95–6, 104, 110–112, 122
labour process theory, 29, 46–7, 53, 95–6, 101
labour relations, 53, 110–23
lap dancers, 47–8, 49, 111, 112, see also erotic dancers
Laurier, E., 226, 234
Lawler, J., 37
Lee-Treweek, G., 19, 94, 95
legal issues, 53, 61–74
legal protections, 18
Leidner, R., 48
Licoppe, C., 157
local authorities, 70, 71, 98, 100, 224
Lopez, S., 149, 208, 235
Lubheid, 171

male breadwinner model, 62, 71
male sexuality, 11
manicurists, 38–9, 160–72
Marchetti, G., 170
Marx, K., 9, 46
masculinity, 37
massage, see Holistic Massage
McGregor, M. J., 95, 105
mechanization of feeding, 213
media, 129
media technologies, 130
medical care, 34–7
medicalization, 207
men
   as clients, see clients
   manicures for, 165–7
   with physical impairments, 16
   as sexual voyeurs, 132
   as workers, 11, 175, 184
migrant workers, 52, 95, 172
migratory flows, 14
mind/body dualism, 79, 89
mobile workers, 226–7
multi-scalarity, 55
mutual intimacy, 16

nail salons, 160–72
National Assistance Act, 70
National Health Service (NHS), 70, 71, 93, 224
neo-liberalism, 6
Nevada brothels, 78–90
NG tubes, 210–13, 218–19
non-human labour, 13–14

nurses, 34–6
nursing homes, 93–107, 208–21
nutrition, biomedicalization of, 207–21

O'Connell Davidson, J., 45, 55
Oerton, S., 11, 175, 179
offshoring, 14
online pornography, 130, 133–4
on-the-job training, 8
Ott, U., 30–1

pampering industry, 6
Pateman, C., 47, 62
patient relations, 15–18, 35–6
Patmore, C., 224, 225, 226, 231
Paules, G., 31
PEG tubes, 210–13, 218–19
personal services, 110
personal space, 32, 35–6
Pfister, G., 199
Pheterson, G., 246
Phoenix, J., 44, 45
phone sex work, 4, 10, 17, 146–58
physical contact, in sex work, 239–51
physical labour, 81–2
plastic surgery, see cosmetic surgery
politics, of sex work, 43, 52–6
pollution, 243
porn aesthetic, 137–42
pornography, 4, 6, 14, 129–30
post-industrial society, 9
power, 9, 49, 54, 63, 72–3
power relations, 67–8, 72–3, 130, 153–4
privatization, 6, 94–6, 104–6
production, 30, 45–6
professional intimacy, 35–6
professionalism of feeding, 214–19
profits, 13, 94, 95, 104–6
prostitution, 4, 43, 65–7, 77, 239–51
    see also sex work
protective clothing, 215–17
proximity, 110, 208

race, 20, 44, 47, 50, 54, 68, 79, 138, 161,
    167–72
racialized sexualization, 162, 164–72
racing stables, 193–205
radical feminism, 45–6, 53
Raghuram, P., 15
reality, 147–8
reflexivity, 153–7
regulars, in sex work, 16
regulation, 53, 61,74, 123
reproduction

bodily, 18
social, 3, 52, 62, 74
resilience, 19
resistance, 18–20, 22, 53–6, 86, 89, 95,
    103, 105, 153–7, 234
risky bodies, 208, 214–19, 220–1
Ritzer, G., 30
role playing, in phone sex work, 150–7
rotas, in domiciliary care, 223–36

saliva, 239, 241–2, 245
Sanders, T., 16, 43, 48, 146, 158, 197,
    202, 239
Savage, W., 36, 37
Scotland, 175
self-employed workers, 8, 13, 15, 110–23
semen, 242–4
service economy, 63, 70
service-recipient, body of the, 31–41,
    see also clients
service work/workers, 28, 29, 79, 110
    interactions between consumers and,
        15, 29–31
    number of, 29
    sexualization of, 10–12
    by women, 63–4. 123
sex industry, 4, 6–7, 14
    see also sex work
sex tourism, 14, 51
sexual harassment, 11
sexuality, 4, 7, 10–12, 54, 140–1
sexualization
    of adolescent girls, 129
    of body labour, 162–3
    of nail salon work, 160–72
    in phone work, 146–8
    in pornography, 129–38
    racialized, 162, 164–72
    of workers, 110–11, 142–3
sexual labour, 43–51, 77–9, 132
    economy of, 139–41
    interactive, 48–9, 84–6
sexual leisure, 139–41
sex wars, 9, 44
sex work
    see also specific types
    body practices, 88–9
    body technologies used by, 130–3
    body work in, 48, 118–20, 77–80, 81–5
    caring practices, 86–7
    clients' legal position, 64–7
    client-worker relations, 16–17, 48–51
    criminalization of, 53, 66–7
    exploitative relationships in, 64–9

sex work – *continued*
  interactive, 48–9, 84–5
  intimacy in, 16, 1
  intercorporeality in, 49–51, 54–6
  labour practices, 77–90
  manufactured persona of, 10
  occupational risks of, 239–51
  polarization of, 44–5
  politics of, 43, 52–6, *see also* resistance
  range of activities included in, 4
  regular, clients 16
  sexualized presentation in, 10,
    129–145, 150–3
sex workers
  activism by, 53, 54–5
  appearance of, 47–8, 129–45
  autonomy of, 46
  bodies of, 43, 45–6, 129–45
  bodily management strategies of,
    239–51
  occupational performance of, 130–3
  representations of, 9
  sexual pleasure, 16, 20, 22, 51, 88, 90,
    141, 247, 251
shadowing, 227
Shah, S., 171
slavery, 68–9
social care, 6, *see also* care, care work
social class, 14, 20, 44, 55, 68, 80, 89,
    113–4, 117, 122, 164, 169, 201
social/community care law and policy,
    70–2
social interactions, 147–9
social organization, of body/sex work
    labour processes, 12–15
social services, 70–2
socio-economic structures, 6–7
somological, 37
Southern Cross, 93–107
sovereignty, 28–32, 37, 38–9
space/spatial, 8, 13, 14, 20, 55, 84–5,
    147–8, 176–8, 184–5, 213, 250
  of the strip club, 114, 119-20
  space, personal 32, 35–6, 180
  space within the phone call, 140,
    155–8
stable yard staff, 193–205
standardization, 12–13, 94–5
state, 53, 54, 69, 74
status differentials, 14–15
stigma/stigmatization 8, 18, 52, 68, 78,
    87–8, 123,130, 162–3, 172, 185–6,
    197, 205, 208, 217, 240, 249,
    250, 251

stigmatization, 208, 240
strippers, 47, 48
stripping/strippers, 110–23
Sweden, 176

table dancing, 6
technologies, 13–14
  body, 129–43
  media, 130
  phone sex and, 147–9
telephone sex, *see* phone sex work
temporality, 5, 121–2, 131, 223–36
textualization, 12
time pressures, in domiciliary care,
    231–4
tipping, 11. 15, 65
Tolich, M., 199
touch, contemporary understandings
    of, 180–1
touching moments, 28–41
trafficking, 65, 66, 68–9, 161
trades unions, 5354
training, 8
trust, 16
Twigg, J., 34, 36, 225

Wacquant, L. 198
wages, 18, 49
webcam work, 4
Weber, M., 30
welfare state, 6, 13, 15, 18, 53–4, 69, 74
Wesley, J. K., 129, 130, 131, 132, 135
'whore' stigma, 240, 246, 249–50
Widding Isaksen, L., 32, 208
Wolf, N., 131, 132
Wolkowitz, C., 45, 46, 48, 79, 207
women
  in labour force, 6, 62–3
  in service sector, 63–4, 123
  unpaid labour of, 7
women's ways of knowing, 179
work environment, 184–5
  sexualized, 11
worker-client relations, 15–18, *see also*
    clients/customers
worker protection, 65, 66
workers
  see also care workers; sex workers
  status differentials between clients
    and, 14–15
workers' bodies, 4
  resistance by, 18–20
  sexualization of, 10–12, 110–11, 1
    42–3

see also body/ bodies, intercorporeality, proximity
work-family balance, 72
working conditions, 95
workplace organization, 89–90

x:talk, 54–5

'yellow peril' stereotypes, 170–1

Zelizer, V., 6, 94, 183